Book cover design by Screaming Poodle Entertainment
Cover illustration courtesy of the United States Air Force and
the people of Eniwetok.

A number of people helped me write this book,
whether or not they realized it.
A short list follows.

Mary Elizabeth McNeill, for absolutely everything.

Donald Day   Joshua Culp

Judy Myers   Betty Solomon, RIP

Geoff Wilson   John Crawford

Kevin Pike   Zelma Beaman, RIP

Olga Van Der Werf   Susan McNeill

The author can be contacted through: theendnovel@gmail.com

ISBN: 978-1456392086

The
End

Brought to you by

A Brief Preamble To The Lie

"What is a lie, but someone else's unpalatable truth?"
Candidate Dwayne Swindel in an address to the Petaluma Elks Club, Aug. 4, 2047

In a way this is a book about a lot of things. It is about people and what they did and in some cases why they did what they did, or at least why they thought they did what they did. And it's also about the forces that came into play leading up to what people at the time thought of as 'Armageddon', though it has to be said that they were flattering themselves just a bit, in a cynical sort of way. What they called so grandly 'Armageddon' was really just another pathetic little ripple on the sea of human history. That history is a blink.

This book is also about politics, and if that isn't a thousand things then I don't know what is. And it is about lies, <u>millions of them</u>.

But in another way this book is only about one thing. It is about The Lie. Not all the little facets and intricately worked misnomers that we all see around us every day, and ignore, but the one, great big, lie, <u>The</u> Lie, of which all those others are but minute fragments drifting by in the infinitely broad lie stream.

There is, ultimately, only one lie. We think that we glimpse it from time to time, like when Richard Nixon used to speak about Vietnam, God fuck his lying eyes. Or when you see a commercial that says in no uncertain innuendoes that you will be a better, sleeker, more lovable, and deadlier person, if you will only buy half a dozen of our, cars, perfumes, cigarettes, beers, computers, iguana polishers, you name it. We think then, that the lies are so arrogantly transparent that we are actually staring them in the face, seeing them for what they truly are, but in point of fact, these are only little self-similar and imperfect fractal fragments of the vast four dimensional lie space we call the history of humankind and most particularly, our cack-handed Western Paradigm.

This preamble and this book are too.

Louis Kohut, Beverly Hills, California, Aug 6, 2089

3

The Beginning

It didn't start, as some have asserted, with a grand plan on the part of the American people, spread by SMS and secret messages, hidden in mirror writing in the text of personal ads, in liberal newspapers. Nor, I might add, as has also been claimed, did it start as a conspiracy by evil forces from without. There were no smoke filled rooms peopled by Arab extremists, or mile high sky scrapers, with soulless glass walls, housing tier after tier of plotting oriental despots, issuing orders, through coded channels, to operatives within American industry. And certainly, certainly, not at the ranting behest of that bloated, imbecile, Dagmar Veets. If that had happened—if he had called for it, and it had come to pass—then subversives like me would, no doubt, have been dragged off by our ears and thrown into a camp. And I would certainly never have been allowed to write this.

No—on the contrary, it began, as most things in the world do, quite by accident, and it's a good thing it did or it probably would have been a lot worse. As it was, it was bad enough, that is if you count World War III as necessarily 'Bad'.

-<>-

"—My answer——bring 'em on!"

George W. Bush, Washington DC, July 3rd 2003

-<>-

"If you don't make a down payment here on Earth, you will not have a home in heaven!"

John Dukes Dunivan, Tragerville, Mississippi, July 3rd 1966

-<>-

The Umbutu River wound through the highland jungle like a beautiful blue-green tree snake. It was clear and cold, even in those few spots where the bright tropical sun broke through the forest canopy and made it glow like an impossible emerald.

Later, after it dropped down into the lowlands, it would slow down and warm up for the hippos, but here just five miles from the spring where it gushed from a deep crack in the side of the mountain, it was in a crisp hurry.

A white man, Alan Yeates, stepped out of the jungle, at the edge of the river and looked for a muddy spot along the bank. That, in itself, wasn't particularly sinister, there were a lot of white men in the Burundi uplands then. He was an American and mud was what he was after. What harm could a little mud do?

He was a geology student at Michigan State, doing fieldwork for the summer. He stopped at a likely spot, a muddy one and took a little plastic jar out of his pack. He unscrewed the lid and put some of the mud into the jar.

The white man looked around at the beautiful jungle that surrounded him. It was leafy and complex, there in the glade. At first it seemed as if he only heard the river, but then as he listened, he started to hear a thousand tiny sounds that layered it. He was struck by the way the sun light glanced off the leaves where it filtered down from the hot African sky above, and the wet green smells. He screwed the top back on as he rose and labeled it with the date and the place. He put the jar back in his pack and went on his way.

It was 1980. In 20 years the mud would be analyzed and it would confirm what the satellite pictures revealed, that there was gold, among other things, in them thar hills.

32 years later he would be killed at the fall of Dearborn.

-<>-

"...They're delicious. They're nutritious.
They're the bestest thing we all say!
So go and try `em. Then you'll buy `em.
And you'll eat `em up every day!
Yeah! Snakos! Yeah! Snakos!
You'll eat `em up every day!"

"Snakos, for your Reagan's birthday feast! And remember, Snakos are the only 100% recycled food from Japan. Accept no substitutes! Get Snakos for a greener world, and fun at parties!"[1]

-<>-

Bill Crenshaw was a cynical, ordinary man, a lot like his neighbor, Ike and the Scifos that lived on the other side of him.

His gray hair made an unremarkable mop on top of a thin face, whose kind eyes had seen thousands of people slowly killing themselves. He had served them drinks and listened to their stories philosophically, and without judgment, mostly.

He was not exactly the sort of man that you would call a firebrand, or a radical hell raiser. He didn't even vote half the time, choosing instead to sell his proxy on the market for whatever he could get for it. He didn't go around organizing

---

[1]Snakos™ and the Snakos™ identity device are registered trademarks of Tokugowa Foods Inc. Floatkyo Japan.

5

political movements. He just wanted to be left alone, the same as everyone else.

He was retired now, but he had worked for over 50 years as a bartender, in tropical resorts for the most part.

The experience had not left him with a great love of humanity. He'd had the distinct displeasure to observe something very disturbing to him about humanity over the course of his life—that they never seemed to change a bit. The jackasses that sat at his bar night after night in the 2040s were not one gram kinder or wiser than those that fell off their bar stools before him back in 1999.

He expected a little more from the race that was supposed, so they said, to be the best that Earth could produce. It made him a little sad, that in all that time people had learned nothing at all about being themselves. He had resolved himself to the fact that that was just human nature, to be dumb and violent—to be evil monkeys.

Ever since he could remember, all the way back to the 90s in fact, there had been a steady stream of wars. After a while he came to expect them. Mostly they were, with a few notable exceptions, minor things fought by people he didn't know, in places he had never been to.

Well, okay, he had been to Detroit once when he was a kid, but that was years before the ethnic cleansings there, and he did know someone who had lost a sibling in '42, a pilot flying sorties for the Soviets, who was shot down over Manchuria. But other than that, it was all just the necessary background chatter, in an otherwise, relentlessly eventless life.

He was bewildered as hell, just like Ike, at why Swindel was demanding a tax hike on top of the last three, so that, as he put it, 'world peace could be maintained'. The world had never been at peace as far as he could see and probably never would be, and who gave a damn anyway!

Bill stared sour faced at the TV, holding his martini between thumb and forefinger as a painter might hold up a brush to take the measure of an image. President Swindel's face filled the screen, five times larger than life, smiling.

'The cocksucker was always smiling', thought Bill. And why not? He was in charge of the most powerful nation on Earth.

Swindel looked out of the screen with his sincere look, and paused for that heart beat that told you, in no uncertain terms, that what was about to follow was the Lord's own crystalline truth, uttered in complete and utter honesty, so help me God as I swear on this stack of bibles. He was lying of course.

"Citizens hear me!"

He paused again for the camera to change angle.

"I know that you will support me when I go to Congress and tell them that they must vote this bill and this appropriation for the good of all mankind. For you are the ones, that will have to live in the world that will be, if we do not. It is for the sanctity and the dignity of each and every American that has ever and will ever live, from Alexander Hamilton right down to our great, great, great grand children, that I ask this of you.

"And, it is not just for them.

"You can if you will, ignore those future generations. We may if we wish hang our heads along with them and say that we did not act though we could have. We did not help another in his time of need—though we took such help ourselves once. And we will yet live on, though bowed by our own cowardice. But, if you would do that then you are no countrymen of mine.

"Think not then of yourselves and your posterity. Think not of those brave patriots, men and women both that are fighting and dying everyday in Greater Burundi and the enclave of Snellville the Lesser, while you sit there on your fat asses gobbling hot dogs and beer. It may be too late for them anyway. But think for a moment of poor General Kabingga, and his family."

He smiled a warm folksy smile at the camera.

"Those children of his love horses, like I guess all children do, you know they have one horse named Pablo, that they ride all the time..."

Bill drained his martini and belched. "TV 126."

Swindel was there too, from a slightly different angle. He turned to the camera and continued in mid-sentence.

"...there with Michael last spring. Michael loves horses too, of course...

Bill opened the phone.

"Phone, Ike."

There was a few seconds pause and then Ike's creaking voice answered. "Ike Tanenbalm."

"Ike, are you..."

"Crenshaw, are you watching this shit?! Phone, picture. The faggot is going on about Michael again, like the first boy has something to do with it!"

Ike's face popped into the bottom corner of the TV screen red and smirking. "Jesus Christ, a martini, that's a great idea!"

7

Bill held up the glass. "This is my third idea today, and I still can't make much sense out of Swindel's crap. What's he proposing, that we raise the tax rate to 70%, just so we can keep Kabingga's kids in ponies?! He's off his rocker!"

Ike got up and made himself a martini in the little window at the bottom of the screen, talking over his shoulder.

"I doubt he's that," said Ike. "He's way to calculating to go around the bend before he's out of office. This is a deliberate attempt to get sympathy from that bunch of bone smokers out on the West Coast, and ring more money out of the middle."

He returned to his seat and sat down heavily.

"The way I see it, he'll get the West Coast corridor behind him with this Michael loves ponies baloney and then do damage control in the Midwest, and South. That's no big deal, he holds the purse strings and the big stick out there."

"Yeah," said Bill, maudlin. "But what about us?! What about the Big Apple? Doesn't he care about the East Coast corridor?"

The sarcasm was not lost on Ike. He stared out of his little corner of the screen stone faced for a moment.

"Have a drink, Bill."

"I think I will."

Bill poured another one out of his pitcher.

Ike stirred his drink with the olive and considered.

"I hate that bastard, he knows just exactly what to say to get that bunch of hyenas in Congress to play along. It is just too damned ugly to watch!"

Bill took a long cool gulp of his drink.

"What bothers me," he said, "is not so much how he's going about it, as what it is that he's really going about. Swindel and his cronies are just getting on with it, business as usual. They are supporting the Pentagon and the generals and the arms dealers and airplane makers and so on. And for what?"

"Money," said Ike.

"Some petty bush war in Africa?" asked Bill. "For the 'sanctity of future generations?' To keep the world safe for democracy? Bullshit! There is no fucking[2] democracy anymore! There is no peace and never has been! I don't give a shit if his cum guzzling little boy friend likes horses! I'm not paying for them!!!! He's a

---

[2] In those days anyone could swear anytime they liked, even in public, and on TV! Now of course you have to have a God damned profanity license like me, I have one because I'm a fucking writer.

8

God damned millionaire, let him buy his own fucking horses!!!!!!"

Bill found himself on his feet screaming.

Ike was dumbstruck, a rare thing, and just sat there staring out of the screen.

Bill drained his glass and hurled it at the carpet. "I am abso-fucking-lutly not fucking paying for it!!!!"

Ike was quiet for a moment. "Good idea Billy boy. Me neither."

"I am putting an IRS hold on my account, right now!"

"Me too! See ya. Phone hang-up."

Ike's face disappeared, and was replaced by a tag for the evening news. It was a man in a plaid jacket looking sternly out at Bill. "Tonight on prime seven news at six, the hidden dangers of iguanas." A sinister iguana frame lapped him. It stared out from the screen balefully at Bill, chewing a piece of lettuce. "They're not as cute as you think!"

It too disappeared leaving only Swindel looking beseechingly at him.

"It is for those children and their ponies that..."

Bill shook his head.

"TV off, Phone, Bank of Boston, accounts."

After a moment a clerk came on the screen, she looked harried.

"Accounts, may I help you?"

"Hello," said Bill.

"Hello, your account ID please."

"Crenshaw, William, Thomas, nine eight nine, six seven, one five nine four, Scarsdale."

She read through the screen for a moment.

"Yes, Mr. Crenshaw, how can I help you today?"

"Place an account hold on all IRS transactions till further notice. Please," he added.

She punched a few keys, and read some more.

"Okay, you have an IRS hold in place effective one o'clock today. There will be a one hundred fifty dollar fee, your account will be debited."

"Fine, thank you. Phone hang-up."

He smiled and was gone.

Tanya, hit pause and sat back, stretching her arms up over her head. Damon was on break, smoking a cigarette next to her.

"What," she asked, "is up with this IRS shit? I've had nothing but holds for the last twenty minutes!"

Damon blew smoke out of his nose and ticked at his thumbnail—a nervous habit.

"Yeah, me too, I haven't the foggiest."

He leaned forward and tapped up an activity profile on his screen.

"It's not just us though, honey, everybody in the bank's getting it. It looks like April 15th."

Joan, an older woman that sat across from them chimed in sagely, "Yeah but it's worse. April 15th is always just the protest hold, and it's just 15% or so, maybe 20 tops, this is a lot bigger! Something's going down."

Damon shrugged. "Beats me."

Jason, their supervisor, came down the row and stopped at Damon's station for a moment. He looked at the screen, waving the smoke away from his face. "It's Swindel, he just made a speech saying he's going to raise the tax rate by seventy percent so he can buy Michael a pony. I've held _my_ account."

Damon was aghast. "A pony?! I'm not buying him a pony! I want a pony! Why does he get a pony?"

"Because, he's blowing the president," said Tanya.

Jason shook his head. "That's not worth a pony."

"Do weasels _have_ dicks?" asked Joan.

"How about if I blow the pony?" asked Damon. "What do I get then?"

Jason smiled. "A full tummy, and hoof prints on the back of your head."

"Oh not again!"

Tanya brought up her own account number, and put an IRS hold on it.

And so it went. All over the country people where placing holds on their accounts, so that the IRS couldn't debit their funds out from under them. It wasn't anything startlingly sinister, or subversive. It was just the only patriotic thing they could think of to do.

They had had their democratic institutions eroded away to the point where they saw their Government as a freight train full of cigar smoking pickpockets running out of control. They were right. And so, at long, long last they did by accident, what they should have done years before, on purpose. They said no.

A law after all, is just an idea written down on paper and the money to make it happen. No money, no law.

On that day, between the end of President Swindel's speech, which was noon in Washington, and bank closing time on the

10

West Coast, about eight hours later, three in five bank accounts had IRS holds placed on them. The trend was picked up on the net by CNN and they reported it as a rather minor side note at the end of the lunchtime feed from Atlanta. The other networks checked on the report, and seeing a trend themselves, duly reported it as well.

Apparently, the news that there were others out there that felt the same spurred on the less stout hearted to action that they would normally have thought precipitous. Once the snowball got rolling it was hard to stop. By three o'clock in Chicago the seemingly minor trend had grown to an outright mutiny. NBC broadcast a special bulletin that interrupted the daytime feed for the entire nation in the middle of One World to Live. Now, that made people sit up and notice! Among them was Dagmar Veets.

-<>-

Veets, who in later life was revered and hated as a razor studded blimp of a talk show host, whose grating, acrimonious, banter both amused and horrified his audiences, started out in life as the skinny, conniving victim of his parents, the school system and all boys older than him. As a youth he wanted desperately to be left alone. This was natural enough—the only attention he ever got was being beaten, or yelled at—or worse, pointedly ignored. This, in spite of his aching need to be nurtured, and he taught himself a hundred clever ways to handle people, so that they would do just exactly that, leave him alone.

By learning those skills, he was able to build himself an almost faultless system of complementary psychological damage, like a great bulwark of crutches, cut from Kevlar armadillo plates. They were exquisitely intricate in their interlocking and co-supporting structure of fucked up buttresses. Even in the sweaty blackness of his insomniac nights he could barely pry them open far enough to peek in at the angry frightened child crouching within, scheming. He hated that child.

Two of his best and most used armadillo crutches were humor, which he found he could use to round the edges of people into softly curving forms that he could slip smoothly around, and the blatant aggression that he later became so famous for and that he used as a great bludgeon to sweep aside those lesser beings that felt themselves equal to stand against him.

By the time he was thirty he had pushed and shoved and bullied his way into a slot on a small radio station in the Midwest. It was there that he keenly honed his wit and first started beating his great armadillo crutches into the swords, concertina wire,

11

claymore mines and the like, that he would later use, not to defend himself against, but rather to make war on the world. They loved him in Des Moines. He hated them back.

"And do you know America, Mom and Dad and all the kids, I say <u>do you know</u>, DO YOU <u>KNOW</u>? I mean absolutely positively one hundred percent sure is sure, that your teeth are as white as they can be? Well? Are ya?" Dagmar paused for impact.

"Well frankly America, if you're sure or if you're not, if I were you, I'd get down to the store today. I don't mean tomorrow, but <u>today</u>, and pick up a tube or a box or even the <u>new</u> handy liquid squeeze bottle of Ultra Teeth. Yes that's right I said it and you heard it and I mean to tell you, this is the absolutest whitest toothest tooth whitener available on the market, and it is because and only because you are Americans that you have the opportunity to purchase this amazing product for the low low-price of just twenty-nine little dollars a tube! That's right just twenty-nine dollars a tube, at a retailer near you. Remember, everybody wants a big white smile on Reagan's birthday!"

Dagmar shot a finger at his producer, Philus. She brought up his header music and set the news chip on standby. Veets got up and signaled her that he had to pee.

"Okay, five minutes," she said. "Oh Dag, you might like to hear this."

She put a copy of the IRS hold report off the net onto his speaker. He listened, and as he did a cynical smile spread across his face.

"Yes, hold that back for me, I want to jump it a bit, I'll be right back."

He went down the hall to relieve himself. He grabbed a bag of Snakos™ on the way. When he came back Philus had the copy up on his screen waiting for him. The news was just winding up.

"...White House said that the allegations of complicity were completely unfounded. More news in one hour."

He waited for his header to play again before he started.

As the last few bars played she gave him a five count on her fingers. When she pointed at him he started.

"America, hear me!" He paused. "What I am about to tell you may shock some of you and it may well hearten others of you on to action." He paused again.

"This country has been taken over by a gang of thieving, conniving, self-congratulatory brigands that think, quite frankly, that their pooh doesn't stink. This is certainly not news to most of you. No, we have known about their little conspiracy for a long time now. That is not news, but take heart, for this will be to you.

"For years now we have been at the mercy of these scoundrels and their boot licking lackey apologist lawyers in Washington. And all that time, while many of you have been asking, what can we do? What on Earth can we do about these filthy thieves?! These bandits?! These second story men?! Well, the answers have been few and far between. Haven't they?

"Except, of course, if you have been listening to me! I have been saying right here on this very show what we must do. I have called again and again for the people of this great nation to stand up and tell their elected representatives just exactly where they can stick their PACs and their privileges and their European 'fact finding' junkets. If you have been listening right here, then you know!

"Because in all that time I alone have been a voice in the wilderness. I alone have pointed the way forward, and I alone have had the courage, and wisdom to speak when others were silent.

"Well citizens, some of you have, it seems, been listening, for some of you, have finally taken my advice and put an IRS hold on your accounts. Now I'm not just talking here about the piddling little protest hold that a few of you put on each April 15th, though that token resistance has been appreciated, and I might add noticed in the halls of Congress, if only by the janitors.

"NO! And again I say NO!! This is not that. This is something completely different altogether. What I am talking about here is an outright tax revolt of the first order, and it's happening right now!

"A small group of patriots on the Eastern Seaboard started it, communicating, no doubt in secret, to time their attack exactly as our 'Boy-loved president' spoke today.

"By now of course you have heard about his little pony speech, about how that man loving lawyer is going to raise your taxes and mine by a whopping 50% so that he can go buy ponies for his special friend General Kabingga. And, how he and the first boy had such a great time out there last year playing in the tropics on our money, while you and I could barely afford to eat[3], that he wants to buy him another ten years in an office that he was never really elected to in the first place, with the lives of

---

[3]According to Veets' 2049 tax return, his total remuneration was well over 43 million dollars, including salary, stock options and taxable perks.

our American men and women in uniform!

"Well ladies and gentlemen, those civic minded individuals on the East Coast stopped their accounts from being plundered by the lackey dogs of the Intolerable Rip-off Screws, and do you know what? Do you? They weren't alone! No-siree indeed. In fact they were in the company of over 30 million people! And that number is growing even as we speak! That's right we are not done yet! Swindel look out, 'cause here we come, boy!

We'll be back right after this."

Philus brought up his header again.

"Nice, Dag—very nice. Maybe later you could take credit for the Grand Canyon."

"Do you like it?"

"Yes, Dag, it's very beautiful, particularly at sunset."

"Thank you very much, I picked the colors myself."

Philus punched up the ads and got a cup of coffee while they ran. Dag's little rant would cost the station at least $50,000 in fines, but it was worth it, after all, that's what the public tuned in to hear, sedition. They could probably up their rates by ten percent without even hearing about it. Dagmar ate his Snakos™. They were bland and crunchy.

The ads ended and she ran the header, holding up her hand for the five count. Four, three, two, one, and.

"Hello America! —Or what's left of it..."

Click! Harvey killed the radio. He hated that man with a blue passion, almost more than that bitch Dahlia. Hell, almost enough not to listen to him! Almost.

The right Reverend Harvard Washington Jr. was not stupid enough to not listen to the broadcasts of his sworn enemy, just because he couldn't stand the sound of his voice. That would have been amateur, and if there was one thing that he was not, it was an amateur.

Harvey, or rather the Reverend Washington as he preferred to be called, was a thoroughly professional shit disturber. In fact it was one of his strictest rules, he never, under any circumstances, caused a ruckus unless he got paid. He even went so far as to stand by while a distant cousin was beaten senseless by three high school football players with tire irons, because one of them threw a twenty at him!

The reason he turned off the radio was not that the grating squall of Veets' voice annoyed him more than usual. Or, that his boastful credit taking for other people's actions was so deeply offensive to him that he couldn't stand it. No, he just had to park in the lot at Santa Monica City hall, where he was going to a press conference that he had called, to do exactly the same thing.

By the time he was through he figured he would be able to get at least three million dollars in additional grant money for his South Central Up™ project alone.

Harvey was the son of the Right Reverend Darnel Washington, a middleweight evangelist, who had dedicated his life to swindling people who lived south of the Mason Dixon line. Darnel fell into the profession by complete accident one day in 1966, when a medicine show came to town.

The proprietor, a snake charmer and faith healer named John Dukes Dunivan was setting up his raged little tent on the outskirts of Tragervill, Mississippi, when the young Darnel happened by on his way to get some milk for his mother. Dunivan, a thin, lazy man offered Darnel a dollar an hour, to help him put up the ungainly structure. Darnel of course, jumped at the chance to make a week's allowance for each hour worked. He forgot all about the milk.

As they put up the tent they talked, and Dunivan told him about the show and how wonderful it all was, how it helped people with their faith in the Lord and so on. He did this as a type of free advertising, thinking that the boy would go home and tell his family about it and they would attend, perhaps bringing some friends.

Darnel was a bright boy who saw right through Dunivan, but he liked the man no less, for his easy grace and sloth-like friendliness. He went home at the end of the day with seven dollars cash in his hand. His mother, Lisa, was ready to beat the hide off him for neglecting the milk, till he showed her the three dollars he had made. After that she was as sweet as pie, and said she would hold it for him in safekeeping.

That night Lisa said they couldn't afford to go to the medicine show, besides it was all just a lot of smoke and mirrors anyway. She sent him up to bed.

He, of course, snuck out and went to the tattered tent at the edge of town. As he slipped in under the canvas he could hear the show already in progress. Dunivan stood in the center of the tent, with a microphone in one hand and a snake in the other. He held the snake over his head and sang Rock of Ages to it. It was a rock python, a completely non-venomous snake. At the end of the show he hissed at the snake and it bit him on the neck as he quoted from the Bible. Unhurt, he put the snake back in its box. People were amazed!

"Now," he said. "Is there someone here that must be healed?!" He looked around the small crowd.

"Well, I feel a presence here, who is it? Who is the one that must be healed by the word of the Lord?!"

That was all the prompting that Darnel needed, he limped into the center of the tent stumbling on an old man's cane.

"I am blind and lame," he said. "I need the healing word of the Lord. I do!"

Dunivan didn't miss a beat either. He stood Darnel in the center of the tent and drew out the audience for a full half hour before he slapped him in the forehead several times with the Bible, saying, "Demons be gone!!"

Darnel looked around the tent smiling in wonderment at the people assembled there.

"I can see! I can Seee!!!!" He jumped up, clicked his heals, and did a cartwheel.

"Hallelujah Jesus saved me!!!!"

He ran from the tent, yelling, "Mama, Mama, Mama!"

Although everyone there had known him his entire life, they all swore that he was the boy that they had seen hanging around down in Hattiesburg, or maybe Tupelo.

After the show he ducked back under the tent and smiled at Dunivan. He smiled back.

"Ha ha. By God, boy, you're good. Real good! Here." He held out a handful of cash. "You earned this tonight."

Darnel smiled bigger.

"Tomorrow, we'll do 'Sea Of Green' on 'em," said Dunivan.

Darnel died a millionaire at seventy-nine. He sent his only son, Harvey, to an expensive private boarding school in Switzerland, and lavished presents, including a Corvette for his eighteenth birthday on him. He wanted him to go to Harvard or Stanford and would gladly have paid the high fees. But Harvey was as thick as pig shit, a fact he managed to cover up till graduation by paying other, gifted students, to do his homework for him.

Harvey had his whole life's road smoothed for him by his father's hard swindled money. He had never actually worked a day in his life, though he claimed to the contrary. Like most people who are born rich, he just expected life to serve up everything he wanted, when he wanted it. And sadly, it usually did.

He parked his Rolls in the mayor's slot and got out. The Santa Monica police by this time were gun shy enough of him after no less than sixteen lawsuits, that they wouldn't ticket his car if it were parked across the entrance to an emergency room. Harvey liked to think of it as a perk.

He got out of his car and walked toward the courthouse sweating. It was only 20° there at the beach, as it was almost all the time, but still he sweated. He always sweated, even on very cold days, and this was something that was noted by just about everybody that he ever came in contact with.

This was partly due to his being way overweight and partly due to the fact that he was so out of shape that even moving around normally was an extreme exertion for him. Over the years the sweat had become part of his look, and it, along with his legendary orangutan-like walk had become a trademark of trouble on the way, for politicians and news people alike. At one time it had even led one incautious reporter to make reference to such on Television.

He raised hell about that one, along with his shyster lawyer, Mel Smeeton[4], to the tune of just under ten million dollars[5]. He speech-made loud and long about the dignity of the black man, and how this was all a vicious plot by the slave-taking, white, Judeo-Catholic[6], media to discredit him in his struggle to free the oppressed inner-city Negro[7], (he pronounced it inter-city Negra), from the chains of economic servitude, and on and on and on till the network finally caved in and paid them off.

As he approached the building some of the camera people started shooting his arrival, all but the greenest of them were careful to take him from the shoulders up so as not to get in any trouble. While this strategy managed to cover up the fact of his decidedly orangutan-like walk, it necessarily meant that they were up close on his face, and that was no pretty picture either. His relaxed curls dripped greasy sweat down his neck as he made his way up the stairs, panting.

Harvey entered the building and waved away the few

---

[4] Mr. Smeeton was the lawyer that helped GM sue the Boy Scouts for recycling newspapers at the same Flint Michigan land fill that GM used to dump dioxins for twenty years in order to make them pay half for the clean up.

[5] The exact figure has never been released.

[6] Most people taken during the African slave trade of the 16th, 17th and 18th centuries were actually kidnapped by Moorish Muslim slavers, who later sold them to satanic Caucasian fuckheads if they survived the journey to the coast.

[7] A group he cared nothing about whatsoever.

questions thrown at him. He made his lugubrious way through the lobby and finally stood in front of the display of seals for the several governmental agencies that were housed there.

He waited patiently as the camera people got set up, looking around at the small crowd that was there, through his sullen little pig eyes. He had put out the word through the usual channels that he would be speaking today, and he found it strange that the turn out was so small. Usually his network would trump up hordes of angry people for rallies at the drop of a hat. He made a mental note to have a word with Cecil about just exactly why managers got 10%. After all, this tax hold thing had just dropped into their laps out of the sky this morning and if they didn't jump on it right away, then the initiative would get lost. Harvey expected a lot more bang for his buck than this, and if Cecil couldn't deliver, then he'd damn well get someone who could.

"Ladies and gentlemen, please," he said. "If I might have your attention. Thank you."

A few of the reporters continued to chatter in the background.

"Please. Your attention, please."

They shut up and looked at him finally.

"Thank you," he said, giving them his evil eye.

"I have called you here today to make a special announcement—an announcement about our great victory against the hateful racist, white, homosexual regime that has infested this nation's capitol.

"For too long now they have squandered this nation's money on French benefits for themselves and their special friends, for insane technical programs that benefit only the wealthy few and on the elitist military machine. It has always been their aim to tax the inter-city negras into the poor house so that they can live in their mansions on the hill![8]"

He paused and pointed up at the IRS seal that hung just above his head.

"This was the target of our anger! The lap dog of the oppressors! This was the focus of our rage! And just rage it is! For this was the snake in the Garden of Eden! And we killed it! We choked it to death like a chicken!"

He sucked a big yellow goober out of his sinuses and spat it theatrically on to the seal, where it stuck and slowly dripped

[8] Harvey's house was a 71,000 square foot rococo revival palace overlooking Hollywood.

down across the shield. Several of the cameras zoomed in on the mucus for a close up.

"For years now I have been calling for a revolution in this country. A revolution for the <u>people</u>! A revolution <u>of</u> the people! And a revolution, uh, <u>in</u> the people!"

He looked lost for a moment, and then he seemed to remember himself.

"And now it has come to pass. Oh, at long last the people have spoken! And they have spoken my words. And my words are no. No I say. No to the unjustice and intolerance of this country! No to the hateful racist policies of the homosexual president and the carpet bagging Congress! No to the squalid quagmire of law upon law designed to keep Americans of African Lineage[9] on the bottom of the social heap! No I say, and no yet again!"

A gob of mucus dripped onto his shoulder.

"But that is all behind us now! Now we have spoken! Now the worm will turn!"

He reached inside his gaudy pink coat and pulled out a piece of paper.

"I have here a list of policy changes that I will be taking to Washington..."

"Excuse me Mr. Washington," interrupted a reporter. "All reports that we have had seem to show that the Hold was a spontaneous event triggered by the president's pony speech. Are you trying to tell us that you are responsible for the Hold? And if so, just how did you manage to engineer an action of this magnitude, completely unbeknownst to the American public at large?"

Harvey was stumped for a moment. He just stood there staring at the cameras with his jaw hanging slightly slack.

"The pony," he said at last, "is just a symbol of the greater problem, and that problem is the blight of the inter-cities, the racist policies of this administration and the international conspiracy of the Jew bankers to keep my people down! Does that clarify the issue for you?"

"Yes it does. Thank you."

"Now this list..."

Another reporter stepped forward. She was dead serious.

---

[9]Americans of African Lineage was the accepted term for black people that week, in spite of the PC movement being declared unconstitutional some thirty years earlier.

"So, Mr. Washington, referring to your earlier comment about the IRS, what you are saying is that you are responsible for America choking its chicken. Is that correct?"

He looked around paranoidly. This was dead air. The clock was ticking! He had to say something!

"Yes. That is correct," he said pompously at last.

A gob splattered on his head.

"Uh. Now, this list..."

The cue lights on the cameras started to blink off one by one.

The new video wall in the Dearfield mall switched over to the CNN feed out of New York, where Dagmar Veets was about to speak. His crew cut and gray bearded jowls gave him the appearance of a pinhead. He looked out of the enormous screen over his reading glasses for a moment as he went over his notes, then quickly put them away and turned his shoulders toward the camera.

"Hello America!" he said over the ambient Mantovani.

Bill stopped walking and stood there looking up at Veets' huge face. He sneered at it. He had never cared for this asshole Veets to begin with. In fact he usually shut him off as soon as he started into one of his tirades, but now, to be accosted by his rhetoric, fifty feet high while he was trying to remember all things he had to get was just a bit much.

"Hello America!" said Veets waving. "At long last the people of this great nation have stood up on their hind legs and looked their elected representatives square in the eye. The people did not blink. Oh it took a while and there are those who will still not hear them, but the word is out. They have said quite clearly that they want a change, and that they want it now.

And, now that the people have finally spoken, it is time for that change. It is time for a new America. An America of home spun values. An America of Mom at home cooking and cleaning and raising the kids to be model citizens. An America of Dad out earning his family's income in a fulfilling career, free of burdensome taxes put on him by those effeminate pseudo-intellectuals in Washington."

Bill shook his head. This guy was off in dreamland someplace. He looked around at the other people that had stopped to watch. They looked like fish staring up at him with their mouths open.

"It is time for an America in which a man can walk down the street without fearing for his life. Where the under classes will stay where they belong. An America were Congress will be subservient to the will of the people, as it was intended to be, and in which the police will have new and broader powers to protect us. All this and more has been called for by me and now the people have spoken too.

"I have waited a long time for this day. God bless you American patriots that helped me make it possible."

Bill said, "Lying asshole," to no one in particular.

Veets pulled a piece of paper out of his coat and unfolded it.

"I have here a list of constitutional amendments, that I will be taking down to Washington with me to show President Swindel." He gestured dismissal. "Oh, I have no appointment. No, I have no cronies prying open the door for me there, and I have no special friends to smooth my way[10] but I am going nonetheless, as a citizen and as a patriot, to demand a meeting with him. If he can be pried away from Michael for ten minutes that is. I have a crow bar for the purpose," he added as an aside. "These changes, these fundamental changes must, be implemented, immediately, or I will pull the purse strings tighter still." He closed his hand theatrically.

Bill laughed out loud now, at Veets blatant hypocrisy. He had been glued to CNN for the past 24 hours watching to see what would happen next. One thing he was certain about was this—Veets had nothing to do with it.

At first Bill had been quite worried about his hold, thinking himself mostly alone. He figured that the IRS would be calling him sooner or later to find out what was up, and he would give them a piece of his mind before releasing it, as he knew he must eventually do, after all he was dealing with Them here. But, as the hours passed and they didn't call, he was heartened. Watching the running tally that CNN set up, of the Holds being placed all across the nation started to actually make him smile a bit.

He felt cocky. This was going great. America was coming apart at the seams! But now, as he stepped out to buy a few things, to have this overblown jackass come on the air stealing all the credit and trying to capitalize politically on something that he had nothing whatsoever to do with was a hell of a lot more than he was willing to sit by and take!

Feeling surly and belligerent, as he hadn't since he was an adolescent, Bill looked around for something to stand on, so he could get above the crowd and give them his opinion of Veets,

---

[10]Veets was one of the best-connected people in Washington at that time.

loud and clear. There was nothing to speak of on the polished stone floor of the mall to drag over and stand on. The place was modern and efficient, not designed for people to live in. He was getting frustrated. He shook his fist at the screen.

"Shut up you lying bastard!" he shouted.

A few people turned to regard him coolly for a moment but that was about all that it got him. He was too lost and small in the crowd. Bill looked around in mounting frustration, and then he saw the cleaning lift parked at the corner of the screen. That would do. It would have to.

He made his way through the throng muttering excuse-mes as he went. When at last he got over to the lift he could see that it was locked out.

He climbed up into the basket and started kicking the control box, trying to crack it open. At first it held up, taking his blows without any sign of giving way, but after a few fruitless attempts, he got up on the top rail and jumped as he stomped down on it with all his weight. The thing made a loud cracking noise as it came in half, and clattered down onto the floor of the basket.

Bill picked up the half with the wires trailing out of it and examined the inside. He could see that the key was just a switch and he pulled the two wires and shorted them together. The lift hummed to life.

Holding the front of the box in his hand, Bill started experimenting with the controls. There wasn't much to it, really. One button made it go up and down and the other made it move from side to side.

He started climbing and moved out toward the center of the colossal screen. He could hear people calling to him from below. There were whistles and catcalls, and one woman who just kept saying. "Get out of the way you fucking idiot! Get out of the way!"

Bill climbed further till he was in about the center. There he stopped, and turned to address the crowd.

"Citizens hear me!" he tried experimentally.

"Fuck you!"

"Shut up!"

"Get out of the way!"

"No God damn it, I won't shut up!" he said nasally. "I won't get out of the way! And fuck you too! Listen to me! Listen! This man is a complete fraud. He is a lying self-congratulatory dickhead!

"Yeah?" said the woman, "Tell us something we don't know!"

Bill pressed on. "He didn't have anything to do with the

Hold. He is just taking credit for it!"

"So what?" asked the woman. "What did you do?"

Bill paused, holding his hands out beside him for a moment.

"I helped start it!" he said. "I was one of the first, I put my hold on at 12:34, but that's not my point. We all did it, all of us! We all spoke and now this moron wants to steal the credit and shove his fascist agenda down our throats like a shit covered prick! He wants to take us back to the dark ages of the 1950s for Christ's sake. Doesn't that irk you? Doesn't that piss any of you off? The 1950s sucked! What the fuck are you, a bunch of sheep?!! This cocksucker is trying to fuck us! He's trying to steal the revolution! Well I say no fuckin' way, Jose! I say fuck Dagmar Veets! I say fuck Dwayne Swindel! I say fuck 'em all!!!!

"What do you say?!"

The crowd was utterly silent now and the only sounds were Veets yammering away behind him about his agenda for a new America, and far off, Mantovani. Bill couldn't believe how docile they all were. He shook his head and tried again.

"I said it pisses me off! How about you?!"

The lady elbowed her way forward through the crowd till she was nearly under him.

"Well, anyone?" asked Bill, cupping his hand to his ear. "Any of you sheep dare to hold an opinion?!"

"Yeah I do," said the lady, a lot louder than Bill would have guessed she could. "I say FUCK Veets! Fuck Dagmar Veets right in his pink little asshole!!!" She shook a speckled fist up at him.

A cheer went through the crowd, spreading out from the woman. As it spread it grew, louder and louder till it was ringing off the rafters like beautiful, violent, choral music.

"Hey, yeah, fuck 'dat Veets asshole," it started.

"Yeah, Veets, fuck 'em!"

"Yeah fuck Veets!"

They began to chant.

"FUCK VEETS!"

"FUCK VEETS!"

"FUCK VEETS!"

"FUCK VEETS!"

People started clapping time, and stomping a rhythm to the chant. It was a booming deafening wave. It was powerful and beautiful.

Bill felt a tear come to the corner of his eye unbidden. He was all choked up, and in that moment he knew, that no matter what they tried to do to him, no matter what, it was worth it. They couldn't touch him anymore. It was like flying.

Bill chanted along with them for a while till it started to calm down a little. Then he held up his hands for their attention.

"Listen, listen people. I say we clean out our accounts. Get your cash and keep it on you, so they can't take it off you. In a couple of days the Insufferable Robbing Swine will have a court order that will let them impound all the money in the country. You know they will! We have to beat them to the punch, or this will all be for nothing!

"I say we do it! I say we don't let this Veets jackass fuck us anymore than we will let the president! Or Congress! Or the IRS! I say piss on Veets."

With that, Bill yanked down his zipper and pulled out his penis.

"Piss on Veets!" he reiterated, wagging his wrinkled old pecker around like a party favor. "Piss on Veets!!!"

He turned to the screen and started hosing it down with a stream of hot, salty, urine.

The urine spilled down the face of the bright screen. Well, actually it was four screens that divided the image in quadrants. His water got to the seam between the screens and wicked into the crack by capillary action, as liquids will do. This was no big deal really, just simple physics.

Now, back in those days, public address screens of this sort were made to be as bright as the engineers that built them could possibly make them, so they usually used a plasma discharge panel as a backlight for the banks of liquid crystal elements that made up the picture. This was just the sort of scheme that was employed by the engineers at Matsushita when they built the screens that Bill was pissing on. And to power these very bright plasma discharge panels they needed pulsed bursts of one million volts to kick the outermost electrons of hydrogen atoms out of their orbits for a moment to make a plasma, that would then subsequently decay, giving a very bright flash of light. To get these million volt bursts they used banks of thousands of really big capacitors, ranked in rows just behind the screen, which was just plain tough shit for Bill.

The urine gushed down the backside of the panel and across a bank of charged capacitors. The electrons in the capacitors, having found a much easier escape route than had previously been available to them, (salt water is a great conductor), flowed up the urine at nearly the speed of light, and through Bill on their way to ground.

One instant, Bill was a hero pissing on Veets' giant face, with the crowd cheering him on, and the next he was a great arc of lightning passing through his penis and trying to fill the universe with light and pain and the smell of smoking monkey meat. There was a screaming noise. He was gone.

The woman looked off screen for a moment and then straight into the camera.

"The guy up on the lift shook like hell for few seconds and then he screamed like a banshee and the lift started slamming him all over the place! It was really cool!"

The camera held on the anonymous woman for a second more and then cut to the charred and blacked remains of the public address screen with the lift imbedded in its base.

"Yeah Bobby, that's good. What else you got for me?"

Bob Ryan plugged the amateur videophone card into his laptop and played it for his boss. The screen showed an odd angle looking up at an old man on the lift in front of the PA screen, yelling at a crowd of people about politics. After a minute or so of this, he turned around and started peeing on the screen. The old guy peed for a few seconds and then started convulsing, as smoke started billowing out of the screen.

The lift he was on started malfunctioning, and slammed him into the screen several times as it bounced him down toward the camera. Finally it smashed into the base of the screen and the camera was knocked for a loop, coming to rest with an out of focus picture of something lumpy. The camera phone focused, it was a blue tennis shoe.

"That's it so far, Miriam," he said.

"Okay. You say the guy survived?"

"Yes. They said he was taken to County Med. If they don't kill him before I get there, I'll try to get an interview."

"Good," she said. "If he's inco try at least to get something dramatic with a doctor. You have one hour."

"Will do."

Bob hung up, and concentrated on driving, traffic was starting to clog up a bit.

-<>-

Blackness. Whiteness. Pain. The white pain was thick, like supersaturated air. It precipitated and Bill rained down out of it as the morphine drip responded to his shredded nervous system. The fog of pain started to lift a little and disperse as the magic poppy serum washed it away.

25

There was a white room with machines in it making beeping noises. There was a curtain. He stared at the curtain for a long time. Eventually, a woman's face poked through it smiling. She was wearing a paper hat.

"Mr. Crenshaw, you're awake."

Bill thought for a moment, trying to figure out what she meant by that, then it all made sense at once. He was Mr. Crenshaw and awake was correct, he was, awake.

"Yes," he said.

Her face disappeared behind the curtain again.

The sheets felt cool against his legs. He moved his toes. He had toes—that was good. There was something wrong with his pecker though, he couldn't feel it, exactly and there was a dull ache in his balls, like he had been kicked.

He lay there for a while looking at the ceiling. It looked ugly and efficient, with lighting panels at regular intervals between acoustical tiles. It occurred to him that he was in a hospital. Bill thought about this, that he was in a hospital. He tried to remember why he was there. Nothing. Then he tried to think if he remembered ever being anywhere else than in a hospital.

Yes! He distinctly remembered making a Singapore sling for a vulgar German guy in a Panama hat. In his mind the German kept picking up his cigar and then putting it back down, as he said again and again, "No, no, no. I want a lobster and a Singapore sling, and get me za fucking telephone! Immediately!"

It ran like a tape loop over and over in his mind's eye. He forced it into the background, and tried again to remember what had happened. For some reason, that he had absolutely no way to explain, a giant pinhead railed at him there in his mind. It was very confusing.

His musing was interrupted by a man, who stepped in through the curtain, smiling. Bill didn't recognize him. He continued to smile and walked a few steps closer.

"Hello," he said.

"Hello. What's so funny?"

"I am Bob Ryan, with Continental Broadcasting. My I ask you a few questions, please?"

"Well, that depends. Can I ask you a few?"

Bob smiled more genuinely.

"Sure, go ahead. You mind if I set up a camera?"

He didn't wait for an answer, but started folding legs out of a small black box that he had with him. Bill watched him for a moment, and then asked earnestly, "Who is the German guy that wants a lobster and a telephone?"

Bob looked at him for a moment.

"I don't know."

"I keep getting this picture in my head of a German yelling about a lobster and a phone, and I'm making him a drink, a Singapore sling, as fast as I can."

Bob shrugged and regarded a piece of paper that he had with him.

"It says here that you are a retired bar tender. Maybe you knew this guy once. Can you remember anything else?"

Bill considered for a moment.

"Yeah, I get a picture of a giant guy. A pinhead. And—— Dagmar Veets? Something. He's yelling at me too, but I can't understand him. What happened? Why am I here?"

Bob pressed a button on the side of the camera as he looked at the back of it.

"You are Bill Crenshaw, a retired bar tender. You were at the Dearfield mall today and Dagmar Veets..."

"Yeah Dearfield, who is this Dagmar Veets character anyway?"

"A conservative radio talk show host. Do you know what radio is?"

"Yes, a, a machine that talks to you, and plays music."

"That's right. Anyway, Veets was making a broadcast, in which he took credit for the Hold..."

"Hold?"

"Yes, there is a tax revolt going on at the moment. And anyway, he read off a list of demands that he is taking to Washington, to give to the president."

"Swindel!"

"Yes, that's right, President Swindel. Apparently, you took extreme exception to Veets' speech and took it upon yourself, according to over three hundred witnesses, to get in a cleaning lift in front of the video wall there and make, uh, well, a little speech of your own. They say you were quite inspiring. At the end of your speech, you turned around and pissed on the screen. And, well, you were electrocuted when your urine leaked down onto some electronics. A million volts so they tell me.

"Would you like to make a statement for the viewing audience at this time?"

"I did that? Wow that's pretty spectacular!"

Bob smiled broadly.

"That's what we thought. Would you like to see an amateur

27

video of yourself?"

Bill nodded. "Oh yes please, that would be great."

Seeing the card brought back a lot. He remembered his anger, and why he felt it. He remembered the lightning bolt that felt like a hammer blow. He even remembered the lady down in the crowd that had jeered him.

Bob double-checked his shot and then Bill began.

"You know, I've never counted much in people that get up to speech making," he said. "I'm not the type to take up with politics myself, in fact I sold my vote most of the time, not caring a thing for what might come of it. But not anymore. Those days are gone now, and I hope that they never come back.

"Yesterday, when I heard the president give that cynical, betraying, pony speech, about how we had to keep the world safe by pouring our money over people's problems like chocolate syrup on cheap ice cream, I decided.

"I thought to myself, you know Bill, you're pretty old now and there's not a hell of a lot left that they can do to you, so why not stick your neck out for a change. I thought, why not make a stand? That's what it's all about isn't it, making a stand for something? So I put a hold on my accounts, so that the IRS couldn't steal my hard earned money like it was so much chewing gum.

"I have to say that no one was more surprised than me when I turned on the news and found out that other Americans all across this great nation of ours were doing the same thing! Not because they were told to by some loud-mouthed jackass in a blue suit, pulling their strings like a bunch of puppets, but just because they felt the same way I did. They've had enough!

"All the time you hear people say, when is it going to stop, when will that bunch of carpetbaggers in DC wise up and listen to the people that earn every God damned dime that they ever spend just like it was water. Well, we all gave them an answer for once, and the answer was <u>right fucking now</u>!

"The bucks stop here! We are not going to pay for your dirty little wars anymore!"

Bill readjusted himself in his pillows, and set his jaw scowling a little.

"That's why I did it," he said. "That's why I got all fired up in the Dearfield mall. I saw that hypocritical son of a bitch Dagmar Veets stealing credit for, and making political hay from, something that he had absolutely nothing whatsoever to do with! That man is a complete fraud! Don't listen to him!

28

"So I got up on that lift, so I could be heard by the people over his idiot ramblings, and I spoke to them. And all the time I was trying to talk, he wouldn't shut up. He just kept yammering about his agenda. What he was going to do with the country, once he was in power! Bla. Bla. Bla. And you know what? It pissed me off! It got me really angry that this country has come to the point that dorks like him get listened to, and the average guy is completely ignored, so I relieved myself on his face.

"I guess you could say, that I thought he was so full of shit that I mistook him for a toilet!"

That was it. That was Bill Crenshaw's prime moment.

-<>-

"You know, I find it interesting what people are always saying in your country, about Africa—that we are somehow guilty of a unique kind of corruption for handing out millions to our cronies and lieutenants. Tell me, have you ever been to Wall Street? How about Washington?"

Joshua Kabingga to Bob Ryan, NBC News.

-<>-

Matsune Suzuki popped the seal on the nondescript jar and fished out one of the lumpy tan morsels inside. He looked at it and made this kanji—pleasant surface—on his note pad.

He popped it in his mouth, and chewed. It was crunchy, and tasted like monkey shit. He made a note of this too and tried another one, this time with a dash of shrimp flavor.

His pet mouse, Hirohito[11] looked up at him from his cage, twitching his nose. Mat gave him a bit of the shrimp morsel. He ate it, and glowed his thanks with his ears.[12]

They tried chicken next.

---

[11] My mouse father.
[12] His ears glowed, because 50 generations before he was born, one of his ancestors was part of a cancer study conducted at Stanford University in 1996, in which mouse and fire fly genes were spliced together.

What to do?

"...That snoodling subversive will never, so help me God, be president of these United States of America as long as I have anything to do about it! In fact as far as I'm concerned the felching faggot aught to stay the hell out of politics all together."

Dagmar Veets, June 13th, 2047

-<>-

Dwayne Swindel was the only son of a divorced schoolteacher from Compton California, who drank herself to death at the ripe old age of forty-eight. Ann Swindel graduated valedictorian from Compton High School. Admittedly, owing to the girl who would otherwise have had that honor, being killed by a crack head gangster named 'Snoop' Johnson, because she didn't feel like giving him a blowjob at a party, but still, she was quite bright.

She had tried very hard to be a writer, and failed. Words came easily enough to her. She wrote poetry and short stories and had produced over a dozen novels in her short, frustrated life. Some of them were very interesting. Most were well written, and funny, or sad or whatever else they were supposed to be, and all quite original, but she could not get a single publisher to even read her work. The problem was, she wasn't already famous for something else and her stories were <u>too</u> original. They weren't 'the next' anything. They didn't fit the market. They were literature, what <u>was</u> she thinking?

That is why, by the way, the world is the way it is, people. Too bad.

So one day, she thought that she would have a drink. She drank bourbon that day, and every other day too as it turned out. She liked it a lot—it enfolded her in a warm numb blanket. She was lonely, and though the bourbon couldn't actually keep her company—it couldn't laugh at her jokes or spoon with her at night—it could help her hold her loneliness at arms length.

She always tried to instill her anger in Dwayne, the fear of failure that she had, and a sense of the bitterness that she felt toward "The fucking world." She would say little things to program him to fail, like, "You can't fight City Hall kid." She said that to him all the time, till he hated even the rests between the syllables.

She would also do this—she would get loaded on her

bourbon, and then corner him in obscure logical arguments, that went around and around in complex loops, with ultimately no right answer to be made. It was a sort of sport with her.

She would say things like, "You know, Dwayne——your mother loves you."

"I love you too, Ann." He called her Ann.

"Good," she would say blearily, "because——I've done a lot for you." It was a flat statement.

"Haven't I?"

"Yes, Ann. Yes you have."

"That's why you love me——isn't it. ————Because of, all the things I've <u>done</u> for you."

"——Yes, Ann, I'm very grateful."

"You're grateful." Another flat statement.

"Yes, Ann, very grateful."

"Yes, Ann, very grateful," she would mimic. "So really, it's just gratitude, isn't it?——Because I'm <u>useful</u> to you. Just sort of a domestic convenience!"

"No, Ann, not like that. Not a convenience."

She would stare angrily, weaving slightly.

"Oh, so now I'm inconvenient to you! Is that it?!"

"No, Ann. No."

"No?! NO?!! Do you know how tired I am of being told no!!! I'm your Mother, you ungrateful little bastard! I carried you inside me for almost a year, nurturing you, making you from my own body. And now, you tell me no!!! NO!!?? You're just like all the rest of them!

"I worked my fingers to the bone for thirty-nine years for you and what's my reward? Insolence!"

"I'm only thirteen."

When at last he could make no answer at all and sat in stone still silence with her watching him, wishing, praying for her to disexist, she would point her weaving finger at him and shout like a very unfunny comic book hag, "What's the matter, nothing to say? You haven't even got the balls to argue with me! You're just like your father, you son of a bitch!"

!

On her deathbed she looked up at him through her yellow-whited eyes and said, "Dwayne, I love you."

He said nothing. What was there <u>to</u> say? He farted, turned, and walked away.

Growing up like this, Dwayne learned at a very young age, the finer points of argument. He learned to twist the words of

31

others, into Gordian knots to strangle them with, as he looked into their beseeching eyes. He learned that most people don't really want to fight, and so you could use that as a lever to pry them away from their point and bludgeon them to death with it as they wandered lost and alone in the wilderness of ideas. And he found, that the easiest thing in the world was to flatter someone into thinking they had the upper hand, and then cut their lags out from under them as they preened.

These lessons and a thousand like them had gone to make him. And by the time he entered college, he was an unbeatable debater, and a very scary date. He was a natural lawyer.

Law school would give him the ammunition, but he had inherited from his mother, the weapons with which to make total war on the world, and probably, to win.

After law school he worked for one of the 'best' law firms in San Francisco.

Yakamoto, Snell and McCraken were willing to pay him more money than he could spend, think of that, to do what he did best and loved most, which was to burn people down. He loved it, especially the David and Goliath cases that pitted an individual against a corporate colossus. He could win those regardless of the merit of the person's case. Not because the corporation had vast funds with which to attack them, though this they surely did, but because he was a secret liberal, and always had been. He could get inside the head of his openly liberal minded opponent, and knock the feathers out of their arguments with ease.

He liked the life style there in the fog bound jewel of the West Coast. There was an easy grace to the city, an elegance that was out of proportion to its compactness—and lots of attractive men.

He never let on to anyone, even in college, that he held other than the most conservative views and even took part in some minor 'counter cleansings', across the bay in Richmond. He was able to make considerable political hay out of this strategy later in life, garnering a large chunk of the un-aligned conservative vote in the Midwest and South during the '48 elections, while all the time talking the crypto-liberal line out of the other side of his face in the big coastal cities.

It was just enough to win, and at the age of 46, he found himself in the unlikely position of being the 55th president of the United States of America.

His legendary homosexuality was actually a misnomer. Except for a few abortive liaisons just after college, including the occasional Cleveland steamer[13], he had not made love to another human being, much less a man, for twenty-five years.

Michael Farber, the man that all the world called his lover, and he had never had sex at all, technically. That is, they had never touched each other sexually. What they were, to be most precise, were co-auto-homo-erotics. They were both attracted to men, and especially to each other, but they both had boxcars full of baggage about touching people. So instead, they would kneel together naked on their bed, with corny violin music playing on the stereo, and masturbate for each other, till they shot their goo onto satin pillows.

The subtle distinction was, needless to say, lost on the vast majority of the American public. He was, nonetheless, elected fair and square in '48.

Of course, his opponent was none other than the infamous Norbert Hosakowa, the butcher of Shaker Heights[14]. Next to him Dwayne was a shoe in.

His administration had been a controversial one, marked by Alpha One, by far the most expensive and hotly contested space program in history, the support of General Joshua Kabingga, the vicious Hutu separatist in East Africa and the institution of a broad expansion of the welfare state among other disputed decisions.

He didn't really care very much if people hated him for his policies. If some people detested him then he took it as a sign that he was doing something very right indeed. But it really fried him when people actually took action to stop him in the implementation of his vision of what America could become. Just because he hated it, didn't mean he could do anything about it.

80% of moneys held by the US population were, by now, beyond his reach. He could always print more or declare a national emergency, but the Secret Service's assessment was that he would probably be assassinated within 48 hours of such action.

---

[13] When one person shits on another person's saran-wrapped face it is called a Cleveland steamer. People really do this stuff.
[14] Hosakowa's televised executions of prisoners during 'the siege of Shaker' made him tremendously popular with a small minority of the electorate but painted his name in blood in the minds of most ordinary people. If it had not been for the general amnesty at the end of the war he would surely have died before a firing squad.

Anyway, he had a plan to turn the thing around and make a huge advantage out of it for himself and his vision.

The cameras were waiting just through the door to the next room.

He was a tall man, broad in the shoulders, with dark, wavy hair that was graying at the temples. He looked like a president.

Michael straightened his tie for him, and gave him a smile.

"Go get 'em, Tiger."

Dwayne smiled and winked.

"Here I go."

He turned and walked into the pressroom with an easy confident stride.

Harmony, his press secretary, was at the podium waiting for him. She spoke to the Press Corps.

"Ladies and gentlemen, the president of the United States, Dwayne Swindel."

She stepped aside presenting him to polite applause.

He stepped up to the lectern and fixed the crowd with a sincere look. The cameras were on him.

"Thank you very much for coming today. It is with mixed feelings that I call you here." He paused for emphasis. "I had hoped a few days ago, to be delivering a speech outlining our plans for the continued, and expanding support of General Kabingga, in his brave struggle for freedom, against the tyrant McDermott, but that, alas, is not to be.

It is, it seems, that sort of struggle that will fall instead to future generations, if there are any such, for the people have spoken, loud and clear, and I have certainly heard them.

"The time has come, in the course of human events, that the American people are no longer willing to pay for democracy to flower in the far off fields of foreign lands——though those fields are surely our source and solace. They have said no, that they do not care for the fate of others. That they basically don't give a rat's what happens. Instead, they will keep their hard earned money for themselves. This is their total right and I acknowledge that.

"They have said enough. And so enough it is. Now our adventures abroad will end, and we will concentrate on ourselves. We will ignore the plights of other, like-minded peoples, and they will either flourish or die according to their own might. This is not how I would make policy, but the people have spoken.

"So now we will build this country into an even greater nation with our money. We will at last see to it that each child has not only a right to an education, but also a hot meal three times a day, and transportation to and from school. We will feed them all, and their parents too, whether or not they can afford to pay. We will build the greatest public transportation system in the world, and it will be free to ride for all the citizens of this great nation. Tourists too," he added.

"Everyone will have a great library right around the corner from their house, maybe some of us will even use 'em. And great art museums will sprout up out of the ground like mushrooms, even in modest communities[15], and we will fill those museums with the great art of the world, both ancient and brand new, for we will pay any artist in this country to create art for the public.[16]

"The streets will now be safe, with a brave policeman on every corner protecting our citizens from the ravages of crime, and people will once again be able to walk the streets at night safe in the knowledge that they are secure because we will put a million new policemen on the streets of America[17]. All this and more will come to us, this I promise.

"And, it won't cost the American taxpayer a single dime, in fact there will be a slight drop in the present tax rate."

He paused for a moment looking around the room at the looks of stunned silence on the faces of the Washington Press Corps, probably the most jaded people on the face of the Earth.

"How, you ask, are we ever going to be able to do this? How will this miracle be worked? Will the money fall from the sky?"

He paused for a moment.

"No.

"Since the American people, in their infinite wisdom have decided that it is no longer necessary to pay the price for freedom of constant vigilance. Since the rest of the world can get along by itself for a while, then we don't need the enormous defense establishment that has existed in this country since the middle of the last century. And so, I have decided that that is where we will get the vast capital needed for this social revolution of ours, from the military budget.

"Effective January 1st. 2051, the Pentagon will cease to exist as a Government entity. This morning I signed Executive Order

---

[15] Ghettos.

[16] Welfare for undeserving art bums to enflame the reactionary right.

[17] Fascist goon squads to suppress the population to infuriate the reactionary left.

4129, divesting the United States of America of all its armed services, save the Coast Guard and a small militia, to be established out of the 1st Infantry Division at Fort Riley, Kansas. All our present acquisitions have been canceled by this order and some 95% of our war making materiel will be moth balled at a few sites scattered across the various states. The entire military budget for fiscal year 2051, minus 3% will be allocated to these new programs starting in April of next year."

He looked around at them. They swallowed and blinked.

"Now, I put it to Congress," he said. "The United States of America has, for the last hundred years or so, made policy more or less, according to the rule of might. Now it's a new age. The Congress of the United States will be required to set new policies concerning a thousand things, and each and every law maker will have to ask themselves this question—'what diplomatic course can we follow in order to accomplish my end?' How can I convince people, who owe me nothing and who are not afraid of me, to cooperate with me?

"If Congress is up to the job, if they can use their intellects where lesser people would use the force of arms, then there will truly dawn a new age in the world, an age in which there is no room for war, a world in which war is an obsolete concept relegated to the history books along with the theory of a flat Earth and the PC movement, and Institutional Communism.

"I put it to Congress, I have put down our weapons—you put an end to war.

"The people are tired of it, and they won't pay for our adventures anymore, so let us, quietly and in an orderly manner, like adults, graduate from kindergarten into the first grade. If the American people will support me on this, and release the hold, then I will do their will."

He looked into the cameras in openness so complete that only Michael and Harmony could read it for anything else.

"Thank you for your time today."

The Press Corp's questions erupted like a crashing wave.

He turned and walked away from the podium. Harmony looked like a cornered rabbit. As he approached the door Michael opened it for him, smirking slightly. When the door was safely closed behind him Dwayne smiled too. Even Spandale would have to bail over this one.

-<>-

The
Burundi
Directorate for Central Planning

Announces a general bid for survey work in the Umbutu River Basin. Bidders will have Mine, Survey, Geological, or related experience, fluency in English, and capital resources of at least 271 Bn. BFr (1 Mil. US$) The term of the initial contract is one year, with an option to renew for an additional five years at the Directorate's discretion. The closing date for all bids will be April 1, 2022. All inquiries should be sent to The Economist c/o Snellville Mining and Minerals, Umbutu River Project,.

The Economist Aug. 1 2021

-<>-

"What's crunchy fun for everyone?"
"Hey, Snakos!"
"What tastes tasty good like a snack food should?"
"That's right, Snakos!"
"And what do picky Moms pick to give their kids a nifty kick?"
"You guessed it, Snakos!"
"They're tasty and round, so pass 'em around!"
"They're ab-Snako-lutely delicious!!!"
"Get some Snakos today!!! They're tasty crunchy good!"
"Just for Columbus day, and every day."

-<>-

"...reported today that thousands of villagers have fled into the bush trying to avoid the advancing soldiers..."

-<>-

"Treason pure and simple," said Veets. That's what it is! Betrayal absolute, at the hands of that man loving, tax squandering nincompoop that squeaked into office with the help of his blood sucking, which is a lot better than what he's sucking, commun-nazi, sponsors in San Francisco and Greenwich Village! This is an outrage! He will not, I repeat not get away with it, that I guarantee you!

"To think that this lawyer has the unmitigated cojones to try

37

and hijack the tax revolt for his own ends and strip this great nation of its magnificent arsenal, so he and his cronies can waste billions mollycoddling the slack-asses, ne'r-do-wells and other human garbage that they so adore, while we sit like ducks in a barrel with our pants down around our ankles, is flabbergasting! It was against him and his asinine policies that the whole thing was directed in the first place! The people will rise up against you Swindel, they will grab you by the throat and ring you like a rag doll. They won't be swindled by you, Swindel! They won't stand for it!

"Can you hear me Swindel? Are you listening to me?

"I'll tell you one thing boy, you and your <u>boy</u> both. Mr. and Mrs. Normal American with their 1.6 children and their modest million dollar home in the suburbs that you find too boring to consider are. They can hear me loud and clear, and they are not just going to sit by and take it from you the way Michael does.

"Are you Mr. and Mrs. America?"

Philus ran a wild track of a crowd of hoodlums screaming NO!

"Well, are you?"

She ran the track again, but much louder.

"That's right. That's absolutely righty right as right can be!"

"Now that they have spoken, now that they have shouted down your throat, the American people have gotten quite a taste for it. They aren't just going to sit by anymore and let you do it to them. No-siree Bob, I mean to tell you. No ma'am, no how, no way, not at all!

"We are not going to cower with our heads in the sand along with you and your special friends in Washington. We are not going to let you take away our guns so that the world of evil men can dictate terms to us as to just exactly how and when we will surrender to them.

"You may wish to go out into the world as a willing victim. That would be right up your <u>alley</u>, wouldn't it? But we certainly are not going to follow you down <u>that</u> garden path.

"Wake up Mr. President! Socialism died sixty years ago, and you are not going to use <u>our</u> money to bring it back from its well deserved grave for <u>your</u> nefarious purposes. The dark ages have passed, Swindel. There is a new light in the land, and its name is NO WAY, JOSE! Its name is Bill Crenshaw, and we will be right back after this word from our sponsor with Mr. Crenshaw <u>him</u>self, and you can hear from him <u>your</u>self!"

Philus ran his header and opened her mic into the booth.

"He's here, Dag. You want to have him wait outside till you announce him?"

"No, no. Send him in! I'd like to meet the man."

"You bet."

After a few moments she buzzed him in through the door.

Bill made his way a bit gingerly to his seat. His posture was a little bent over and he kept his legs apart as he walked making him look geriatric. As he sat down he put out his hand across the console.

"Hi, Bill Crenshaw."

Veets shook his hand neutrally. "Dagmar Veets, at your service."

Veets was a large man and Bill's hand felt small in his, something Veets noticed too.

"I'm very pleased to meet you, Mr. Crenshaw."

Bill smiled, but said nothing. The silence dragged on, and then Veets held out a plastic packet.

"Snakos?" he asked.

"Thanks, don't mind if I do," said Bill.

He took the packet.

Dagmar's monitor played his header again, after the commercials, and Philus held her hand up giving him a count, three, two, one.

"Hello America, and welcome back to the show, or welcome to it, if you just tuned in, you're always welcome here on the Dagmar Veets show. I'm Dagmar Veets, and today we are talking with a great American patriot, a man who puts his, well, let's just say his money where his mouth is for the moment. Ladies and gentlemen please welcome Mr. Bill Crenshaw to the show."

Philus played some caned applause that she ramped down after a moment.

"Hello, Bill, and welcome to the show."

"Hello, Mr. Veets, I'm happy to be here."

"Please, call me Dag. That's what most of America calls me, Bill, Dag, you might as well too," said Veets, trying to put his guest at ease for his own ends.

"Tell me, Bill, you were one of the first thousand people or so to put an IRS hold on your accounts. Isn't that so?"

"Yes that's so, Dag, so they tell me."

"Well—I'd like to thank you, Bill, and all of the other thousands and thousands, heck millions of Americans like yourself, that took the chance and told the Government that enough was enough, that you weren't going to pay for their little

39

game anymore. It's because of good people like yourself that this country is still solvent and still a beacon of freedom for the whole world to look up to. Well hey! Thanks!

"You're welcome, Dag. I'm glad you like it.

"On behalf of myself and all those other Americans that started the Hold, I'd just like to say, that you had absolutely nothing to do with it. We acted spontaneously, just doing what felt right to us at the moment, it was just that we all felt the same way at the same time, and not as you claimed, because you said so."

"Yes! Did you hear that out there, Swindel? They all felt the same way at the same time, and just did what they <u>knew</u> was right! You can't pull the wool over our eyes anymore!

"Tell me, Bill, has the IRS called you up to ask you for an explanation as to your actions?"

"Well, you know, Dag, that's what I can't really figure out. You would think that they would just go down the list of who put on a hold, and when, and shake 'em down for their money like always. They can't be so inefficient as to have just not gotten around to me yet, so I guess that they are just so shell-shocked from the thing that they don't know what to do! I haven't heard hide nor hair of them, and so far as I've heard, neither has anyone else!"

Veets winked at him.

"That's great! Keep it up, America! Show them that the president and his IRS lap dogs can't push you around! Let them know..."

"Tell me, Dag," interrupted Bill. "Have you joined the hold?"

"I'm with you 100%, Bill, because this country has had enough, and I can only support your actions."

"So then, you have put a hold on your accounts?"

"...Absolutely.[18]

"Tell me, Bill. What went through your mind, exactly, when you heard that pony speech of the Swindeler. Did it anger you? I mean did it really get under your skin like a chigger and irritate you?"

Bill succumbed a bit to Dagmar's folksiness, lapsing into the easy Middle American accent that was never a part of either of their childhoods.

"You know, Dag," he said. "I have never been one to go

---

[18] Veets' accounts never actually had a hold placed upon them, as he feared reprisals from Internal Revenue more than anyone.

burning the barn down every time I hear tell of some damn fool shooting his mouth off up in Washington. After all that's what we send folks like that up there to do, shoot off their mouths someplace where they're out of earshot, but that speech by the president, it was something else.

"I mean, I sat there in my living room, I'm retired now, or else I would have been at work, of course, and I watched that bastard's smarmy mug lie to me about war and peace and ponies. Ponies for Christ's sake! He sat there and said that he and Michael had seen that General Kabingga's kids loved ponies, like he guessed every kid did, and so we had to go and fight for freedom in Africa!

"Africa! Ponies! Most kids in this country nowadays have never even seen a pony! They don't love them. They don't know what one is!

"How would he know what kids love or hate or don't give a shit about?! He's a turd burglar! He's never had kids, and it looks damned unlikely that he ever will.

"So what if he and his boyfriend went to visit with this Zulu fascist and his kids had ponies?! Does that mean that you and I have to pay for that—that that is worth defending with American money and American lives? I don't think so!"

"You're not alone, Bill, go on please."

"I said to myself, look Bill, you're pretty old now and what the hell are they going to do to you anyway? Take away your birthday? So I just went and did it. I phoned up the bank and told them to hold my accounts back from the IRS. At least we still have that right in this country. At least they haven't managed to take that away from us yet. Our money is our money.

"And you know what? Everybody else did the same thing. They felt the same way, and they did the same thing, and the president of the United States of America got caught with his pants down!

"I just felt surly when I put on the hold, but after that, when I heard about everybody else too, I felt, well, something you don't often get to feel. I felt triumphant, like a Caesar coming back into Rome after making war! It was glorious!"

Philus was lightning fast with her console, and brought up a triumphal blare of trumpets, just at the end Bill's statement.

"Hail Crenshaw!" said Veets.

"Did you hear that, Mr. and Mrs. America? Did you hear that, Swindel? He said it was glorious! Glor-ee-us!

"So, Bill, now that you have helped start the revolution,

what's next for you? Maybe a stint on the rubber chicken circuit? Tell us, Bill," he said conspiratorially. "Have you had any offers yet?"

Bill smiled self-consciously.

"Well, Dag, first I think I'll just spend a little time recuperating before I go shooting my mouth off in public again. After all you have to think of your health first you know, especially as you get up there in years like I am. As for offers, well I had a few phone calls, and I might consider them but only after I am sure I'm okay."

"Yes, Bill, it seems you had a little mishap the other day. It seems like you might have shot off a little more than just your mouth. Care to share it with our listening audience?"

"You sure you want me to tell about that on your show, Dag?"

"Bill, we have no secrets here. This show is an open book, please proceed, you have earned..."

"Well, okay, Dag, if you insist.

"The other day, the day after the pony speech in fact, I had to go to the Deerfield mall to pick up a few things, and while I was there, I had occasion to walk through the main gallery. I don't know if you are familiar with the Dearfield mall, but anyway, in the main gallery there is a huge video display to entertain people and also to give important information to the public. The kind of thing you see most places nowadays.

"Well, as I happened past on my way to the pharmacy, I saw you, Dag, up there, on the screen, sixty feet tall. You were making a speech about how the president was going to have to listen to the people for a change, how things were getting turned around."

"Amen brother!"

"Yeah well, that's the thing, Dag. There you were one minute, saying all this great stuff, and the next you started talking about wanting to keep women in their place and having America slip back to the dark ages of the 1950s! A time, just by the way, according to my Dad, Bill senior, that was not nearly all it was cracked up to be. He said that the '50s were a Cadillac full of manure!"

"Now hold on a minute there, Bill, I never..."

"No, Dag, you hold on! You asked me and now I'm telling you. You can refute whatever you like when I am done. Okay?"

Veets smiled a patronizing little smile.

"Okay fine, Bill, after all this is a free forum."

"Great, Dag, thanks.

"Okay so there you were gassing on about good old American values and all that bullshit, and then you started taking credit for the whole thing! You started saying that you had been behind the Hold and that you were going to Washington to read a list of demands to the president of the United States of America! As if you could dictate terms to your sponsors much less make demands of the president! He may be an asshole, you might hate him like an ingrown pubic hair, but he is still the president.

"The American people did elect him, Dag. Who elected you? And just by the way, Dag, did you get to see the president without an appointment, like you were the Pope or something? I never found out because I was knocked out cold on morphine."

"No, he would not see me, an honest tax paying citizen![19]"

"Well, there you go, that's Washington for you. So anyway, there I was watching you speak up there, about how the American people had spoken, and how you were going to tell the president what's what, and, well I just plain got mad as hell. I thought that you had no right to try to hijack the 'revolution', if you will, for your own political ends, regardless of how well intended they may be. And so I went up on a maintenance lift and made a little speech of my own.

"I got up there and I started talking. And after a while I got up a pretty good head of steam. You know how it is, Dag. And I started calling you a charlatan and a faker, and saying that it made me angry. In fact I got a bit carried away with myself and said that it pissed me off! I guess I was swept up in the moment. Then I turned around and urinated on your giant face, to show my disdain."

Dagmar started laughing at this.

"So tell me, Bill, what happened then?"

"Well, Dag, it's funny you should ask that particular question. It seems that my pee leaked down behind the screen and trickled across a high voltage circuit, sending a million volts up my pecker!"

"OH NO!" laughed Veets. "How did that feel?"

"Beats me, Dag. All I know is that I woke up in the hospital with a snake eye the size of my index finger!"

"Man!" said Dagmar. "That's got to hurt!"

---

[19] Veets' 2047 tax return had to be 'amended' no less than three times due to subsequent 'disclosures'. He paid a total of $2,256,954.14 in fines that year, which equals 1.346 times his actual tax burden.

"I wouldn't know, Dag."

"We'll be right back after this and take some phone calls, also I'll have a rebuttal, and much, much more, please join us. Won't you?"

Philus brought up the header, giving them a big okay sign.

Bill ate his Snakos™ during the break. They were tasty crunchy good.

-<>-

Alpha 1 was a quarter mile long aluminum cylinder 100 meters across with a 150-meter thick asteroid glued to its butt. It rotated at 4.2 rpm giving it a 1 G acceleration on the inside skin. It contained 1000 people and 384, 5-mega-ton, F-F-F type H-bombs as a propellant. There was a bright star in front of it and a brighter one behind, and every month the two stars traded intensity a little bit. Pretty exciting stuff, eh!

-<>-

His head was square to begin with, and it sat like a pale block on top of his squat, slightly wrinkled neck. The effect was all the more enhanced by his regulation crew cut and square, black framed glasses that he had sported for over four decades, though they were quite unnecessary even in that day and age. His shoulders too were square, bolstered by the epaulets, and always held at right angles to his path of travel, except on those, now rare occasion when he had to snap his head to the right or left and salute a superior officer, (there was only one), at parade. And, if you had seen him from behind, in the shower at the Officers Club pool for instance, you would not have been able not to notice that even his ass was square, in an organic, hairy sort of way.

General Harlan Baisch stood at the window filling its rectangle with his square, gazing out at Washington.

He was a soldier's general, rising through the ranks by hard work, personal bravery and an uncanny ability to blunder upon the right solution, while all the scheming tacticians were keeping their heads down and quoting theory to each other.

Baisch first distinguished himself as a young lieutenant during the battle of Dearborn in 2032. His unit was pinned down in a junkyard that was squeezed between an apartment building and the bus depot. His men were being picked off in ones and twos by the Black Cells of Islam Black Africa[20], who had taken the apartment building by stealth and murder the night before in order to lay this ambush on the one side, and a gang of 'free

---

[20] Formerly, the FTWB.

44

lancers' led by none other than the, now legendary, Shit Bone Johnson, himself on the other. Seeing that their position was deteriorating rapidly as the sun started to set behind a warehouse, and knowing that the choppers didn't dare fly at night, he decided that either they got themselves out or they would wind up as 'listed'.

He sent his best 'man', a twenty-year old sergeant by the name of Tanya Mortenson out into the street, with a bazooka flair and a .50. Mortenson made it, under cover of their fire, to a Buick that was up on its side and waited for the signal. At the same time Baisch and the rest of his men were preparing to set a ring of charges around the base of the apartment building with the last of their Cordtex® [21].

Baisch gave the first signal, by hitting redial on his cell phone, and Mortenson let fly with the flair, right into the center cupola of the adjacent bus depot. There was an extremely bright light there for about three minutes. It wasn't a hell of a lot, but it was just enough.

As the last of the charges was set against the supporting abutments of the apartment block, he hit redial again and they started running. Mortenson opened up with the .50, fanning it across the face and side of the apartments. She only had about two hundred rounds, and she laid it down in short bursts, nursing her meager supplies.

Baisch and the others spilled out of the junkyard that lay between the buildings and into the street, taking what cover they could find behind cars and mail boxes and so on. Mortenson's ammo ran dry and she yelled as loud as she could, "NOW!!!!" Baisch flicked the detonator switch as he dove behind the carcass of a dumpster.

The cutters did their deadly work like a giant samurai sword, chopping the legs out from under the apartment block. There was a muffled bang and the ten-story tower fell down like a concrete wave into its rising dust cloud. It washed across the narrow junkyard, screaming, and took out the bus depot on the other side. Everyone that ran out of that junkyard made it. Baisch's unit was credited with over 460 confirmed kills that day, a record that stood for the rest of the war.

It was this sort of quick thinking under fire, not fancy tricks that his superiors recognized as the mark of a born leader, they were as rare then as they are now and by war's end he made

---

[21] Cordtex is a registered trademark of Orica World Group.

captain.

Ten years later, in Manchuria as a major, he had devised simple effective plans that spared his men, both Russian and American as much as possible, and at the same time played absolute hell with the ten million man Chinese Army. General Shevlenko had personally recommended him for promotion after the Shan Shang valley campaign. He lost only twenty men all winter, while holding almost half a million infantry pinned down in the valley below. They were leaderless, and very intimidated by his holding the high ground, and so they froze to death by the tens of thousands, without him barely having to fire a shot. And after they had eaten all the corpses they could thaw enough to chew, they killed each other for fresh meat, by order of descending rank. He was a hero for having caused unimaginable human tragedy among the enemy.

Baisch turned around and paced the floor, away from the window—he was tired of the view. He was tired of looking at Washington, and knowing that all his skills and all the men under his command, and all the ordnance of the combined armed forces of the United States were utterly useless against the stupidity of just one man who happened to live there.

He had called the president himself personally after he had made that speech, but had been unable to talk sense into him. The idea that America was going to throw away almost three hundred years of military excellence, its preeminent position as the policeman of, judge, jury, executioner to and merchant for the entire world, so that HE could buy the next election from a bunch of welfare bums was too stupid to think about. And yet Baisch was sentenced to stand by and watch with his hands tied. Swindel had even laughed out loud at his protests, saying, "Don't worry Harley, everything'll be fine, you'll see."

He had been racking his quite ample brain for days trying to think of something that could be done, but short of a coup d'etat, he was completely out of answers.

"What are we going to do?" he asked the room, looking around. "Anybody? Guesses, bullshit stories, conjecture?"

There were eleven other people there, and not a word was spoken. They were all sitting around a big table looking hang dog at each other and thinking about what they would do for a living next year.

John Dunivan[22], Baisch's legal counsel folded his hands behind his head and sat back in his chair.

"You know, Harley sometimes when you're fucked, you're fucked, and it's just a bit unbecoming to sit around crying in your beer about it. The president is well within his rights to decide that the Military is too expensive and has to be slashed, by whatever amount he feels fit."

"Thanks for sharing with us, John. I though you were working for me. Maybe you could go the extra mile and earn your corn by thinking of something."

"Okay, General Baisch, it is my advice, my legal opinion, as your counsel that you either, A—change the president's mind, B—get Congress to impeach him, C—find the clause in the constitution that has eluded the greatest legal minds of our time, that says that the president takes orders from the Chairman of the Joint Chiefs of Staff, or, D— get another job."

Joan Filbert[23], Baisch's secretary was there, pouring coffee and taking any notes that might be generated. She made a round with the pot checking cups.

"Coffee, John?"

He looked at his cup.

"No, thanks."

She went on around the table.

Dan Carstairs from Navy was there. He was a Fleet Admiral who had served most of his career in boomers. He was a pointedly informal man, with a shaved head, sharp features and green eyes that never quite managed to stop smiling.

"John," he asked, "can't you put an injunction against the president, just as a delaying action, till we can find a lever?"

John shrugged with his eyebrows.

"Sure, I can do that. It will have to wait in line of course, behind the other sixty odd actions against the president that have thus far been generated by various and sundry departments over this, and which are mostly being sat on by Justice. Shall I have my staff start wasting time on that right away, or can it wait till after the meeting?"

"Cazzo," said Carstairs.

Milt Stanburg, the Air Force liaison, a three star with buckteeth and a comb over, sat forward gesturing with a pencil at

---

[22] Grandson of the aforementioned snake charmer and evangelist.
[23] Née Robertson

47

Carstairs.

"There you go again thinking without authorization, when are you squids going to learn that that is strictly an Air Force prerogative."

He turned and looked at Dunivan.

"Change the president's mind? How do you propose we do that?"

Dunivan shrugged theatrically.

"Yeah. Beats the fuck out of me! Maybe we could reason with him. Maybe we could reason with a water buffalo."

Joan freshened Stanberg's coffee for him, saying, "Maybe we could advertise."

Stanburg looked at her for a moment.

"What? Ah, thanks, Joan."

She nodded and continued on around the table.

Baisch spread his hands on the table, looking at the man at the other end of it, Frank Quigly. He was a tall gaunt man in the obligatory blue suit and conservative tie, held in place by an FBI thirty-year pin.

"What about the spooks?" asked Baisch. "Does The Bureau have anything, on, Swindle?"

"The Federal Bureau of Investigation," he said calmly, "does not have any information that I am aware of, with which to leverage the president's decision in this matter. What, after all, can you use against someone that they have used in their own campaign to get elected? It's not like he is going to be threatened by us denouncing him as a queer. Is it?"

"You mean to tell us," asked Carstairs. "that Dwayne Swindle got to be the president of the United States of America, and the only thing he ever did wrong on the way up was suck somebody's dick? Sorry ladies."

Quigly's eyes smiled a little.

"Well, Dan, according to testimony in front of a Federal judge in Atlanta, he did that rather well, and, he did engage in three incidents[24] during the spring of '33, in Richmond California. However, both those facts are not only a matter of public record, he actually used them as major chips during his campaign, if you will recall.

"There is nothing else in his background that I know of, that we are aware of, that will be of use to you in trying to get the

---

[24] Two ambushes on the Black Cells and one lynching of a rapist, murderer and 'Inquisitor'.

president to change this particular decision."

Joan got around to Quigly's cup and topped it up.

"Sugar?"

"Thanks, two please."

"Here you go," she said, dropping two lumps into his cup. "How about a disinformation campaign?"

"No, just ate, thanks."

He looked at Baisch reasonably.

"I hate to suggest such a thing, but can't you cut some kind of a legitimate deal with the Executive. You know, like it was 1950, you scratch my back and so on?"

Baisch shook his head.

"Basically, there's nothing he wants from us or anyone that owes us much. We have a few feelers out in Congress, but what's not corporate vote, is mostly uninterested in or is openly hostile to Military. Aliesha's been talking to Failsworthy and a couple of others but so far no dice."

Aliesha Sarson pounded her head back against the seat in frustration.

"Faircloth is a sure thing, and Failsworthy might be willing to go to bat for us, but he wants to be president himself, so he's not going to shoot himself in the foot over this. Not for us! If he can be persuaded to get enough Corporate Bloc votes together to stop the appropriation for the overhead, then maybe we can slow Swindel down long enough to bury this thing, but we run two dangers there. Either way the corporations make money, so they don't really care whether we have a Military or not. They can't be trusted to do the wrong thing. And if we do try to slow or stop the president's action too much, he will probably take it to a direct vote of the people. If he <u>does</u> call a referendum then we are in even deeper shit. He's still very popular in the cities in spite of Alpha 1's cost. And when was the last time you heard about a group of people turning down life time welfare when it was offered to them?"

Joan offered her some coffee by holding up the pot.

The Congressional liaison held out her cup without comment. Joan filled it, speaking softly, as if to herself.

"If we advertised our position to the public, <u>they</u> might well come to our aid in this matter."

"The big industrials," Aliesha continued, "are so diversified that it will be quite difficult to get them to even give us token support on this one. Tanks, refrigerators, it's all the same to them. They're starting to try to sell themselves as an alternative to

49

conventional Governance, God help us all!

"Our inquiries in that quarter have met with stiff rebuff so far. And, if Swindle takes it to the people directly, they, the industrials that is, are in control of almost 32% of proxies don't forget, then it's kinda like asking the crocodile to dinner, as far as we are concerned."

Baisch nodded.

"Well, keep hammering them anyway please, you never know."

Aliesha nodded assent.

"What about, Swarthmore, the VP?" asked Aliesha.

Baisch smirked sardonically. "Yes, what about him?"

Aliesha and the others laughed a bit darkly.

"That's what I thought."

Joan poured a cup for Rick Stern, the boyish, but lethal political analyst.

"How about running a front page ad in the New York Times? Sugar?"

Stern's eyes met Joan's and held for a moment.

"How about running a full page ad," he said, "right on the front page of the New York Times, Wall Street Journal, and Washington Post. That ought to get his attention!"

Joan smiled at him.

"If we can turn the people our way, he'll have no choice," she whispered.

Baisch look up at him.

"And say what?"

"Well, we can make our case against him in our own terms and turn public opinion against him. If it works it will take the wind out of his sails. Why should he be the only one that can use public opinion as a weapon?"

Baisch considered for a moment.

"Run a news paper ad."

Now Rick ran with it.

"Yeah, look. He's got the populace behind him, that's what makes him such a tough nut. That's why Veets and Senator Kayhill and all the rest of his detractors are all just so much flap in the wind. That's why he can get away with this if we don't act, because when all the middle American values crap has been said and done, the majority of the electorate is still city dwelling, white collar and liberal. They will back him if he tries to drop the Pentagon, unless, we can convince them that there is a real threat, a real reason to have a Military. The American people have always been leery of too big a Military, especially in peacetime. If we can show them that the world is not the soft warm fuzzy place that the companies have been selling them that it is, they might just give Swindel's leash a yank. And, oh yes, it costs us practically nothing."

Baisch looked at him for a moment.

"Do it. But get some pros on it, I don't want any of us writing this stuff, there are people who specialize, they know their trade a lot better than we do, let's use 'em."

Rick smiled at Joan. She smiled back.

"I'll call Cassy," she said.

-<>-

"If anyone in this country can name me a fucking politician that is worth the price of the bullet to execute them with, I'll eat my hat!"

Celebrity, Bill Crenshaw, 2050

-<>-

"America is a country founded upon the idea that the Government works for the People, and not the other way around."

Candidate, Dwayne Swindel, Des Moines, Iowa, Jan. 3 2047

Hello There!

P. Worthington Yeates & Associates is what it said on the door, in gold trimmed black lettering. The decals that made up the words had that minute asymmetry to them that let you know without shouting about it, that the name had been meticulously painted onto the glass by very skilled and expensive hands.

That was just what Yeates[25] wanted you to think when you looked at the door, that behind it were people who could afford to pay for hand lettering and all that it implied—the fast cars, and dachas in Vermont, the raw success. The letters told you that these were people to be reckoned with, which is just exactly what you were looking for in an ad agency.

'Worthy' put them on himself. He was nothing.

Yeates, a 'B' student at college, did have a head like an encyclopedia. It was thick and square and crammed to bursting with useless data. He could do good work at art school, witty, original work that was detailed and finely finished.

The mechanics were easy, but as a freshman he had come across the works of the 'Wiseass' School and that had caused him no end of trouble with his well meaning but pointedly conventional professors.

The Wiseass School was an art fringe, made of brainy, tongue in cheek performance/painters that faltered its way onto the gallery scene for a couple of weeks in San Francisco just before the turn of the 21st century. They were interested in poking fun at the art establishment, and particularly what they called, in their 'Fuck-ass Manifesto™', 'The Fagot Jew Mafia that controls the art market!'

The best-known work from this school was, Self Portrait With a Gorilla, by some guy named Ignat Flaubert that depicted the screaming artist, naked and being played wheel barrel with, (actually being sodomized), by a vicious gorilla, wearing a mask of the art critic, Clement Greenberg. Flaubert sold it at his one and only one-man show for $372.28, a pittance at the time, to an alcoholic nightclub singer from Bakersfield who thought it was a picture of two acrobats. The gallery took 60%.

The movement caused a minor scandal when it was first foisted upon the 'Fagot Jew Mafia that controlled the art market!'

---

25 Alan's grandson.

and then quickly faded into obscurity, much as you would expect. Worthy almost didn't find out about them at all, but he did.

This accident of history bent him.

There was the condom ad. It was a class assignment his senior year at Central Arts. His campaign was a series of ads with slug lines like, 'Use a condom, so you don't get bugs up your wang!' and 'Stick yo' dick in some rubba' fo' you stuff it in da' bluba,' Buba.' the first having a picture of a condom stuffed full of roaches, and the second featuring a picture of Bob Marley smiling away with an enormous erection. He was very lucky to graduate.

His portfolio was full of this stuff, so he worked for himself most of the time, which wasn't most of the time.

He made no bones about his work, so people who hired him couldn't really say too much when they got what they got. Some of his customers where quite happy with his off beat take, especially a radio station out of Austin, KJIZ. They loved his campaigns and kept him in groceries, sometimes.

KJIZ was a cowpunk station that broadcast out of the basement of the University of Texas with only ten kilowatts of power, so it wasn't like he was getting rich off of them. But at least they didn't complain about things like 'There's bull spew on your radio!' or, 'Next to sex with a goat I like KJIZ best!'

He was graying a little at the temples and his gut was starting to show in spite of his clothes. He didn't mind except for his strike out rate at the bars.

In his 30s he could get women interested by talking to them. They liked his wit, and sense of humor, he even found the occasional friend among them. But nowadays every time he told a joke, it was met with a blank stare, or worse, nervous laughter. They didn't get it, and most of the time the situation was reciprocal. He had started to become 'a little creepy'.

It was okay. He felt soiled a little, every time he woke up next to someone who was unaware of who Chairman Mao had been, or that there had ever been a place called Czechoslovakia, or that pomegranates were a type of rose, or whatever. Sometimes when he got very drunk he made speeches to them about it. Then it was really ugly.

Don't get me wrong. He did the deed when he got the chance, but at least he felt bad about it afterwards, kind of.

Yeates sat with his eyes shut, daydreaming in his chair by the sunny window. After lunch he liked a little pause to digest and think about nothing in particular. Out the window was the Brinkner building. 1970s ugly, he didn't really want to see it on a full stomach anyway.

It was nice in the sun, just letting his mind drift from one thing to the next, like a jellyfish in a warm sea of ideas.

He thought about how chicken's knees work, and if they would have made bicycles the same as people do if birds still ran the world. He thought about the Earth, how it was such a nice place to live, in spite of people. He thought about clowns. Clowns were people. Clowns worked with children. He wondered why. He thought that clowns must be very patient, not to become angry and piss on the kids, though many had it coming and worse, for all their manipulation and abuse of the adults they found around them. He thought maybe he'd become a clown someday and see how long he lasted. He imagined himself hosing down a crying brat that would not stop screaming and eat the broccoli that was in front of him, just because he knew that sooner or later the adults would once again cave in and give him a cookie. He blamed the parents.

In his mind the piss splashed off the little tike's cranium like a lawn sprinkler, making an almost perfect circle. It was a funny image, and he laughed quietly to himself with his hands folded behind his head. It was great to be alive, and not in charge of a daycare center.

The phone rang, breaking his train of thought.

"Phone, open."

There was a little click, and he spoke in a mild New York accent.

"Hello, P. Worthington Yeates and Associates, how may I direct your call?"

"Hello, this is Rick Stern with the Pentagon, I'd like to talk to the president of the company, please."

"Just a moment please, he's been in meetings with Coca-Cola all morning, I'll see if he's available. What shall I tell him this is concerning?"

"A job."

"One moment please. Phone, hold."

Worthy sat up in his chair and straightened his clothes. He checked his hair in the mirror. Satisfied, he stood up half way out of his chair.

"Phone, picture, line one open," he said sitting down.

"Hello," he said in his flat California accent. "P. Worthington Yeates, How may I help you?"

The wall of the office changed from its 'Wall paper' to a picture of a black haired man of medium build with no-bullshit eyes.

"Ah, hello, Mr. Yeates. My name is Rick Stern, I'm with the Joint Chiefs of Staff at the Pentagon, and we were given your name, as someone who could help us out with a problem that we are having at the moment. Would you be free to discuss it at this time?"

"Yes I am, as a matter of fact, I've got some time between meetings right now, if that's convenient."

"Great. Mr. Yeates, I'm sure, ——I'm sure that you are aware by now of the president's speech, well, concerning the Military establishment in this country."

"Yes, Yes I am." Worthy smiled.

"And tell me Mr. Yeates, how do you, uh, feel about his proposal?——Personally I mean."

Yeates thought about who he was speaking to for a moment.

"Well, I think it's quite a dumb idea, myself. I mean——it's kind of like being in a Mexican standoff. Yeah? And saying, 'Oh fine then, if you're not going to play it my way, then I'll just go home', and stuffing your pistol in your pants." He paused. "I think he's going to shoot himself in the balls, at about the same time he is gunned down by the opposition." He smiled more now.

"How do you, uh, feel about it?"

Stern looked quite serious.

"Well, I don't know that I would put it quite so, colorfully, but I think that there's certainly a consensus here at the Pentagon, that it is not in the best interests of the United States of America to throw away our ability to defend ourselves for the sake of a domestic policy of, questionable worth."

The two men looked at each other for a long moment, neither speaking.

"Right," said Yeates. He paused again. "What did you have in mind?"

Stern had a pencil in his hand and he started twirling it slowly around as he spoke.

"What we would like really, is to change the president's mind on this issue, if that is possible. And, well, it has been suggested to us that advertising might be one route to pursue in that cause. What <u>we</u> think is a logical first step, is to run some full-page ads in major papers around the country, stating our position—stating our side of the argument directly to the people of the United

States. We think that they will agree with us, if they can be properly educated on the, downside arguments, of the plan."

Yeates nodded.

"Yes," he said. "And since the Hold there's not a hell of a lot that the president, or anyone else in Washington for that matter, can do, without their direct consent.

"It, sounds like a good start, to me——how about a full page ad with a picture and a slug-line, and two boxes of text below? I can have some of our associates start work on it immediately—— if that suits you."

"Yes, yes that sounds good, but we'd—we'd obviously like to see a couple of examples before we go ahead with a whole campaign. Can you send us something, by say, tomorrow say?"

Worthy let him hang for a second as he pretended to think.

"Yes that would be probably possible. Do you have something specific you want in the ad?"

Stern nodded.

"Yeah, we have some ideas in that direction, we could send them over to you right away, if that helps. What's your E-dress?"

"PWY @ PWY&A dot com. and yours?"

"Stern @ JCS/PENT dot mil."

"Great. I'll send a contract for you to look over, and get our staff started right away."

"Fine. I'll look forward to receiving it and have my secretary send our ideas to you forthwith."

Worthy smiled.

"Thanks for your business, Mr. Stern, good-by. Phone, hang up."

Stern's picture blinked out and a McDonnell's ad replaced it. It was a singing dancing Big Mac.

"Volume down."

This had no effect—commercials were 'Volume Independent'. The thing sang on about the fabulous features of the burger for another twenty seconds, ending in their newly revived retro tag line "You deserve a break today, at McDonnell's."

The picture disappeared and was replaced by his usual wallpaper.

He thought about what to do next.

-<>-

The Umbutu River system comprises the watershed of the Rusizi, Katanga, and Qu'ue River valleys as well as the Great Umbutu itself. It is over 900 miles long and is visible from low earth orbit. It is a good place to live if you are a hippo.

-<>-

Effective 3/5/2049 Employee # 324J76DS1231 (Matsune Suzuki) will be transferred from Snack Food R&D (T.F.13) to Genetic Cosmetic and Identification Services (I.B.1) at Tokugowa Industries Facility, Flotkyo Japan.

DFDC CC Hiroki-san@ChoubiHonshuJapan.COM

-<>-

He was only twenty-two when 'The shit went down', as the 1st American Race War was referred to amongst the more free speaking brothers of the Black Resistance. He witnessed its birth, saw it flower and laid it to rest along with almost a million other of its victims. The war had been his second mother, and a part of him died with her.

Back in '32 he had been just another black gangster nearing the end of his run—twenty-five year olds were ancient warriors there in the mean streets of Detroit, and Islam had had only a bad death or prison to look forward to.

His gang, Fuck The White Bitchez, was not interested in him anymore. They had already used him for their purposes and now it was getting time to discard him. He was increasingly on the outs, particularly amongst the younger, more violent members. Some of them had even begun to challenge his right to use the FTWB tag on his territory, think of that!

They were starting not to return his gang sign. He knew what that meant. The option of 'going out big time'[26] was starting to look more attractive to him everyday. He probably would have gone that way, as another self-styled martyr to the spurious cause of Afro-American freedom[27], and been promptly forgotten, but there was a change coming he couldn't have known about.

It was hot August and the streets were so tense that even <u>he</u> was starting to feel uncomfortable. Everyone in town was nervous, and the brothers were keeping the safeties off, like it was war already.

---

[26] Making one last suicidal stand against the authorities, that could give him enough money to retire, like robbing the mint or kidnapping the Governor or what ever.

[27] 'Freedom' had not been the issue for American blacks for many generations, but that was what all the popular bla bla was about at the time. Probably enfranchisement <u>was</u> the issue, but it, like competent administration, was difficult to sell in a sound bite.

He was two blocks away when the first sirens came wailing down Coeur d'Alene street, in hot pursuit of a '26 Cadillac. He looked that way and saw the Cady start to make the turn into Republic Avenue. It was moving too fast and as it started to heave over into the turn he could see sparks coming out from under it as the car's skirts skidded across the pavement. The car flipped up onto its side and stayed there, as the police slammed on their breaks. In seconds the cops were all around it holding their guns out in front of them like impenetrable shields.

A sergeant spoke to the driver over the PA system—he could hear it still in his mind as he though about it years later.

"We have you surrounded William James Robinson. There is no escape. Come out with your hands up. Leave the girl in the car. This is your only chance."

Willy was his neighbor. There was no way *he* was giving anything up to the white policemen.

A blond girl, about sixteen stood up out of the window of the car with her hands over her head, she was pretty.

"Don't shoot me," she pleaded. "Move away, or he'll kill me!"

The cops were stuck, he could remember them look at each other for a moment. Then he heard Robinson's voice from inside the car.

"Do it mutha fuckas! Do it now or the bitch i'dead meat."

The sergeant shouted an order and the police pulled back a little. Robinson stood up and climbed out of the car with the girl, Barbara Vicars, held close to him. He stuffed an UZI up next to her temple. She was crying. He remembered that quite distinctly, her eyeliner made a little black rill down her cheek—she was looking at the gun.

"Back off, all of you!" he said, gesturing with his head. "NOW!"

The cops moved back to their cars grudgingly, on and only on Sergeant Mendez's order. He was the only one that stood his ground and tried to reason with the gunman.

"Give it up Robinson. We know who you are. You're right in front of your house, man! Come on—let her go. Let her go, and, we can negotiate. What do you want? You name it!"

Willy thought about his predicament. He had just knocked off a liqueur store up in New Seoul, killing the proprietor and his two daughters for $126.50. He had taken the white bitch as a hostage when the squad car pulled up out front and had blown the head off one of the cops making his escape. There was no way they were making any deals.

Robinson smiled and put a burst of three through Barbara's head. Then he opened up on the sergeant, hitting him in the chest and shoulder. They both went down in a hail of bullets from the twenty or so police officers that were there.

The cops would probably have done better to pull back and cut their losses, to be 'tactical' about it, but they couldn't _really_ do that. After all, they had the law to uphold.

The sergeant was correct, they were right outside Robinson's place, an armored crack house, with twenty-three members inside. They would have done better to just let it be and get their evens on the next one, but this was _their_ hood, and either they owned it or they didn't.

They opened up with small weapons, and a few of their rockets, nothing compared to what they could have done, but they did manage to kill sixteen of the officers in a matter of thirty seconds or so.

That's when Islam's life had changed. Instead of doing the smart thing, instead of doing what you or I would have done, and running the other way, he had watched himself, like it was a video of someone else, run to the nearest dead cop and pick up his weapon. He ducked behind a squad car and made his way around the back of the remaining officers. They were far too busy with the crack house to notice him, and he had very little trouble shooting them in the back as they fought for their lives in the other direction. After ten minutes, they were all dead where he dropped them. He stepped out from behind the Cadillac.

"It's okay!" he shouted up to the house. "It's all okay! They're all dead now." He gave sign.

That one short incident bought him a new lease on life in the hood, for while the other members had shot from cover, with the height advantage, he had been seen by the whole street to shoot it out with the police face to face, and against stiff odds. After that, people started asking _him_ what _he_ thought they should do.

He heard the choppers coming, and ducked into an alley. The Detroit police, having lost so many at one go, reacted like the Russian Army. Helicopters poured into the projects landing on the rooftops and deploying snipers all around the sight of the original gunfight. They drew down on the crack house, that contained most of the upper echelon of the FTWB, and enough ordnance to defend itself for weeks, which was what they intended to do.

The police laid siege to the building for days, trying both to dislodge the 'criminals' as they called them, and defend their backs against an increasing onslaught by FTWB 'Rebels' as they called themselves led mostly by Islam. There was a media circus, of course, and black militants seeing their brothers under attack by the hateful racist monsters that were the mayor's lackeys, came from as far away as Philadelphia to fight what had become the first battle of the war. Red neck militia from all over the country soon followed them.

The FTWB was pitted against under gunned National Guardsmen, SWAT teams and a couple of units of Marines from the Great Lakes Naval Training Facility at Larchmont. By week's end, the three remaining members were 'liberated' from the crack house, and the battle of the Republic Projects had turned to a running street fight, with the rebels shooting, and most significantly, looting their way toward the city center. The Detroit police et all just tried to stay alive long enough for Mayor Tiegler to decide whether he was first and foremost, the mayor of Detroit, or a down trodden black man, finally seeing some justice for a change. Fortunately Governor Harkness took the situation out of his hands while there was still a Detroit left to defend. He called up the sixteen National Guard units under his command, complete with armor, air support and satellite intel. They ringed the City Center making a safe haven for the 'Caucasian white people' that fled there from the 'burbs.

It was then that Islam and his FTWB 'Guerrillas' as the press had coined them started what would soon spread to every large city in the United States, 'Ethnic Cleansing'.

They went about it methodically, searching from house to house, for any 'Non-Blacks', and they found thousands.

They hung them from lampposts with coat hangers and executed them for the TV cameras by slitting their throats, hoisting them by an ankle and letting the gutters run red with their blood. From behind his ubiquitous ski mask he made pronouncements, delivered demands and called for wholesale insurrection on the part of all people of color throughout the nation, and always, as Islam Black Africa, leader of The Black Cells.

The war spread, first to the region, and then to the whole nation. And as President Risedail poured reluctant armies into the fray and began deputizing heavily armed neo-Nazis, Islam's importance began to lessen, but in those first critical days and weeks of the war he was a major player. There were others, later, such as Ace Washington in Camden that would eventually supplant him as the voice of the Black Resistance. It was just as well in the end, when he considered how they ended up, but still he'd had a shot at it long enough to make himself a name before he faded back into the fabric of America and was lost.

He had checked the records and was officially listed as presumed dead at the battle of Dearborn, in the collapse of an apartment building.

He had stepped outside onto the roof to take a leak when the charges went, and the concrete slab on which he was standing acted as a sort of giant surfboard, riding over the death and destruction below. He was horribly injured, but at least he was alive. Johnson's men, the few that survived, had dragged him with them on their hasty, murderous retreat into the hills and by the time he was able to fight again, the war was all but over and they were trying lesser figures for war crimes, and executing them, or worse.[28]

He was thought dead, and he let it stay that way, posing instead as one of the collaborators, a simple, unassuming man that had lived in a rural area and was not interested in the Black agenda, a 'Good Nigger'.

After the war, during the reconstruction, he had a short career, as the step and fetch it rapper, Malcolm Why.

That adventure earned him a little money, and what his agent didn't steal he squirreled away, but he had to let it go. He started to see people that he recognized from the war. They could finger him as Islam Africa and that was not worth any amount of money in the world.

He faded from the scene again and worked at odd jobs here and there, biding his time and waiting for the day that the revolution would rise up again, to take back the world from the white racist devils that had stolen it from its rightful owners, the Black African Man. When that day came, and he knew with absolute certainty that it must, he knew that he would be the one called upon to lead it. He would not hesitate—it was destined to be.

In '41 he stumbled onto publishing in a round about fashion[29], and began to pursue that as not only a means of supporting himself, but also as a way to help foster the next phase

---

[28] Ace Washington was cloned for perpetual punishment by the CIA after his death, for blowing Reisdale's brains out of his head with his shot gun, Louise.

[29] He won a failing printing business in a rigged poker game, from Sid Mornstein. Mr. Mornstein subsequently committed suicide after reading Islam's first edition.

of the glorious renaissance of the Black African man.

He founded the Voice of Black Islam, a militant newspaper that featured among other things, 'Booty Call', a black male, all-race female date section, and Black Light, a series of commentaries on contemporary society with a distinct predilection for blaming whites for everything. He even went so far as to blame the death of Virginia Simms, a ninety-one year old black woman who was raped and beaten to death for her color TV by a twelve year old Haitian psychopath named Jakarta Sexoil, on her, for having been a race traitor. It turned out that she had once worked for Ford Motor Co., a white owned carmaker[30].

His paper was quite a hit in the inner cities of both coasts and around the Great Lakes during the years leading up to WW III, particularly after he started laundering money for the mob through it. That really gave his circulation a boost, and lent him the penetration he needed to use the paper as a coded message board for the new black resistance movement. The Black Cells of Afrimerika—it was a name that he coined himself.

A lot of their rhetoric, much of which he wrote, was based on misquoting, and paraphrasing Dr. Martin Luther King Jr.—the saint of the legitimate civil rights movement of the previous century, and Ho Chi Min, the father of Vietnamese communism, so the rest of the press referred to them as the King Kong. They were a minor terrorist group that specialized in blowing up Elk's clubs, Shriners conventions and other such Masonic manifestations.

If the Mafia had discovered this connection he would, needless to say, have been rubbed out immediately, but he always hid the BCA messages in the Booty Call section, following a Percy Sledge lyric, so he remained safe.

It was through his paper that he first met Yasad Al Hazier, a little known Shia Muslim cleric. Hazier had seen his paper out in Los Angeles, where he lived and approached him about running a paid column every weak called 'The Voice of Allah'.

At first he was skeptical, but Hazier could afford to pay top dollar for the space. Besides it was all in Arabic, a language that Islam couldn't read or speak, and cared little about exploring. So what harm could it do? Also, he liked the way it made the paper

---

[30] In reality, at the time she worked for Ford, it was a publicly owned company, with a high level of subscription by black shareholders, herself among them.

look to have this big column of Arabic script running down the front-page, all, Islamic and everything.

Hazier was backed, of course, by Iranian and Saudi money and was passing coded messages from his masters in the Middle East to Hezbollah and Al Qaeda terrorist cells in and around the cities of the US. He could have afforded to run ads in the New York Times, if had wanted but that was too big a risk for his bosses on the other side of the Atlantic. Also he liked utilizing The Voice of Black Islam as a conduit for his schemes against America. It was elegant using those that took the name of Islam in vain, to destroy the 'Satanist State' itself.

The day was fast approaching when the sword of Islam would rise up and take back the world that was rightfully its to rule, and when it did, he would be in a position to hold that sword over the necks of the Jews and their proxies in America, he would not hesitate—it was destined to be.

The phone rang on Islam's desk. He put down his Snakos and picked it up by hand.

"This is the Voice of Black Islam, may I help you?" he asked, in a deep tenor. It was Hazier on the other end.

"Hello my friend," he said. "I wanted to call you to say that I will be in town next week, and I was wondering if we could get together for a meeting at last. After all we have been doing business for over a year now and I have never even shaken your hand."

"Why yes, of course," said Islam. "When does your flight arrive?"

Hazier told him, and he noted it down.

"Seven-forty-five at Kennedy, great I'll buy you dinner."

"Oh, that would be excellent," said Hazier. "I have something to discuss with you that I think you will find most interesting indeed. I look forward to our meeting. I'll see you at the gate, I will be wearing..." He paused. "Is this line secure?"

"Yes, I pay a fee to have it checked once a week."

"Ah, well then, I will be wearing a green jacket with a gardenia in the lapel."

"Okay, see you there."

He hung up and made a note on his computer, wondering what Hazier's concern with security was all about.

-<>-

"Hey, Janey, what are you so happy about?"

"Oh, nuthin' much."

"Come on now, you don't smile like that every day, girl!"

63

"Okay, Suzy, I'll tell ya'. You know that new internist, Dr. Michelson?"

"A-haaaa!"

"Well, he was looking at my chest X-ray and he saw my Inner Beauty mark!"

"Oh yeah. Isn't it a kitten or something?"

"Something like that, it's on my pericardium.

"Well?"

"Dinner tonight and afterwards, who knows?"

Inner Beauty, the ultimate intimacy.

For details call 1-700-4-INNER-BEAUTY.

A Tokugowa Industries Company

© PWY INC. 2050

Here's My Plan

Kwang Zu Cola is very delicious! And also good for you!! It is very lucky to drink—Kwang Zu Cola! Buy Kwang Zu Cola today! Made in China to export standard.
Three dollars only!

-<>-

At first, Worthy though very hard and long about playing this one straight. About doing the smart thing and restraining his sense of humor—of filling his bank account with the thousands of dollars that he knew the pentagon had and was very willing to part with in order to get what it wanted. All he had to do was forget about all the ideas he liked, all the deliberately provocative, wise guy assaults on the customer's delicate sensibilities. Instead he could do the straight thing like anyone else in his position. That would make him so much money in so short a time that he would probably be able to take a vacation in the tropics for years. That would be the 'smart' thing to do. That would be the 'right' thing to do. That would certainly be a self-treasonous little way to win.

He couldn't do it.

Every time he thought about the problem, with his deliberate, up front mind, like an ad clown, the other part of his head, the sarcastic joker that lurked beneath would step out, dust off its gloves meticulously and slap the living shit out of his seriousness with a rubber fish.

He tried to think stoically about America without its defense system intact—about the dangers of being exposed in a world of scoundrels. He thought about American families walking in the park with the sun shining and a sincere voice over reading the constitution. A little girl looks up at her father wide-eyed and open. There is a bright flash that resolves to a hydrogen bomb. How poignant, he thought. How fucking stupid.

He thought about a hapless looking Uncle Sam with a ball in his mouth, bent over, with his striped pants down around his ankles, and his hands duct taped to his legs. Uncle Sam looked at Worthy, bewildered. Worthy smiled back and gave him a big thumbs-up in his mind's eye. Behind the distinguished gentleman was a pack of militaristic hyenas and baboons dressed in epaulets and general's caps, sporting ludicrous sex toys on the charge. He liked it. Worthy grinned to himself.

In fact he had Timmy working on just such a picture at that very moment. He was struggling with the caption a bit. He was torn between "Don't let this happen to you." and "Do you really trust that bunch of dildo packing hyenas out there to back you up when push comes to shove?" He thought he would probably show them both and let the generals decide.

He went all out on this pitch, making seven different ads to present to the Pentagon. Timmy, his photographer was over the moon about it, he hadn't had that much work all at once in ages. He had Anna Kohut, working on a media plan and he was just now finishing the copy writing. His meeting was in three hours.

The copy that the pentagon had sent him was okay. It was quite dry and unmoving stuff, but full of useful figures that he lifted and sprinkled liberally into what he wrote to replace it. He even quoted whole passages here and there from some of it, as sort of a tribute and sales technique. People liked to feel involved.

That was the biggest obstacle to him or anyone working in advertising, the customer's input.

People who made widgets, and knew widgets, called on the services of other professionals from time to time, as their needs dictated, and then they let those people get on with their job.

When they called an engineer to fix the elevator, they wouldn't dream of telling them their job, of suggesting they hang less weight on the counter balance or use a different kind of grease on the rails. That would be dangerous and stupid. What did they know about elevators? But these same people wouldn't hesitate to suggest a different and daft campaign to the ad guy or change their copy, making hash out of it.

I'm not trying to suggest that your average ad smack is something other than a malodorous sack of fertilizer, screaming out to be stymied, but they are good at lying. If you want to sell your useless plastic crap to the public they are best left alone to do so.

He hoped the people that he was about to meet weren't that kind of 'helpful' idiot. If so, then he would try to work around it. He knew he could smooth them for a while, but sooner or later someone would say something so stupid he'd just have to tell them what he though about that suggestion. When that moment came, and he knew it would, it was time to give 'em the bill and walk away before the blood sport started.

Timmy was starting to worry him a little. He did good work, but he took his time about it.

"Phone, Tim Akins."

The speaker purred and then a click as Tim picked up, the screen stayed black.

"Yo!"

"Yo, Timmy, I'm dyin' here!"

Tim said nothing for a long moment. Worthy could hear the sarcasm pouring out of the silence.

"Perhaps," said Tim at last, "you could eat shit and die. Uh, Don't forget to swipe your card on your way to the morgue."

"Fine. When will the picture be ready?"

"Now, phone, picture."

Tim's smirking face popped onto his screen nonchalantly, holding up a print out of the Uncle Sam shot. It was perfect, he got just the right look of sappy vulnerability on the model's face, and the animals were magnificently raucous and predatory.

"Warhol?" asked Tim.

"Gauguin! It's great, I'll send you two captions, you can please lay them below as indicated and I'll pick them up on my way to the train."

Tim nodded. "Thirty minutes, okay? I got a date tonight."

"Okay. Phone hang-up."

The phone went dead right away. His new software was working.

He gathered up the other mockups he had scattered around his desk. If he and Cassandra could convince the Pentagon guys, then he'd be happy to do them, but he wasn't getting his hopes up. Even Cassy was going to have trouble selling these.

Cassandra Robertson was an account executive he knew from college. She was fast and slimy, and pretty smart. She was like a linguistic ameba. She could feel the direction of a conversation and change her line on the fly to match the other person's without them usually noticing. She always seemed to agree with you. She was a great spin-doctor when she decided to be. Her ex used to say she could suck up to a screen door when she wanted.

He would need her talents to get the pentagon to bite and even more once they did. She was due any minute to pick him up.

He slipped the last of the mockups into the case as the doorbell rang.

"Yes?"

"Cassy."

He hit the buzzer.

"I'll be down in a second, come in."

The latch clicked and she pushed the door open. Cassandra was glad to be in off the street. It wasn't even sunset and Worthy's office wasn't in a really bad neighborhood, but she felt nervous standing on the street in New York City.

'He's going to keep me waiting again' she thought.

She hated that about him, he always kept you waiting while he dicked around with details. She checked her watch.

Worthy came down the stairs with his portfolio under his arm.

"Okay. We have to stop at Timmy's for a couple of things on the way."

She held the door for him. "Today then eh?"

They just got to the train, as it was leaving. It was an hour ride down to Washington on the maglev and that gave them enough time to go over the comps and plan a strategy. They drank scotch instead. They would think of something when the time came, they always did.

-<>-

As the population ages, and habitation density increases, it is highly likely that peoples' tolerance level for crowding, as well a general angst surrounding dying will increase too. Angry frightened people tend to make hasty and ill-considered decisions. Therefore it may be in the national interest to supply various means of "soothing" the general populace.

A partial list follows:

Legalization and dissemination of certain dopamine producing drugs.

Soft music can be supplied in crowed public places.

Aerosol agents ca...

Massage fragment recovered from a malfunctioning paper shredded in the pentagon basement.

-<>-

Anna hefted Louis up onto her hip and pushed her way through the crowd toward the gate.[31] She was a little late for dinner already. The damned Subway! She loved and hated it the way most New Yorkers did, like a rich old pederast of an uncle— its utility was almost outdone by the wretchedness of the thing.

A thousand people jostled against her, pushing and buffeting her around like a cork in a stream. She flowed with them holding her arms around her son like a stiff protecting basket. One man, a

---

[31] There were a lot more people back then, don't forget.

thin, sweaty looking, Chinese guy kept shoving her back as he pushed his way forward with his briefcase held out in front of him like a sword. He was a real belligerent jerk.

"Move aside everyone," he said. "I have to get through here! Madam! After me, I'm very important—a very important man!"

He shoved at her again, this time harder than before. She tried to shift around his hand and flow through his resistance, but he wouldn't have it. He turned and looked at her.

"I said, after me, woman!"

Anna smiled and tripped him. She didn't like the way he said woman, like it was a swear word. As he went down she stepped nimbly over him, trading Louis to her other hip. She glanced back over her shoulder at the guy. People walked over him like a rug. He was gone. The theme from 'A man and a Woman' was playing softly over the PA system.

She passed through the gate with everybody else who wasn't special.

As she came up to the street she could smell fresh baking, and there was the sound of someone playing a guitar, mixed with the constant sound of the street, children talking, cars and a man yelling at someone in broken English.

"What fuck you are doing like idiot? Poosh! Poooosh!"

"Yeah fuck you I'm poosh!"

There were people standing around smoking cigarettes and talking, she felt safe. Louis was quiet and alert.

It was only a short walk to Sergei's place through little Moscow, and as she went she listened to the night trying to understand what was going on around her.

"I said poosh, goddamnit!"

It was chaotic, a jumble of sounds, that she couldn't make tell one story. Instead it was like hundreds of people all telling similar stories at the same time in their own words. Most of the words were Russian.

She didn't speak much Russian, just a few phrases, but she loved to listen to it. It had an odd rhythm, like a different sort of machine clanking away in some foreign but familiar place.

There was the man with the guitar. She often heard him when she came there. He was singing something about Kraznioyorsk. And mingled with it were the sounds of people working in a kitchen. She could hear them banging pots and pans around, and calling orders. There was a woman calling too, for someone named Bill. She pronounced it "Beel" Then she stopped. The streetlights were green there.

She crossed the street and came to the stairs that led up to Sergei's door. They were cast concrete that was rounded off at the edges from a million foot falls. He lived in a row house that dated from the 1860s, along with six other families. There was always the noise of children there, and of people living, and warm humid smells of cooking and tobacco, and sometimes, other less pleasant things. It felt like a home to her.

She mounted the stairs and rang the bell. She waited, hearing the street around her and watching.

Somebody started banging on a car fender with a claw hammer, meticulously, with a two second rest between beats. Bof!. . . Bof!. . . Bof!. . . Bof!

"Hey! Shut the fuck up——down there!"

Bof!, "I'm almost" Bof! "Finished!"

"Shut! The! Fuck! Up!!!!"

Bof!. . . Bof!. . . Bof!. . .

Rat!,Ta!,Ta!,Ta!,Ta!,Tak!

Louis laughed, there was a pause and she heard brass hitting the ground like tinkling raindrops.

"Hello?"

"Hi, Sergei. It's Anna."

"Da come up."

The door buzzed, and she pushed it open.

Bof! You missed me asshole!

SHUT! THE! FU—

The door closed behind her. She went up the stairs with Louis.

There was a rat,ta,ta,ta,ta,ta,ta,ta,tak!, far away.

Sergei was standing at the top of the stairs smiling. He held his arms out wide.

"Anna darlink, we've been waiting for you."

She got to the top of the stairs and he hugged her like a blanket.

"Work," she said.

"Work. In this house there is no work, only is vodka. You will have eternity to work in hell with the rest of us."

He looked at Louis who was asleep now.

"Snoozing as usual, you are missing life."

"Sergei, a sleeping baby is a blessing. Be happy."

"So is secret policeman," he smiled. "Till he wakes up. Join us."

He swept his hand down the hall.

They walked toward his door past Svetlana's kitchen. It

smelled like garlic and boiling potatoes. As she passed, Anna could see Svet's husband, Danny asleep on the couch. He held a crushed beer can in his hand. It rode up and down on his tummy like a tiny ship.

Svet and Danny met in Manchuria where they fell in love killing Chinese people. They were young and beautiful then, and it seemed they would never run out of ordnance or sex. Now they weren't so young or beautiful anymore. Now they were middle aged and a little dumpy. They fought like ferrets.

At the end of the hall was Sergei's place. It was a large apartment that faced back onto the park. Its door made a warm rectangle full of people's voices. She could hear them talking and recognized them even though she couldn't make out the words.

The first one was Mort's, of course. It was high when he laughed and low when he was talking, and always sounded like he was smirking. He was her husband—he was also her best friend. He was a stubborn man.

She could also hear Nadia's alto dropping articles like beads from a broken necklace. She couldn't understand her from there, just, but she could hear the missing words in the severed cadence of her speech.

They entered Sergei's and she was washed over with the smells of cigarette smoke and vodka, and rich food kept warm on the stove. It was kracha, cabbage soup from Belarus. It smelled a little like wet earth and onions.

"Go sit down," said Sergei, smiling. "I bring you soup."

Anna went into the dinning room with the others. There were four people there, Mort, Nadia, Igore and Stan. She caught Mort's eye and he pulled out a chair for her. He also pulled out the next one and she hung Louis' papoose on the finials of the back.

They kissed.

"Hi," said Nadia. "You would like maybe, drink?"

"Da, please. Beer."

Nadia got up and went into the kitchen.

"So tell us," said Stanislow. "What brings you to us so late this evening, dear Anna?"

"Work and work, we are very busy right now. Worthy got a big pitch for the pentagon."

Igore nodded sagely.

"So Worthy consorting now is with the Devil."

Stan carefully knocked the ashes off his cigarette, speaking sardonically. "Is more like down on knees giving him a blow job."

"The Pentagon," said Mort, "has fifty-three percent of the federal budget at its disposal, you can hardly blame Yeates for going after a piece of that, even if it is only crumbs, it's still a hell of a lot of money."

Stan looked at Igor. "Americans."

Igor started gesturing with pouched fingers. "Money, money, money. All is money! What about principle?"

Stan smiled wisely. "Principal is money you actually borrow, cumulative interest may be substantially higher over life of the loan."

"So," asked Anna, "if you were offered work for the Defense Department at something like ten times your normal wage, you wouldn't take it?"

Igore considered for a moment.

"Well," he said, "is maybe different if you are putting it like that."

Everyone started laughing derisively.

Mort looked at Anna. "Russians!"

"It doesn't take much money to buy their principles," she said.

Stan asked frankly, "How much did you actually get for your grand mother?"

Igor shrugged. "Fifty thousand rubles, but she was still alive, it makes discount by maybe half."

Nadia came back with the beer. "Here, is house made."

Stan looked at her. "Learn to speak English, your new language, is <u>home</u> made!"

Nadia sat down backwards on a chair. "Fuck you, learn to make your own beer."

"What do I look like, old babushka?"

Nadia, who was an absolute knockout with almond eyes and a figure like a centerfold lifted her breasts arrogantly. "Is looks like babushka to you?"

Stan just smiled.

"Trust me," Igor said to Stan. "You look more like scrotum than babushka."

"Scrotum?!" He looked to Mort and Anna for support. "Help me out here!"

Mort looked at Anna. "Scrotum?"

She appraised his face for a long moment.

"I'm afraid Igor has a point, though it depends on whose scrotum exactly."

Sergei came into the room carrying a tray. He set it down next to her and served Anna her soup with a thick slices of black bread.

"What is the topic?" he asked sitting down.

Nadia gestured to one of her brothers with an open palm.

"We were discussing whose scrotum Stanislow most resembles."

Stan turned to present his profile to Sergei, who regarded him gravely.

After a moment——

"Zhirinovsky I think."

The others looked at Stan as if he were a melon that they were considering for dinner.

Mort squinted, turning his head slightly.

"Really? You think the jowls are floppy enough to resemble Zhirinovsky? I think more like George Washington."

Sergei was most adamant. "Absolutely not! Washington had wooden scrotum. Look at the strange asymmetricality of the forehead, the way jaw sags allowing the skin to hang in ugly folds. It is definitely Zhirinovsky's scrotum."

Igore looked at Mort, and then at Sergei.

"Holding on," he said. "First of all, how do <u>you</u> know what Zhirinovsky's scrotum looked like? And secondly, I happen to have it on good authority that Zhirinovsky's scrotum was quite hairy. This man doesn't even have a beard!"

Nadia looked at him, incredulous. "Good authority?"

"Well, reasonable authority, yes."

Everyone waited. It started to get awkward.

"Wiki...," he said at last.

No one said anything for a moment—they all just looked at him.

At last, Sergei broke the silence. "Stan, please to, invert your head."

Stanislow stood up and turned his head upside down over the table smiling.

Sergei shrugged. "See? I rest my case."

Igore had to admit that the resemblance was a striking one. He made reasonable. "Okay, so maybe you have point."

Stan's face was starting to turn red, thought Anna. No one else seemed to notice.

"Stan, will you please pass me the mustard?" she said.

"Da," he said amiably, handing her the small jar. After a second he thought of something and handed her a small spoon.

"Is for serving."

"Spasiba," she said.

Sergei poured a shot of vodka and handed it to his brother in law. "Thank you Stan, you can sit down now."

"Just second," said Stan, taking the shot. He held the glass to his upper lip and started gingerly to pour it into his upside-down mouth.

Everyone started chanting and clapping time. "Stan, Stan, Stan, Stan!"

He drained it, swallowing hard and rolled out into his chair all in one smooth move.

Anna applauded.

Louis's eyes fluttered open at the sound and he looked around at the people there.

Anna looked at him as she ate her soup. He seemed happy enough just to sit there and observe.

At this point I was about six months old and did little else than watch and eat and sleep and make unspeakable filth in my diapers.

"So tell us about this work you are doing," said Sergei.

Anna tore off little bits of her bread and nibbled at it as she spoke.

"Worthy's pitching the Pentagon for a campaign to counter Swindel's proposed 'Peace Budget'. I spent all day making media plans for various options. The really silly part of all this is that it's the Pentagon we're talking about. They can afford anything in the world, and they are talking to the entire American people here. So who needs a plan? They should probably just confiscate NBC."

Sergei poured himself a tall tumbler full of red pepper vodka, frowning.

"Ah yes, the peace budget, is shitty idea."

Anna took a drink of her beer. It was cool and strong and very malty—then it tasted like sour walnuts.

"Well," she said. "That's what the Pentagon thinks, for obvious reasons. They would, wouldn't they? And that's what Worthy is going to try to sell all of us on, if they go for his——

style. I think it might not be such a bad idea to spend our money on this county for a change and see if the rest of the world can get along without us, at least for a few years. They seem to get along well enough without our opinion most of the time. There are a lot of problems, right here in River City that could use fixing with endless money."

74

Stan and Igor looked at each other, and then Stan got up and went to the bookshelf that was across the room.

"Yes," said Nadia. "But are you saying that the world is safe place without Military?"

Mort answered for her. "It's maybe as safe as it is <u>with</u> the Military, but costs less to maintain."

"Ah," said Sergei. "So then you trust the Chinese to behave themselves, just like that? And what about the other Asians, and the South Americans? There are eleven billion people in the world and most of them are hungry and armed to teeth. You are rich and fat and you throw away your gun? Freedom costs something. Right?"

Anna looked at Louis, who was watching the conversation alertly.

"I'd still like to try it as an experiment, in spite of the risks," she said.

Igor lit a cigarette thoughtfully. He blew out a cloud of smoke, thinking.

"Is moot point, yeah, the Hold, remember, is still in place, and shows no sign of being released in near future, not that this helps Pentagon, necessarily. But is Swindel sitting on hands and talking out of ass too?"

"How is spelled River City?" asked Stan staring at the index of an atlas.

"Da, da, da," agreed Nadia. If Hold stays for another six weeks the Government will be broke anyway, so maybe Army just cuts to chase and we have little coup d'état, like maybe Kennedy."

Sergei turned to his wife. "Ugliness."

" Da, ugliness," she replied.

Louis started to fuss a bit and Anna gave him some soup.

"River City..." asked Stan.

"Is just an expression," said Mort.

"Da." Stan looked lost.

"So Mort," he asked after a moment, "what do you think, is Hold coming off or is American people going to put screws to Washington till it chokes like diseased chicken?"

"Well, that's hard to say. I can tell you I am not going to release <u>my</u> Hold come hell or high water till I see the Senate beaten naked in the streets and the president swinging from a lamp post, but then I am quite a bit more militant than the average guy.

"You also talk a load of shit," said Anna sweetly.

75

"If, on average," said Mort ignoring her, "people are only half as pissed off as I am, and only half as willing to risk their worthless cowardly necks as I am, then I think the Hold will hold, at least for another few weeks. The longer it stays the more the pot boils and the more the shit floats to the surface.

"Did you see the allegations flying around about Faircloth and his cronies?"

Stanislow laughed out loud at this. "Ah yes, Failsworthy's speech and all that. Amusing idea—threatening to 'impound' the money of the American people. That will get him thrown out of office at very least, if not shot."

"Exactly!" said Mort. "If they try to pull that shit, I may get my way sooner than I would have thought possible."

Sergei shook his head emphatically.

"No, no, no, you don't really want that to happen. Trust me the fall out would be disastrous. Thousands of innocent people would be killed needlessly, and for what? So that 'nother bunch of criminals can surreptitiously hide salami in their place? It is much better the devil you know."

"Sergei, I think you're wrong. When you have been held down and fucked once too often, it is time to turn around and cut off the bastard's dick, even if there is another one right behind him in line. Maybe the next prick will take note!"

Louis looked up at his daddy. He recognized his daddy, and remembered his voice.

Louis filled his diapers with fetid stinking shit and grinned up at his daddy. He grinned back.

"Elegant turn of phrase there," said Sergei. "Tell me do you kiss Louis with that mouth?"

-<>-

Commander Dave Tomlinson was about the calmest man that you ever weren't very likely to meet. First of all he was very far away from most people, and the few he was relatively close to were, with one exception, asleep. He was the sort of a man that you could walk up to and say "I fucked your mother with a meat ax, and she dug it!" and he would just think you sad.

He was a tall man with coffee skin and steady green eyes.

It was thought by the mission planners that his sort of patience would come in handy in the gulf between the stars. After all, he was not going to have a hell of a lot to do out there for eight years—get up once a week, set off an H-bomb, and then go back to sleep. Pretty routine.

When they started they had 384 of the things and now he was

76

down to 320.

Dave sighted down the scope at the sun. It was a very bright star against the background night. The cross hairs exactly framed it, dead in the center of the scope. He checked his numbers.

"Knute, will you please give us a burn sufficient to gain three hundredths of a second on number four? On my mark."

"How much would that be?"

Dave looked at his lieutenant for a moment.

"My numbers show 100% for 1.5 seconds. Do you concur?"

Knute looked at his readouts. "If you say so."

"Yes, I do. Ready? Three, two, one, and, mark"

Knute punched a button. There was a tiny nudge.

Dave checked his scope again. He glanced at the readout. "Firing," he said.

Knute turned his key. "Ready," he said.

Dave turned his key and armed the switch. "Three, two, one and mark." He pushed a large red button.

Nothing happened for a heartbeat, and then the nuclear equivalent of 5 Million tons of dynamite exploded behind them.

Alpha rang like a bell, and the cushions took up his brief new weight, enfolding Dave in a vinyl marshmallow.

After a while he could breath again and focus his eyes. He looked at the accelerometer. It read 5.7 Gs. All his lights were green.

"All okay here. How about you?"

Knute got out of his chair holding his hand over his eyebrow. There was blood running down his cheek.

"Yeah, every things fine here too."

He looked at Dave. "I left my pen on the console!" He pointed at his chair. The pen was buried in his headrest.

-<>-

Senator Daniel Failsworthy, was what those who wished not to offend, if not actually to flatter him, euphemistically referred to as a 'portly' man. Or more often, as 'That fat assed carpet bagging son of a bitch,' by those he dealt with on a daily basis. He had earned the latter appellation through years of connivance, throat slitting and bribe taking, as the boot licking pony boy of one industrial task master after another. He was hated, but he was 'in'.

There was a lumpy asymmetry to his posture and a perpetual sweat stain darkening his arm pits. He was balding and sneered a lot.

Back in the old days, before the Corporate Enfranchisement

77

act of 2041[32] he had sucked up to various private sector meglomorates[33], in and around his district. These had been mostly defense and space systems suppliers and the occasional health care provider or logistics concern, all of them as large and as 'generous' a set of sponsor as he could find.

In those days, he had spent a lot of time justifying his votes to his constituents in New York and greasing political bosses at the local level to smooth his way. Not to mention the fact of his authoring several scurrilous bills of his own, including the 'Park Land Budget act'[34] and the 'Social Security Reduction and Redistribution act'[35]. He had been good at the 'old game', and made alliances fast amongst the other shysters that lived under rocks in and around the nations capitol.

Then, when the 'act' was passed, and the 'new game' fell upon Washington overnight, he had leapt into the power grab hewing limbs right and left from his fellow blood sucking leeches to secure for himself a consolidated position amongst the privileged cronies of the new corporate order. That established, he stopped justifying himself all together, and concentrated

---

[32] This little talked about act, that was rushed through Congress in the heat of the first days of the Second Sino-Soviet war gave corporations with more than 10,000 employees, 'Voting Stock' in the American political system by giving them a representative in the house. Buried in clause fourteen of the act was a provision that allowed these corporations to buy a citizens vote proxy for life, for lifetime welfare. And it was a pittance at that.

[33] Before WW III, cavalier as it may sound to you now, companies were, with a few notable exceptions, allowed to get as large as they liked, without a second thought being given to the matter. Such monster companies, complete with political wings were called Meglomerates

[34] This act voted 13 billion dollars of Federal moneys to the Park Land Acquisition Fund, which in the words of the act put these funds 'At the sole discretion of the members of the House and Senate to use as they see fit.' The 13 billion dollars lasted all of six months.

[35] The infamous SSRR act of 2036 pilfered 14% of all moneys collected for Social Security benefits that year, and put them in a bogus 'Money Market' account, that was meant to pay high interest. The account was actually a method for the five largest banks in the US to 'loan' the money to other 'banks' in the third world, that were really thinly disguised organs of themselves. The default rate actually toped 102% on these loans, a fact that no one has ever really been able to explain fully. Undaunted by this fiasco, Congress covered the overage with a 'special appropriation.'

entirely on sucking money out of other peoples budgets to shunt to his new masters pockets, skimming heavily for himself, of course, and building new alliances with the other turd smoking butt boys of the new order.

He had been doing this for the last nine years and was quite expert at it. Although he was reviled by nearly everyone in the capitol, he was still an essential part of every shitty deal that went down there. He didn't mind being hated—he liked it and took the widespread animosity held for him, as a hard won badge of heroism. He had earned every ounce of that hatred, by God, and he was damn proud of it.

He was the man that not one but three different 'sponsors' had turned to within hours of the Hold being placed. What they had in mind, was the corporate takeover of first the US political system, and then the entire world economy. If they could get away with it, and at last drop all this expensive political posturing about 'government' they could get on with business as usual at a fraction of the cost.

The man they called on to do the deed, was the most slippery eel they thought they could dupe to get what they wanted. They would betray him later, of course, but that would be in their own good time, and only if he succeeded. If he did not, he would take the fall for their ropey schemes as placidly as a lamb, whether he liked it or not.

That's what they thought at any rate.

Of course, they didn't go around blabbing about this stuff in public, or callously calling him on the carpet to do their biding like the feckless chore boy that he was. No. On the contrary, they wheedled and cajoled him with subtle flattery and promises of power and riches beyond even his prodigious imaginings. They spoke in public of corporate helmsmanship and creating a new order, captained by those most able to lead. This nauseating horseshit was sucked up by Failsworthy and the upper 30% of the salaried public like opiated mother's milk.

They didn't even have to prompt him much on the main points, their subterfuge was so internalized in him that he wrote the rap himself, only having the final text of his speech vetted by the chairmen of the boards.

They passed it with only the most minor changes to a word here and there, really just the occasional turn of phrase. He held this speech in his hands now as he walked to the podium, to address the Senate.

All week they had been trying to figure out what to do about the Hold, without reaching so much as a consensus on what the problem was. For the most part, both sides of the aisle had spent the week pointing fingers at each other and screaming like a bunch of purple assed baboons on methadrene.

Actually, this analogy is less than accurate as baboons usually have something important that motivates them to scream at each other besides simple co-hatred and nay saying, like sexual dominance or the need to secure a food supply. These people wouldn't have dreamed of securing a food supply when they could just steal somebody else's children and eat them. Some of them <u>were</u> on speed though. He could feel their eyes on his back as he walked up the aisle. They hated him—he loved it.

He mounted the few steps up to the podium and nodded his hello to the speaker. Behind him, he could hear people talking among themselves, as a kind of dull rumble. He turned around, and the rumble died away.

Failsworthy regarded his colleagues through squinting porcine eyes. He felt old and powerful, like a blunderbuss full of rusty nails and cat shit, as if even the minutest scratch from his words would eventually kill his listeners. This feeling was utterly illusory of course, but it made his balls hang pendulously down like a great warrior, and his voice deepen into a rumbling, authoritative timbre, that rattled glasses, and put peoples teeth on edge.

"Fellows hear me.[36] I am here before you as a humble citizen and servant much the same as you all. I ask you to set aside your partisan politics and listen to what I propose with new, open ears, like children, unencumbered by old idea and old ways. If you can, then there may still be hope for this great nation yet. If not then we might as well all just go home and put our feet up to wait for the inevitable end to overtake us in our sleep.

"We are at a crossroads here, and there are trucks headed our way. We had better wake up and step out of the way pretty damned fast or we will become the political road pizza of the twenty first century.

"I don't have to tell you what's at stake here, I'm sure. Each and every one of you knows full well what we stand to lose if we do not have the courage to come to a new resolve about this. This

---

[36] It was all the rage just then in political circles to use such affectations, particularly as a pop, at the beginnings of insincere speeches. This fact was not at all lost on the American People, though <u>this</u> was, apparently, on their politicians.

is the greatest nation on earth, possibly the greatest that has ever been, and not inconceivably the greatest that ever will be. We have built an infrastructure that is the envy of the world, made a life style and a standard of living that is virtually unmatched, and even now, as we speak, are sending brave men and women to another star. Ladies and gentlemen, it isn't likely to get any better than this, certainly not in our lifetimes."

He looked around at the chamber. He had their attention for the most part. He liked this, it was like playing a fiddle, not that Failsworthy could have begun to play a fiddle, but that's how he imagined it.

"Now," he continued philosophically, leaning on the podium. "All this greatness, all this 'Progress' to use the old term, was not come to by accident and happenstance. It didn't fall on our heads like manna from heaven.

"No. It was wrested from a wild and unyielding continent, bepeopled by savage Indians and inhabited by wild animals, one grueling step at a time. In short it was a complete bitch! People died! Horses were worked to death, and great forests hewn down by sheer will and singing steel.

"The people of this great nation all had to pull together, or they would be pulled apart.

"Then, as now, for it is just such a time as that, that we are now faced with, the United States of America is being pulled apart at the seams from within, by a few selfish individuals[37] that can't seem to get it through their thick heads that this is a collective effort or it is nothing at all. They seek, so it seems, to take all our great works, all the blood, sweat and tears that went into making this great nation of ours and dashing them against the stones of their indifference, like so many unwanted kittens. They can not, or will not see that they owe a huge debt to this nation, to their forebears, and to this very body itself, for is not a nation defined by its laws? And are not those laws made right here in this very room? That's what it's all about, isn't it? Law!?"

There were some nods and grunts of assent at this last.

"They would ignore their obligation to pay their rightful taxes in order that we, their governors, might get on with the important business of governing them, so that they can make an annoying little stink about fund allocation. A subject, I might add, that they, the taxpayers, have not the foggiest notion how to conduct. We cannot be held to ransom by these brigands. It is

---

[37] As he spoke the number was 91.7% of the US taxpayers.

not their place to micro-manage the affairs of Congress, so I put it to you. Have we not an obligation to this great country, to take back the reins of government from these interlopers? Can we afford to sit by hoping for their eventual benefaction after we have bent down and kissed their feet? How do we know that they will not instead free our heads from our encumbering necks?

"Come on stand up with me! Stick your necks out while you still have them to stick out, and let's take this country back! Let's stop all this bickering back and forth and do something about it!"

This was the cue for Sam Tiendale, one of Failsworthy's cronies to stand up and ask his question.

"Tell me Senator," he said. "What did you have in mind to accomplish this feat?"

"Funny you should ask, Senator, because I happen to have with me, right here, a first draft of a bill that would solve this problem once and for all. Perhaps you'd like to hear some of the major points."

He stopped only long enough to catch his breath.

"Fist of all I propose two amendments to the credit act, *SB 49756*, clause four, such that it read as follows.

"The citizens of the United States of America shall hold all moneys, credits and currency in the Federal Credit System and shall draw upon those moneys, credits and currency as their needs so dictate, except in case of national emergency and at such times as Congress deems fit in its wisdom to disallow. At such times it will be the sole right of Congress to reallocate these funds as needed to amend the crisis, take control of the country's affairs, if it deems such action necessary and make good all debts therein accrued.

"And secondly, clause sixteen such that it reads as follows.

"Anyone who seeks to stop work, circumvent the Federal Credit System, or otherwise stop Congress from carrying out its rightful tasks under the provision, and who is convicted of such under due process of law is guilty of economic treason, and is punishable by death, under the Special War Powers Act of 2041, provision seven.

"Further I propose that these two amendments be coupled to a provision that only the members of Congress themselves be exempt from these acts under the general amnesty provision of 2044, and not the executive and judiciary branches as otherwise set out in that document.

"That is what I propose to stop this cancer from spreading. If you have the courage to vote these provisional changes to the existing laws, we can have access to those moneys in future that have been taken from us so criminally this time.

"For now the problem remains that most of the people taking part in the Hold have actually taken their money out of the banks in one form or another and are holding it mostly in cash, thinking that we can't get at it. Well, maybe we can and maybe we can't. We could try to repeal the 31st amendment[38] and just borrow the money, like back in the good old days but I doubt that either the Chinese or the Street have forgotten the last go round. I don't know who else we could ask, anyway, but I know one thing that we can do, and that is to reissue the dollar. If we do that and declare all 'old dollars' null and void, we can take it off of them when they come to change 'em for new ones. And if they don't want to come to us with their hats in their hands then they will just have a bunch of worthless paper stuffed under their mattresses.

"Now, I know that reissuing the dollar will cost us some, but that should be more than made up for by the offset of having the entire black economy fall flat on its ass, at least for a little while.

"There will be a full copy of the draft legislation in your mail by this evening, God help us all if we haven't the guts to do this."

He stepped down from the podium to applause from both sides of the aisle, in spite of how people felt about him. As he walked up the aisle to his seat Al Faircloth approached him coming the other way. His opponent stopped and shook his hand.

"Wonderful speech Dan. I really enjoyed it, especially the part when you called the electorate a bunch of thickheaded kitten murderers. That was truly elegant."

"Thanks Aluwishus and listen, say hello to your wife and my kids. Won't you?"

Faircloth smiled a big, insincere smile.

"Fuck you Danny. Fuck you very much."

Failsworthy smiled, feeling the inner glow of Faircloth's absolute revulsion for him, like a warm fire on a cold night. He turned away and continued walking.

"Kiss my balls Al."

Faircloth turned and walked toward the podium shaking his head. That man was born a jackass, and he would die one

---

[38] The 31st amendment you will recall was passed after the crash of '26 and forbids Congress from borrowing money. This is why the US is still a cash based economy to this day.

someday, it was just his nature. He felt sorry in a way for him, it must be lonely to be such an asshole.

He couldn't understand how a person could be so graceless as that. After all, there was no reason for it. It didn't smooth his way, or get things done any quicker or more efficiently. If it facilitated matters, he could understand it, at least as a pragmatic, if somewhat objectionable political technique.

He himself had, on occasion, had to resort to less than gentlemanly behavior, as a means of getting someone's attention, for instance, but then only as a last resort. And he never felt good about it, even if he eventually got his end. To him that sort of unpleasantness was strictly whores business, an unfortunate necessity, but Failsworthy seemed to him to wallow in it.

Aluwishus Faircloth was a throwback from a more elegant age, a Southern gentleman—a dynastic politician who had inherited his grace, his money and his seat from his father, just as *he* had from *his*. In fact, his family had held one of the senatorial seats from Arkansas for so long that the office was, at least in the South, referred to as the Faircloth seat. He had only been opposed twice in his political carrier, both times by secular humanists, who had been tainted by the cities and both times he had won easily on the Christian conservative ticket.

His place on the Armed Services committee was also a somewhat dynastic affair, though this was due more to his family's fierce loyalty to the Military machine, than their line of accession. If he had ever wavered in his support for the generals and their corporate Christian machine, he would have been trundled off to the Arts committee like a North Dakota freshman.

He stepped up onto the podium and adjusted the mic to his greater height, eyeing the legislature. His esteemed colleagues were all there waiting to hear his deep rumbling tenor ring out in sincere, authoritative tones.

He cleared his throat and began lying.

-<>-

The Government of Greater Burundi,

(including the enclave of Snellville the Lesser),

Announces the general public sale of **common stock**, and a smaller amount of **preferred stock**, in a new placer mineral extraction program in the **Umbutu River**

Valley. The initial offering will be for **13 Million shares** of **Common Stock** at **BFr 100.00** per share, and **2 Million shares** of **Preferred Stock** at **BFr 250.00** per share. All stocks available through the London Stock Exchange.

Source, The Economist Sept. 13, 2046

-<>-

"Mommy! Tommy won't give me the Snakos, and they're the new ostrich flavored ones. They're my favorite!"

"Now kids, don't fight over the Snakos, there's always plenty to go around!"

"Thank you, Mommy!!!"

"Snakos! Now in 5 de-snak-a-licious flavors! Which one's your favorite?"

"Get 'em before they're gone, supplies are limited!"

Pitching

"...and it is upon exactly those sort of conservative, Christian, American values that this country was founded, not by this bunch of fanatical anarchists, worshipers of the anti-Christ each and every one, that have taken it into their heads to abscond with the rightful property of the American people, but by right thinking, family people like those who live in all our districts. They voted us here and I, for one, think that we owe them, the voters, a debt of gratitude. I think that we owe it to them to take back the controls of this Government that they entrusted to us before it goes down in flames!

"Now, I would reiterate to you, what many of my colleagues here today have said, that this is not the work of the vast majority of the electorate, but the doing of a few trouble makers that have undertaken to swindle the American people out of their birth right. A free democracy! The freedom to vote for the party of their choice!

"That's what all this is about! Freedom! That's why we established Conservative American Christians, as a freedom of choice party, so that all those Americans out there that think alike could vote their choice together, and I do not intend to let that freedom be taken away from them. They put me here, and it is here I intend to stay till they vote me out again, <u>lawfully</u> and <u>legally</u>!"

Faircloth paused for effect, as applause bubbled up from the less gun-shy among the Senate.

"The American people want us here, that's clear, and as we owe it to them to stay and do the job that they hired us to do, we had better get cracking. This is no small threat to our great nation. This is no two-bit dictator in some banana republic rattling his absurd little saber at us. This is a real and significant challenge to our sovereignty, and it has come from within!

"Just like Rome!

"Just like England!

"Just like Russia!

"And by God is my witness, we are not going to just let it happen here! We love this country too much. She is our mother and our father. We cannot abandon her now in her hour of need.

"We, the Government of these great United States of America have to put aside our partisan politics. We must band together and present a unified front against this onslaught from the far out left wing kooks that are seeking to destroy us. We must sniff them out wherever they hide, in whatever dark place they inhabit, crawling amongst the worms and excrement with the other lower life forms that in those fetid environs abide! We must hunt them down like rabid dogs and blast their deluded little brains out of their misshapen skulls as they cringe before our terrible anger.

"We must not stop! We must not let ourselves be turned aside in this sacred quest to rid this country once and for all of the cancer that is eating away at it from inside, for that way lies servitude and death.

"This is a national emergency, and I have asked the president to declare it as such, so that we can get access to the weapons that we need to fight this fight. What we need is the Army, as we have never needed them before! And the Air Force, with their sophisticated spy satellites and the Navy with their, boats, and of course, the Marines with their, uh, famous will to fight. Only these men can save us, only they have the means to do the job and do it right, and it is they themselves that are under the greatest attack even as we speak! From these scoundrels and the president alike!

"He must be made to see that it is the last thing that we should do, to cut money from the Military. We must convince him to support the Military, and to declare a state of emergency, so that we can impound the money of these, bandit few among us and use that money to prosecute our cause against them.

"Isn't that what we want to do? Isn't that elegant, to use the money that they seek to hold from us against them? If we can get the president to move swiftly and decisively against this gang, we can have the last laugh.

"That's why I have proposed the Emergency Funds Acquisition Act. It will make it possible to get to the moneys that have been misappropriated by placing a tax directly on all spending as a value added tax of something like 25%, that will be paid, more or less directly, to the Military for the duration of the emergency. All those millions of citizens that are law abiding tax payers and support us, can claim back part of it off their income tax at the end of the year, as a credit..."

"That's a sweet little fuck he's trying to pull," said Sergei gesturing with his cigarette. "That way either you pay or you pay."

Mort nodded, taking another handful of popcorn from the bowl.

"Yes, and so blatant, like he was talking to a Jr. High School civics class, and no-one was going to notice his dick hanging out."

"And, they can claim back some of it as a credit at the end of the year. Who in fuck he thinks he is fooling?"

Mort took a long drink of his beer, sweating in the hot still afternoon air. There were flies dog fighting in the doorway that led to the kitchen. Mort could see Anna working at the counter making lunch. She had a slender waist, and little butt. Mort thought about her butt. He liked it.

She turned around and came toward him carrying a tray of food.

"Lunch time," she said as she came through the door.

The flies parted to let her pass and as she did the one on the right ambushed the other one with a diving attack from above.

She set the food down on the table and sat between the two men. She took a sandwich and a beer.

"What's he lying now?" she asked.

Mort went for the pastrami on rye.

"He's lying that we need the army now more than ever, and that we must put a 25% sales tax on everything we buy so the Military can have all the money that we aren't gullible enough to just hand over to them so that they can squander it on useless horse shit and more beside."

"You can claim back part at the end of year as tax credit."

"Part?!"

Mort nodded. "Nice eh?"

"Cock suckers," she said.

Anna drained half her beer in one long drink. "He's ugly too."

Faircloth looked out of the TV like a tough but fair god, regarding the audience.

"The American people deserve better than this, and I for one intend to see they get it."

"Give it to me baby," said Anna.

She looked at Mort. "He'll never get away with this you know."

"He's getting away with it even as we speak."

Sergei turned his head to the side, appraising.

"In stolen limousine, with police escort."

Anna held a bowl out to him. "Snakos?"

-<>-

The Office of President of Greater Burundi

Snellville 16/1/2047

Dear Senator Failsworthy,

I am very pleased on this occasion to be writing to you with an announcement regarding the Umbutu River Project. As I am sure you have heard by now, our initial share offer was a great success, and our start up capitalization levels are on target. This is in part due to your interest in the project as that interest did much to reassure our investors.

By way of a small token of my thanks please find enclosed a stock certificate in the amount of 50,000 shares of preferred stock in your name.

Please accept this gift and my grateful thanks,

Sincerely, Joshua Kabingga

The Office of President of Greater Burundi

Snellville 16/1/2047

Dear Senator Faircloth,
I am very pleased...

-<>-

Michael ate his egg watching Dwayne, with a slight smile on his lips. He was a slight man as well, narrow across the shoulders and thinner still in the hips. He was in his early thirties, with big brown eyes and a shock of curly hair that he always made sure to have hanging down coquettishly over his forehead like a soft spring.

He lifted the spoon to his mouth and cupped the rich yolk onto his tongue with the point of his lip. It was warm and smooth and filled his mouth with luscious eggyness.

Dwayne looked up from his papers at him. Their eyes held for a moment, before Dwayne spoke.

"What?"

Michael smiled with his eyes silently, letting him stew for a moment, till just before he was about to speak again.

"What are you going to do?" he asked.

"Do?"

"Yes, do. What are you going to do about it?"

"It?"

"Yes dear man. It. The Hold."

"The Hold," said Dwayne flatly, as if it were a meaningless phrase.

He had a way of doing this, sometimes, that flustered Michael, as it was clearly meant to. Someone would ask Dwayne a question that he didn't want to answer, and he would turn it back around on them, making it sound as if it were the stupidest thing in the world to say, just by repeating it flatly. Michael knew this trick for what it was, a trick and nothing more. Knowing it, didn't stop it from irritating him.

"Yes," said Michael just as flatly. "The hold. You will recall that you are at an impasse."

Dwayne smiled wisely, holding his eye. "No, I'm not. Only Kabingga is."

Michael believed him, sitting across the table from him. Dwayne didn't wear that smile as a weapon, ever. It was his don't worry about a thing smile.

Michael smiled back.

"So then, what _are_ you going to do?"

Dwayne let him stew for a moment as he meticulously picked up his coffee cup and took a careful sip. Michael looked back at him, waiting.

"Nothing," said Dwayne at last.

"Nothing?!"

Dwayne was amused by this. Michael could never play the game out to the end—he was too emotional.

"Look," he said. "On the one hand Failsworthy, et al, whether they like it or not, know that they can't possibly break the Hold by force and expect to survive. They believe from their analysis, and rightly so, that they would quite likely be dragged from their offices and lynched in the streets if they tried. This is all just so much posturing for the sake of their sponsors. They'd never get away with it and they know it.

"And secondly, why should I _do_ anything, when I can just sit by and watch it all happen around me, more or less as I want it to?

"The Senate will wind itself up to near bursting, damaging its credit all the while, as they puff and posture like the pathetic chimp spankers they are. Heedless of the real issues at hand, which are—what price are we willing to pay for freedom, and what are we willing to do to ensure prosperity.

"When they have finally managed to paint themselves into a tight little corner," he said, squinting through his gesturing fingers, "I will step in at the last minute and turn all that energy, all that noise and confusion in on itself like folding up a news paper full of dog do, with the power of a few well chosen, softly spoken words. That is the way..."

He seemed lost for words.

"Forward?" offered Michael.

"Yes, that is the way <u>forward</u>."

-<>-

Dear Mr. President,

Congratulations on your recent electoral victory. On behalf of my entire family please let me say that we were all pulling for you from the very beginning, especially Pablo. I look forward to meeting you someday should the opportunity present itself.

Also please allow me to extend to you an open invitation to come to Snellville for a visit any time you like, you will love Africa's beauty. Enclosed is a token of congratulations in the form of 200,000 shares of preferred stock in the Umbutu River Project.

All the best, and let us know if you need to borrow a cup of sugar.

Sincerely, Joshua Kabingga

-<>-

Worthy sat on the narrow bench next to Cassandra, listening to Mantovani. Before them the hallway bustled with people, even at this late hour. They had been waiting a long time there in the pentagon, with its officious soldiers and other sexless workers.

Worthy thought about how hive-like the whole place seemed to him. He imagined that just behind one of the doors that lined the hallway, there was a vast macabre honeycomb stuffed with colonel pupae. A woman walked past him with a cart full of data. 'Probably food' he thought, 'Human souls coded into card after card to be sucked up by the twisted larvae that pulsated deep within the heart of the building.'

"Souls for the hive," he said circumspectly, gesturing with an eyebrow.

Cassandra eyed the cart. "How would they know what to do with them?"

"Instructions from central control."

A short, efficient looking sergeant walked purposefully up to them and stopped. "You are waiting to see General Baisch." It was definitely a statement not a question.

"Yes, we..." was all Yeates could get out.

"Follow me," she said.

She turned and walked away down the hall, with no further word. Yeates and Cassandra hurried to keep up.

She had a stiff little terrier's walk that carried her like she was hung on short springs. Worthy wondered if she was a robot. There weren't any robots that he knew of other than crude crawling things with simple programs that allowed them to operate in hostile environments. Not, he had to admit, that this wasn't a hostile environment, but he hadn't heard about anyone developing an android of this complexity.

He looked at Cassandra. "Android?"

She regarded the sergeant. "Cybot."

She turned at a side corridor and they followed her.

As they walked behind her, they tried to pick out the wiring of gears, that they knew must be there, from the sound of her heals ticking on the linoleum.

She stopped at a door and opened it for them.

"Enter."

She followed them in and then spoke in a clear voice. "Mr. Yeates, this is the Special Working Group on Sustained Procurement."

Cassandra waited to be introduced, and waited and waited. Finally she elbowed Worthy in the ribs.

"Hello," he said. "This is Cassandra Robertson, one of our account executives."

There were four other people in the room, three at a large table and one, a general officer, looking out the window into the night with his back to them. No one introduced themselves for the moment. Worthy recognized Stern. There was a bald guy with a wise assed look on his face who sat forward nonchalantly gesturing with an open palm.

"Have a seat."

As they sat down, the man at the window cleared his throat.

Baisch stood facing the window, trying to look as though he were gazing into the distance, thoughtfully. He let his ego handle this as a background task, like keeping his shoulders square and his back straight, and all the thousands of other little bits of posture and image handling it did.

Consciously, he let them hang for few seconds more and after precisely enough time had passed, he turned around.

Baisch squared his shoulders to the two advertising people,

and regarded them.

Yeates, the man, was a skinny guy, with thinning hair and too honest eyes. He looked slack and uncomfortable in his suit, like he was lying by wearing it. The other one, Robertson was a woman. She had short straight hair that stuck up off the top of her head like a cocky black brush. She seemed unafraid. He wondered what it would be like to have her somewhere in Mongolia.

"Hello, I'm General Harlan Baisch," he said. "Coffee?"

Without waiting for an answer he spoke to the sergeant without looking at her. "Coffee."

She turned around and left the room.

"So," asked Baisch, levelly, "what kind of results have you managed to produce out of the data that we sent you?"

He looked at Worthy, waiting.

"Jesus Christ, Harly, let 'em have their coffee, will ya? They been sittin' out in the hall for an hour."

Baisch looked at Carstairs for a moment.

"Good suggestion, Dan."

Baisch looked back at Worthy.

"How was your journey down to Washington, Mr. Yeates?" he asked stiffly.

Worthy thought he was like one of his high school dates' fathers. Like, he was embarrassed to be there, or that _he_ should be.

"Uneventful." He just stopped himself from calling him, Sir.

There was a pause.

Cassandra cleared her throat.

"So tell me, General Baisch, How long have we got to sell the American People on our message?"

Baisch liked that. She was direct, like Joan, his secretary. She was clear. He looked at her with his most sincere expression. "A month, maybe six weeks at the outside."

"Okay."

She thought about what that meant to them for a moment, how they could possibly deliver any sort of meaningful result in that short a time. She turned to Worthy. "Don't wait for the coffee."

"Right," he said, standing up and unzipping his portfolio.

He pulled out a thick stack of mocked up ads and set them out on the table in front of him. He flipped the first one out onto the table, upside down to him, so that Baisch and the others could see it.

93

"This," he began, "is an idea that we had for a first approach, a sort of introduction to the consumers of your basic idea. It's what we call a teaser."

There was a picture of Uncle Sam standing sideways to the camera with his pants down around his ankles looking vulnerable, and the simple caption 'America'. Baisch looked at the picture silently. Dan Carstairs sat forward looking too. He looked at Baisch, who after a long pause looked back at him. They both looked at Yeates.

Worthy didn't flinch—he had been here before. "Next we run this," he said, flipping the next board over. It had the pack of dildo packing baboons and hyenas on it with the caption 'The World'.

Now Rick Stern looked over Baisch's shoulder for a while before speaking. "Yeah, then what?"

"Then the next day we run this." He flipped the next board.

Now the pack was right behind Uncle Sam and the lead baboon had a huge spiky dildo strapped on. He was about to pounce. The caption read, 'Our country is about to be Swindeled.' They stood there looking at it for a long time. Baisch looked up at Worthy from under his crew cut.

"Is that it?" he asked.

"No." said Worthy. "It's just the start.

"This first ad is followed over the next couple of weeks by these three campaigns."

He turned over three more boards and laid them out next to each other. One had a picture of a small girl looking up at her father, the second was of a cute fuzzy old couple and the third was a pretty young woman at the beach.

"This one," he said, pointing at the child, "is targeting young parents."

"The second most active group of voters in the country, but they also have the support of various ancillaries—their parents, the press and so on," added Cassandra.

"The story is this little girl walking through the park with her mother," he said, lifting up the picture like a flap to reveal a series of storyboards beneath. "Here they are walking through the park, with all the birds singing and there is happy music playing in the background. It's all very lovely and peaceful." He pointed to the next frame where a man was now with them holding ice cream. "Here, Dad comes up to them with ice-cream cones and the little girl starts to clap and skip around, happy to have her ice-cream in the lovely park with her loving parents."

94

"Yeah, so?" asked Carstairs. "Then what happens?"

"Then here," he pointed, "Mom and Dad have a peaceful, happy look between them, and he gives the ice-cream to his daughter. Mom says to Dad, 'Gee honey, it's great to have more money now that the rest of the world isn't our problem anymore.' and he says, 'Yep, sure is, even though I haven't had a job in three years the state provides for all our needs, even ice-cream!' They smile empty-headedly. There is an airplane coming toward them in the background.

"They look up at the noise of the motors," he continued, pointing at a frame of Mom shading her eyes, "and Mom says, 'Look honey, what's that funny looking airplane up there?' Dad says, 'Gee Baby, I don't know. I certainly don't recognize it.' Here we see the view from inside the cockpit of the airplane. The gauges are labeled in some foreign language and there is foreign radio babble in the background. We see the pilot's hairy baboon hand. The plane noses over and starts diving for the park."

"Uh oh," said Carstairs.

Worthy pointed to a frame of the family being laced with bullets.

"Here the plane strafes the family sending twenty millimeter slugs ripping through them like paper targets. Their ice-cream cones splatter to the ground and are spattered with blood and guts as they die screaming. And then the last frame is a black card. We bring up these words. Fiction? Coincidence? You decide."

"That's a bit harsh. Don't you think?" asked Stern.

"These are harsh realities we are talking about here, and it is the American public which must decide their own fate. They've taken that on and now they have to deal with it."

Baisch looked at the ad man with new eyes. He didn't fold up the way he figured he would. "Well put, Yeates."

"But..."

"Let him say his bit, Rick, you will get your turn in a little while."

Stern smiled an, 'Okay asshole, if that's the way you want it' smile. "And this next, what's up with it?" he asked Worthy.

Cassandra said, "This one is targeted at the elderly, the big bloc."

Worthy lifted the picture and pointed to the first frame. "This one starts out with these two old people. They are everyone's parents. They are lovable and harmless. It is their retirement celebration and they are sitting up on a stage as people cheer

95

them from the floor of an auditorium. There is a Swindel look alike speaking at the podium as the band plays and balloons float in the air. Behind them we can see several soldiers bound and gagged and tied to the posts that support the stage.

"Here he gestures to the old couple and introduces them as Mr. and Mrs. Senior America. He says that the entire country owes them a debt and that without them the world wouldn't be the wonderful place that it is today. He presents them with a check for $3.16 from the treasury and says, 'Stand up and let the people thank you.'"

He pointed to the next frame. "Now the people are cheering and the oldsters are waving, and the Swindler helps the old guy forward to the microphone. As he does we see him lift the old guys wallet. Pop here says, 'Thanks everybody—thanks a lot it was our pleasure, we were happy to do it, to build a world worth living in for our grandkids.'

"And here it's a little later and a line of people are passing Mom and shaking her hand, some are giving her a kiss on the cheek, some are baboons and hyenas. Each one takes something from her. One her cane, the next her purse, then her sweater and so on. The soldiers behind are trying to struggle free of their bonds. Pop turns around and he is half naked as people swarm up onto stage cheering them and stealing everything they have. The pres. applauds with his boyfriend off to one side.

"And here we see a close-up of the old people looking bewildered. We see their bare shoulders, showing that they are now naked. The old woman is crying. Pop holds her to give what comfort he can.

"Here in the end, the old folks are sweeping up after the party and everyone has gone home. The Prez's boyfriend, dressed in an incredibly rich, gay tuxedo stops at the door on his way out, we see a Rolls waiting for him outside. 'Hey,' he says disrespectfully, 'don't forget to turn out the light when you're done.' He exits as we hear the carnival music outside.

"The black card at the end just says, 'Thanks a lot'".

John Dunivan, who up till now had stood quietly and watched, shook his head. "I don't know, we might have trouble over too close a look alike for Swindel. I'll have to have the department check on that."

Baisch nodded assent.

"What about this one?"

"In this one, this young woman is playing volley ball at the beach, with her friends. They knock the ball around and dance to the music and so on. In the background we see boats out on the sea.

"She stops play for a moment, as her friends continue, to go get a coke. Here we see her kneel down to open the ice chest.

"She calls to her friends over her shoulder, 'Hey, anybody want a drink?' They say 'Okay, sure Sandy.' She grabs the cokes and is just standing up with them when, here," he pointed, "the cooler is stomped shut by an army booted foot. She screams, looking up in terror.

"Now we see her point of view. There is a full scale landing in progress by, you guessed it, dildo packing baboons and hyenas along with foreign looking soldiers. They storm up the beach shooting the boys and grabbing the girls and dragging them over the dunes screaming.

"Sandy is knocked to the ground and riffle butted in the face. She screams, spitting out teeth as she too is dragged over a dune to be raped by the vile horde.

"The black card at the end on this one says, 'It could happen.' Fade in a young Marine standing in front of it in full dress uniform, holding his rifle at the ready. He looks into the camera sincerely and says 'Not on my watch.'

"Then we have a voice over saying 'What price freedom?'"

Baisch shook his head, looking at the artwork.

Worthy looked at Cassandra, they were done here.

Baisch looked at Carstairs. "Well Dan, What do you think?"

"What do I think? I think that a lot of people are going to get pretty pushed out of shape by this kind of thing. I think that we ought to run a more conservative campaign, that is set up along much more conventional lines, so we don't alienate the taxpayers anymore that they already are."

Baisch looked introspective for a moment, he inclined his head and then looked at Stern. "Rick?"

"I would agree with Admiral Carstairs' assessment, particularly in the light of recent events[39], that we can't afford to risk turning public opinion against us no matter what, and that these ideas would have a good chance of doing so, especially in the South and Mid-West. I would advise against it."

Baisch stayed Worthy's up welling response with a smile and

---

[39] He was referring to the poll taken surreptitiously by the IRS that showed that fully 90% of respondents indicated that they had no intention of paying their taxes under any circumstances whatsoever.

an open hand. "Please," he said, and looked back at the ads.

"Okay, Rick, anything else?"

"No, that's about it."

"Fine, thank you for your assessment."

Without looking up Baisch said, "Mr. Dunivan?"

The Lawyer took his time speaking, as he almost always did. He looked at the ads again, appraising them, looking for what he might have missed. At last he spoke, with a pointed deliberateness.

"Most of this doesn't represent anything like a big legal problem for us. As I have said before, I will have to check with my staff on how close we can get to a look-alike. Just off the top of my head, I think that if the actor happens to look like the president then that can be put down to coincidence, but special makeup will probably be viewed as libelous. But there is something in this that worries me, beyond the straight legal implications, and that is that we not only risk offending large numbers of people in the Mid-West, but also that there my be large numbers of people on capitol hill that this sort of approach will polarize into two camps, those for us and those against." He looked at Baisch.

"Tell me, Harly," he said. "If they called the vote tomorrow, how many people on the hill would back you up, at risk to themselves and their position?"

Baisch shrugged, "I don't know. Rick, how many?"

"One hundred thirty or so, that we believe are trustworthy under normal circumstances. Which these aint."

Dunivan counted off his points on his fingers. "Okay, so maybe they stand behind you through the storm, most of them, or maybe they don't. Then maybe a few brave hearts in both houses, either like your approach enough that they go for it, or more likely, they cynically decide that you might be a dark horse worth backing and so stand behind you. How many is that? A dozen, two dozen, maybe? In any case I think that it will be far from sufficient to carry the day, and what good will it do us anyway, to have the support of Congress if half the country is against us, not to mention the Swindeler. Don't think that he is going to just roll over and take this from us, to borrow a term. You may say what you like about him, you may hate him like a prostate exam, but don't for a moment under-estimate him. He got where he is on his own back."

Baisch made reasonable with his hands out spread before him like an impenetrable shield of calm. After a moment he said,

"Thank you, John, I get your point.

"Well, Mr. Yeates? What have you to say to these dire allegations?"

Worthy had nothing at all to lose, as far as he could see, they hated it, and he was not going to change their minds by handling them. Not that he was too good to stoop to that. He just figured it wouldn't work. He swallowed the hard lump in his throat and said his piece because he thought he was right and damn the consequences—he was an undiplomatic fool.

Worthy spoke up in a loud clear voice, looking at Baisch.

"Hog wash." He paused for a moment. "You people have no balls.

"What do you think this is, some kind of a debate? Some kind of talk-show chitchat? This is the end of the free world, as we know it! Right here and right now! This isn't fiction, man, it's real!"

He rounded on Stern and the others.

"You think these images are too strong? You think that I might offend someone's delicate sensibilities with disturbing pictures of what it's going to be like after we just throw away what it has taken this country two hundred and seventy five years to build. What about our ancestors? They fought like fiends and died by the millions so that you could walk your days under a free sky, and stand up to vote your conscience without fear of repression. What about your children, and their children, and theirs and theirs? Don't they deserve the same chance you had? What will you say to them? That you threw it all away because you were reticent to fight as hard as your fathers? That you didn't want to offend anybody!? What are you going to do, let your good taste stand between the American people and freedom?

"Wake up, assholes, these are Americans we are talking about here, not some bullshit TV family with lines written for them by blood-sucking cowards in Hollywood. This is still a nation of farmers, you know. Sure, you and your cocksure, college boy, friends may have stuffed them into coffin suits but down inside, under all the excuses and regulations beat the hearts of real live, warm-blooded mammals that will not be bullshitted by you or anybody else! These people deserve better, show them a little respect and tell them the truth for a change! Isn't that what this is all about? Truth? Don't they want to stop being lied to by you Washington shitbags? They will not give their money to you anymore! Not unless you shoot'em straight."

He stopped for breath looking around at their faces, and

99

seeing them for the first time in awhile. They were stone masks. Cassy just sat with her eyebrows arched, smirking. She knew this side of him pretty well, but he didn't usually light up like this in front of customers. Worthy heard Baisch start to laugh.

"'Lied to by you Washington shitbags!' Wonderful."

Baisch took a cigar out of his pocket and started rolling it between his fingers. He pulled out a lighter and played it under the end as he spoke.

"And you Ms. Robertson, do you have anything to add to Mr. Yeates' opinion?" He started puffing on the cigar.

"Yes I do," she said. "To begin with, I have to say that Worthy is right when he says it's honesty that the American people want, not more comfortable lies. That's what the Hold is about. You shouldn't lose sight of that, or it will trip you up. I also agree that there is a lack of moral courage here that will only be a liability to you. You have nothing to gain by caution——if you do nothing, unlike most times, this thing will rise up like a wave and take you.

"There is only one way open to you and that's to fight. Not the backroom politics of the past but a real street fight.

"I also agree with this guy. What's your name?"

"John Dunivan."

"With Mr. Dunivan. Swindel is no push over, so all the more reason to press him harder! If you hesitate for a second he will be at your throat like a pit bull. The American People aren't going to back you if you back down. They don't bankroll losers, they back winners."

Their eyes met.

"If you have the nads to take the reins you might win, if you try to stand tastefully out of the way, you will get killed."

Baisch looked at her squarely with his cigar sticking out of his pursed lips. His mouth looked like an asshole to her.

Baisch took the turd out of his mouth and smiled.

"Thank you, in fact, thank you all. Everybody's had a chance to say what they think. I think that we have all been pretty frank with each other about this. Quite frank in fact."

He looked at Worthy.

"Now it's my turn. Here's what I think.

"I think that these people," he gestured to his staff, "are paid a lot of money to give me their honest opinion. They are expected to be right all the time. They are most of the time too—in fact they are damned good at their jobs. They earn their money.

"And if you want to know, I think you have a hell of a nerve, Mister, coming in here, to this office in the pentagon, and telling

100

them and me that we are all full-a shit up to our eyeballs."

Worthy could see Stern and Carstairs start to smile to themselves now.

"I also think," Baisch continued, "that you're right, and that someone with a hell of a nerve is exactly what is called for here."

Stern and Carstairs stopped smiling, as Worthy and Cassandra started to.

"I want these ads running by next week. John, figure out how close we can play it as soon as you can. Thank you for your time Mr. Yeates, Ms. Robertson. The sergeant will see you out. Let me see what else you come up with."

The sergeant, who was just returning with the coffees set them down and held the door open for them.

"This way," she said.

Yeates and Cassandra picked up their boards, looking at each other.

"Uh thanks," said Worthy.

"We'll call you," said Cassy

Baisch looked at them without smiling. "Fine, we'll get you set up with some capital tomorrow. Good night." He winked at Cassandra and turned around. They left, the sergeant closing the door after them.

Baisch looked out at the lights of Washington, waiting.

No one spoke for a long time, and he could feel the room hanging emptily behind him. He felt very alone then as he watched the cars passing by on the street, like a man standing at the end of a very narrow tongue of cliff.

"Well?" he asked at last. "Any comments, and analysis?"

He focused on the reflection of the room in the window, watching Stern and Carstairs. Dan started to shake his head.

"Gee, Harly, that was really some speech he made there, all full of conviction and anger, Do you really think it's the best way to go, though?"

Baisch turned around and looked at Carstairs. He had known him for twelve years. In all that time he'd never heard him ask such a frank and open question. He was normally an unflappable sarcast.

"You know, Dan, I honestly don't know but I do have to agree with Robertson's analysis—we have everything to lose if we do nothing, we also have nothing to lose if we do this. You know that guy Yeates may have an over-active imagination—he might even be dead wrong, but Jesus Christ the guy's got commitment. Did you see the way the veins bulged out at the sides of his neck like it was a hard on? That's the guy I want fighting for me!"

Rick nodded his head. "Yeah, he did have a pair. My first thoughts still stand, but maybe you're right. I wonder about this honesty angle, it sounds interesting— dangerous, but interesting. I don't think that Aliesha's going to go for it though. She is also one of us Washington shitbags."

"Oh, don't worry too much, Rick," John smiled. "Aliesha can do honest if she has to."

As Cassandra walked down the hall with the sergeant's curt heals tapping out a rhythm in front of her, she turned to look at Worthy. He was trying to fumble his portfolio back together as he walked. She wondered to herself just what the hell all that was about. Worthy looked at her, and answered her silent question with a shrug. "Beats me," he said half under his breath.

The next day at precisely ten o'clock a Mr. Green arrived at the door of P. Worthington Yeates & Associates. He had a briefcase with him.

-<>-

"Hello? Mr. Crenshaw? Is this Bill Crenshaw?"

"Yes. This is Bill."

"Hi, Mr. Crenshaw. My name is Bruce Tilden. I'm with Continental footwear. Bill—how do you feel about socks?"

On their way

His deliberate plainness, the monkey shit brown, four door sedan, the drab clothing with the ill-fitting necktie and the aviator sun glasses were all carefully orchestrated parts of the timeless uniform of his office. They said it as surely as would a neon sign twelve feet high floating over his head with a blinking arrow pointing downward at his cranium, saying SPY.

You could see him for blocks spying his way along through town noting things as he came toward you, like, well, a spy really. It was his very spy-iness that had landed him this particular assignment, in a rather round about way.

The thing was this, he was way to spy-like to actually be an under cover agent, since all he had to do was show up at the airport in Caracas, or Tel-Aviv, or wherever and he was instantly made as a spy. No great surprise there. Now, you would think that these spy-like tendencies of his, would make him utterly useless to the intelligence community—quite the contrary, he was the perfect decoy. In fact he was so useful that he couldn't remember his last day off, or the day before either for that matter.

What they would do was send him on a plane with other, properly circumspect spies, to whatever country the CIA wanted to infiltrate, and there he would disembark the aircraft to be immediately tailed by the secret police. He would go about his business attracting attention to himself with his ugly suit and clumsy questions while the others, unbeknownst even to him, slipped in and blended with the exotic wall paper.

He was perfect, and when the authorities finally ambushed him and dragged him to the little room that they invariably had set aside for his questioning, he could tell them nothing at all. In fact he was unaware of any Government secrets that he might have been privy to, and that was why he had the job today.

The reason for this was that he liked oysters, raw ones.

When he was thirty he was a field manager for Aramco as well as a spy and covert dealer in African uranium, living in Bahrain. There was a restaurant there that he frequented, Abdala's Ocean Kingdom, *an intimate wine bar and eatery.*

When he wasn't out on the rigs, or spying, he would go there in the early evening to sip chardonnay and slide oysters down his throat like delicious fishy mucus, as he looked for attractive foreign women to date.

One evening he was there and the place was pretty empty being a weeknight. He saw Kimeeko, a Japanese call girl that he dated from time to time. She was a lot of fun and always wanted to drink and dance and giggle a lot, as well as make love with him back at his villa. She was like a real date, not like a call girl, with awkward pauses and surprising little details about her family. She always took the money in the morning while he was still asleep.

He caught her eye across the room and she came over and sat next to him.

"Hi, Danny, you want company tonight?" she asked.

In those days he was called Danny Greenshire.

"Yes, please, have a drink, Kimeeko," he said, smiling.

They chatted and drank and she told him a dumb joke about a little boy with welding goggles and a pederast. It was lovely just sitting there wasting time. They ordered a fresh plate of oysters, and Kimeeko picked one up and squeezed lemon on it. She went to eat it and then stopped and made a face at the smell.

"Go on," said Danny, "they're good."

She shook her head. "No, it smells funny."

"Ah ya big sissy, come on give it to me. I'll show ya," he said, tipping back his head and closing his eyes with his mouth open.

Kimeeko didn't like that sissy remark. She shrugged, deadpan, and dumped the putrid bivalve in his mouth just to teach him a lesson.

He had a point to make so he never even chewed. He just let it slide down his throat and into his stomach. He opened his eyes and smiled.

"See, they're delicious!"

She started laughing.

He started to feel a little funny. He smiled trying to put a brave face on it, and stood up to go to the bathroom.

"Excuse me a moment please, I'll be right back," he said.

His stomach tried to jump out of his mouth, but he held it back and stepped toward the toilets. Kimeeko watched him go. He took another step and lost it.

He projectile vomited the offending oyster, several of its partially digested fellows, and a bottle of Côte d' Bourgogne in a gory fount over the Bar man, a potted palm tree and, an Australian geologist named Perry Davenport.

Kimeeko was holding her sides at this point as Danny tried to retch into the palm and apologize at the same time.

Perry, looked down at Danny, bent over puking, he looked at

his new silk jacket covered in unspeakable filth, with the sound of Kimeeko's laughter cackling in his ears.

He hefted a champagne bottle that was on the bar and swept it down through the space where Danny's head was, in one continuous motion, fracturing his skull and causing deep edema to the left side of his brain.

Danny went to sleep, and he never really woke up again.

While he was asleep for six weeks, the virus that was what had made the oyster such a revoltingly putrid object in the first place, and ultimately caused him to become 'sleepy', found a marvelous new place to live. It was warm and there was lots of fatty tissue around to eat, which was a major asset as far as it was concerned. It was his bruised brain.

The virus took particular interest in a minute portion of the corpus callosum, whose job it was to make a complex chemical known as anodene-sufoxilase.

Anodene-sulfoxilase is the chemical that stimulates the brain to build permanent memories out of the transient memories that are the heart of the awareness system. It is the glue, if you will, of ideas that lets the brain build its amazing three dimensional memories, like the first time you made love, if you weren't too drunk, that we so relish. No glue, no new memories.

The virus ate all the yummy tissue that it could find. So when what was left of Danny Greenshire, the part that Perry Davenport hadn't obliterated, sort of woke up he had no ability to form new memories.

He opened his eyes and his mother was there. She smiled and a tear ran down her cheek. "It's okay now Danny," she said, "you're back."

"Mom, What are you doing here?" he asked quite surprised.

She said. "Don't worry about it now son, you get some sleep."

He smiled at her and after a while he dozed off again. It was the fourth time that day that something like that had happened.

He lived with her now just outside Washington, in a big house by a golf course. He could never learn to play golf, but his mom was mad for the game. These were facts that he was usually unaware of.

For the rest of his life he would never remember his thirties. He was aware of his life in high school and later in his twenties. He remembered the Army, and how to drive a car for instance, and as he aged he slowly remembered little bits and pieces, but he could never remember anything new for more than a few moments, except that is, when the Company would inject him with anodene-sulfoxilase, and give him a briefing. Then he could remember almost nothing else!

Today he had to remember to give the suitcase to the guy on the card. P. Worthington Yeates 418 Clavel Street, P. Worthington Yeates 418 Clavel Street... again and again and again. It was clear and tangible, almost stone-like, running around his whacked out brain like a hamster in an exercise wheel.

They had briefed him in Maryland with an injection and a pair of headphones. This memory would fade slowly over the next several days until it was drowned in the cacophony of all the hundreds of other such "briefings" he had been given.

Mr. Green, as he was now called, parked his car across the street from Worthy's office and looked around obviously circumspectly. He made rather exaggerated motions out of moving the rear view mirror around to sneak a peek at the address, even though he could have just turned his head to the left and read the number as plain as day on the door. He remembered to write down the number on his pad. He always kept a lined yellow pad with him and a pencil, which he used to write things down before he forgot them. This strategy often failed, because he would read his notes from a few minutes ago and not know what they were about. Sometimes though, they helped a little.

He looked up and down the street for—something—and seeing it was clear, got out of the car with the brief case and walked to the front of it. He pretended to look at the tire and then, looking around once again, he swiped his card on the meter and walked quickly to the corner, where there was a mailbox.

He stopped at the mailbox and pretended to look for a letter to mail. He patted his pockets as he observed the area. Still clear, he stopped searching and walked quickly across the street. As he got to the other sidewalk a car passed on the next street. He froze. 'Who were they and what did they want!?' He looked toward the objective, P. Worthington Yeates 418 Clavel Street, P. Worthington Yeates 418 Clavel Street... He'd never make it before they came around. There were some garbage cans in a small alleyway about halfway to the address, P. Worthington Yeates 418 Clavel Street... He went for it.

Mr. Green walked quickly up to the cans and stepped behind them. He crouched down and stayed there watching, waiting, observing. No car came. After a while, he wondered what he was doing there. He looked around and stepped out onto the street.

P. Worthington Yeates 418 Clavel Street, He looked down at his notes. 418 it was the same number! He walked along to the next door and looked at the number. 416, no it was just a coincidence. He looked around again. P. Worthington Yeates 418 Clavel Street... He walked on observing the car across the street. It seemed familiar to him, a tan four-door sedan. He came to the next door. The number was 418, he looked down at his notes, 418! This was it. P. Worthington Yeates 418 Clavel Street. He pushed the buzzer.

After a while there was a little voice saying, "Yes?"

He wondered what that was about—then he remembered P. Worthington Yeates 418 Clavel Street.

"P. Worthington Yeates 418 Clavel Street," he ventured experimentally.

"Yes?"

"I have something for you."

There was a pause.

"Okay, come up."

There was a buzz and he pushed on the door, it opened.

Mr. Green walked up the stairs with the brief case, looking around for—something. At the top of the stairs he stopped and looked down the hallway. It appeared empty, so he walked quickly down to the first door and opened it. It was a broom closet. He went on to the next one. It had the name on it. He opened it. There was a man there, sitting at a desk.

"P. Worthington Yeates?" asked Mr. Green.

"Yes. You've come to the right place. I'm Yeates."

Mr. Green stepped in and shut the door.

"May I please see some identification?"

Worthy smiled sarcastically and pulled out his driver's license. He handed it to Mr. Green who looked at it closely for several seconds as the hamster ran around and around and around.

"Thank you" he said at last, handing back his card.

"And your ID?" asked Worthy.

Mr. Green looked at him blankly and set the brief case down on the desk. He flipped the latches and opened the case. Inside was more money than just about everybody has seen before in their life.

Green turned over the card that he had in his hand and read it to him. "With kind regards, please proceed. Your friends."

He opened the door, looked out into the hallway and stepped out, shutting the door behind him, before Worthy could say a word.

Mr. Green went down stairs and walked to his car. It seemed familiar to him. He drove south, toward Virginia.

When he got home later, he was surprised to see his Mom there.

-<>-

There were bright lights glaring in his eyes and somebody stuck a microphone in his face.

"Excuse me, Senator Hackelbraton. Your comments on the floor today indicate that you support the president's policies in spite of accusations that he is ignoring the democratic paradigm. Can you confirm this?"

"No," he said. "These accusations are groundless. He's the president.

-<>-

Snellville the Lesser started out as a place pretty much like it sounds. It was the lesser of the two Snellvilles, at least that is while there was a 'Great Snellville' for it to be lesser than.

That situation ended in 1914 when tensions between the Dutch/German expatriate population and the English enclave there came to a head over a poker game. Pater Van Hool the local powder man for the mine, having lost his family's farm on a single, and admittedly rigged, hand, picked up a chair and crowned Nigel Coppinger, the mayor, with it, breaking his neck.

In the ensuing gun battle most of the people quickly polarized into two groups, the English hunters, and the German hunted. At the end there, in the early hours of the morning, with the entire town ablaze like a candelabra, the good English citizens of Great Snellville, unable to find Van Hool and his armed cadres, cornered 106 cowering people. They were mostly women, children and old folks, hiding in Van Hool's cattle barn. And, without so much as an excuse me please, the English torched them like termites, after first taking care to dump the contents of the communal generator's fuel tank in on them through the thatched roof.

What the blood thirsty mob, and their victims for that matter could not have known, was that old Van Hool was illegally keeping his powder magazine in the barn. So, instead of the English, placidly watching their neighbors burn like kindling in the stone kiln of the barn, grizzly TV show that that would have been, they became a bit more involved.

Mrs. Coppinger had the honor of tossing the first torch. She heaved it over-hand, in through the barn doors as the Boers screamed their pleas to stop. Several more were thrown after it by the pompous self-righteous mob, and after a very still moment, the barn gushed flame out the doors and up through the roof in a great whoosh of orange. Mrs. Coppinger turned around to the assembled English people there and said, "Serves the bastards right." Then there was a very bright and deafening light for a second as the magazine went up.

The explosion killed everything, man, beast, and plant alike within 500 feet of the barn. And, at least for the people, her words rang true for them too.

The few men that survived the explosion, Van Hool among them, did so by being lucky enough to be out in the bush, drinking and killing each other in ones and twos.

As the sun rose, they staggered back into what had been their town. It was just a smoking, rubble strewn plain with a big hole in the middle of it now, and all around the edges of it were scattered bits and pieces of bodies, some of them still recognizable, stuck in the crotches of sheered off tree trunks and pinned up against some of the larger rocks.

Van Hool went alone to where his barn had been and stood there, looking down into the crater. He was holding an Elephant gun in one hand and a bottle of peppermint schnapps in the other. He belted the schnapps back trying to imagine what had happened in a bleary sort of way. 'The magazine' he thought at last.

It was clear what had happened, the English had found his magazine and blown it up, but they had made a mistake and taken the town with it. 'Fools' he thought.

He shook his head and started walking east, toward Snellville's bastard stepchild. When he got to the edge of the great circle of devastation he stopped, and looked down at the head of a small boy that was resting on what was left of a saddle. It almost looked peaceful lying there on its side, like the boy was sleeping. It was his nephew, Jost.

Van Hool walked on, shaking his head. It was all so sad, and such a needless waste of innocent life. 'God, people could be stupid sometimes.'

He walked along down the road that led to Snellville the Lesser, and as he did he listened to the sounds that the veldt made, the birds and the snort of the beasts in the bush. It was odd, he thought he shouldn't feel that way, but still he was overwhelmed by a sense that it was great to be alive, that each single moment of each hour was precious, and had to be savored. He smelled the air, and it smelled clean and vibrant and alive. It was the good air of a good Earth.

Now, all the hatreds of the night before seemed to fall away, like the trivial encumbrances that they were. Good, free, honest men were too good for such senseless folly.

As he walked he could hear the steps of another coming up behind him. He didn't turn around though, and level his gun at whoever it might be. The time for that had passed. He was free of all that. The footfalls came faster now, and he could hear them coming up beside him. It was a man—he could hear that from his gait. Neither man spoke or looked up at the other. They just walked along down the road together in a silence that was both respect for the fallen, and an acknowledgment of what they had all done that hateful night.

After a long time the other man spoke. It was Groves, a man that he would have gutted a few hours before.

"I saw what we've done," he said slowly.

They walked along for a bit more in silence, and then Pater spoke. "Ya," he said. "Me too."

He stopped and looked at Groves. "For my part," he said, "I'm sorry."

Groves nodded. "Yes, me too." He put out his hand.

Van Hool took it and they shook. There was really nothing more to say then and the two men walked on down the road in the peaceful chatter of the early morning.

Cool dust rose up in a cloud from their footfalls behind them as they went and caught the glancing sunlight that broke through the sparse acacias.

"It's all gone," said Van Hool after a long time, "like today was the first day of the world."

Groves, who had lost his wife in the explosion, was silent, thinking about this for a long time. At last he said, "Yes, it's a new day."

Pater heard a tiny metallic click that fell out of time with the rhythmic clanking of the men's stride. He listened, and heard the movement of leather.

Van Hool stepped back and swung the elephant gun around discharging it into Groves' chest. The Englishman kind of exploded from the shoulders up sending his arms flailing and flinging the pistol that he was about to murder Pater with into the bush. Groves' body collapsed into the ditch at the side of the road.

Van Hool walked on into Snellville the Lesser, alone.

The town was little more than a cross roads when Van Hool and the others went there. It was the home of several poor black families, whose hovels squatted about the landscape in an unruly sprawl. At least that's how the white men perceived it. In fact the houses were placed the way they were for very good and complex reasons, having to do both with the resident's animist religion as well as the need to conform to contour farming practices that saved their precious top soil for future generations.

The white men came there and bought people's houses for the cash they had in their pockets, or, if they refused to sell, just kicked them out into the dirt road at gunpoint. Van Hool took a house and settled down. It was the house of a young widow, Sarah Otaro. She took his money and walked out the door. Van Hool walked in and looked around. It was clean and full of brightly painted things. He turned around and saw Sarah standing there looking at him. She had nowhere to go and so she just stood there watching him, with her head cocked a bit to the side. She watched him for a long time. He stared back, wishing she would go away.

At last he said, "Go, get out of her! I have paid you for your house, now get out of here!" He shooed her on with his big white hands. She didn't budge. In fact she didn't even change her expression. She watched him.

He turned around cursing her and went to sit in the only chair in the place. It was a zebra hide sling seat, and his big white ass filled it and then some.

From where he was sitting he could see her standing there. She watched him sitting in his new house, with the sun warming her face, expressionless.

Van Hool reached over next to him and picked up a drinking gourd. He threw it at her saying, "Go on you black bitch, get the fuck out of here I say!"

The gourd bounced at her feet and came to rest just a bit behind her. She turned around and picked it up, and then resumed her stance looking at him.

'This is impossible', thought Van Hool. 'What did she intend to do, just stand there till the ice age pushed her into the sea?'

He took a drink of schnapps and watched her back.

After about ten minutes of this stand off, he got bored and restless. He stood up and went out to her. He walked straight up to her and stopped just centimeters from her, trying to intimidate her. He had to bend down to put his face in front of hers, and then he yelled at the top of his lungs, dripping vitriol with every word. "What the fuck is wrong with you, you screwy black bitch? Why the fuck, don't you fuck off some place else where you are wanted? Eh? What do you want here? There is nothing here for you now, I own it all! What do you want!?"

"A job," she said, her accent like acacia honey.

"A what?"

She never blinked or cringed, not for a second, she looked back into his angry drunken eyes and said, "A job, I want a job. You have my house, but no one to clean it. You have my house but you cannot cook food in it because you don't know how. Where will I go? What will I do with this money? It is not enough to live on." She sorted through the money in her hand and held out a few coins. "I will work for you for this much each week."

Van Hool was surprised at her frankness as well as her English. It was as good as his. He looked at the pittance in her hand.

"For that you will cook and clean?"

"Yes," she paused, "and I will sleep on the floor."

Van Hool thought about it for several seconds. He was hungry.

"All right then," he said, gesturing with the gun that he was still holding. "Get in there, get in <u>my</u> house and make me some breakfast. We'll try you out for a week."

She walked into <u>her</u> house again.

"Couscous okay?" she asked over her shoulder.

"Fine, I don't give a shit. And an egg, two eggs!"

"Big noise last night," she said.

She would bear him six children and die within two weeks of him in 1944. And though he would eventually build her a fine house with many bedrooms in the shade of a banyan tree, she would always sleep on the floor.

For years Snellville the Lesser remained a back water even by African standards. All around it the continent underwent momentous changes, but it remained sleepily tucked away out of peoples notice. The people that lived there kept pretty much to themselves, growing crops and hunting among the seasonal herds of wildebeests. They had many half-cast children, who grew up and had families of their own, and as time passed the hatreds of the past really did fall away. People stopped being 'white people' or 'black people' and just got on with trying to be human beings.

They were medium brown in color with wavy hair and hazel eyes. They were big for Africans, with the thick necks and rounded out shoulders of their pasty white ancestors, and the large teeth and ready smiles of their native ones. They spoke English mostly, sprinkled liberally with Dutch and German words, as well as Swahili and Kirundi.

In the 1970s and early 80s they had a little trouble from Reaganist insurgents, but after a while they stopped coming there for food, probably because the food they had been taking away with them had been laced with mercury and other minerals by the Snellvillans, or 'Villains' as they called themselves. The low hills around there wept mercury in places and there were many oxides in the earth there about that lent themselves readily to the poisoning of crops that would only be stolen anyway.

In fact the hills contained all sorts of minerals that they mined surreptitiously and sold far away, in the markets in Dar es Salaam. They didn't take a lot at a time, just enough to make ends meet when the bandits took too much. And, while the committed young capitalists sat shaking in the bush like palsied octogenarians, eating their stolen, poisoned wheat, the Villains would look out their window to see if the coast was clear, before tucking into their lovely oysters Rockefeller, and fresh green salad.

Later, in the late 80s when all the Reaganists had shaken themselves to death, in hopeless, misaimed fire fights, they went back to farming in earnest, and only sold their gold and platinum and gemstones to cover them for the wildebeests that barely came anymore.

It was at about this time that Landsat got in their way. One day it flew over them without making a sound, and took a broad-spectrum picture of their town and the surrounding hills. Later, several years in fact, a geologist working in Colorado, examined the photo, and saw what looked like little yellow stripes running through the hills. He compared this information with a sample of mud he had taken from the banks of the Umbutu River as a graduate student many years before. It seemed like very similar stuff. He noted it down and went on with his survey.

But the information took on a life of its own and someone, somewhere, pulled it up on a database and low and behold, Snellville the Lesser jumped to the front page of every newspaper on Earth.

The reason for their fame was that the stripes and the mud represented not just mercury, or gold, or platinum, though those would have been news enough all by themselves. No, they were also evidence of the richest deposits of uranium and plutonium ever found.

Joshua Kabingga's house was the very same one that his great-great-grand father had built for Sarah Otaro, his housekeeper and concubine. It was at the western edge of Snellville the Lesser, where the road led in from the plains. In fact the road went straight through his yard and out the other side past the chickens and goats before it crested the hill and went down into the bowl that held Snellville the Lesser proper. He was the chief of police and fire marshal as well as being, more or less, the mayor.

He was fixing the clutch of the decapitated Citroen 2CV that served as his tractor, when a car pulled to a stop beside him under the banyan tree. The whitest man he could remember got out and asked who was in charge around there. Joshua shrugged and said, "Well, I am I guess. I'm the mayor."

The white man smiled and shook his hand. "Hi," he said, "Don Day. I'm from the American State Department."

Joshua smiled back, looking at his suit. "Yes, I guess you are."

He took Day up into the hills and showed him around. Day picked up some rocks and put them in the trunk of his car. Then he sat down on a big log that looked out over the town.

"You know," he said, "very soon everybody in the world is going to be coming here trying to buy your land from you. They will offer you more money than you can possibly imagine."

"I don't know about that," said Joshua, "I have a very active imagination."

Day laughed. "Yes, and you also have what we think is the biggest uranium mine in the world. A lot of those people will want to get the uranium to make bombs. They are dangerous people, irresponsible people, and if you don't sell them what they want they will probably kill you and just take it.

"We, the United States of America, would like to see you keep your land. We would like to see you and your people prosper from your good fortune, and live free happy lives."

"You would like an exclusive deal for the mineral rights to all our uranium ore."

Day had to smile at Kabingga's savvy and candor. "Yes, and a lot more.

"The Government of Tanzania, dedicated socialists that they are, are going to have something to say about who gets the benefits from this treasure of yours, like themselves and other socialist countries for instance. We think that you people around here might like to keep the profits for yourselves. We think that

114

you might not be such good socialists as to want to give away your wealth just like that—that you might want instead to have the opportunity to become rich beyond your wildest dreams, and have your children go to college at Harvard and Oxford, and control your own destiny."

"Ah yes," said Joshua, "our destiny. And are you quite sure that the United States wouldn't want to help us control that too?"

Day's face was open and sincere. "No, you will control your own destiny. We will offer you guidance, so that you might be better informed to make the right choices, but it's up to you."

Joshua looked out over the savanna, it was near sun set and there were storm clouds rolling in from the Indian Ocean like a purple wall of Armageddon.

"So," he said, "what you are suggesting is a coup d'etat, and as long as we continue to make 'the right decisions' then you will support us."

"What we are suggesting is a change in the history of your country, and it is our assessment that so long as people are free to make their own choices, they will chose democracy and free trade over the tyranny of the collective."

Joshua turned toward Day and came up close to him, well inside his invisible perimeter of 'personal space'. His eyes looked at once mistrustful and at the same time almost pleading.

"Okay, so why me, why not some General someplace? Why here, and why now? Why can't you and the rest of the world just go back down that dirt road and forget what your stupid space ship told you?"

Day normally operated in a world so corrupt and self-centered that at first he didn't quite believe the man's simple obvious question. Then, he stepped back, in his mind, and pretended that he was speaking to a complete layman, which he was.

"Why you? Okay, I'll tell you something that I probably shouldn't, but you will find out soon enough anyway.

"The world is changing Mr. Kabingga, changing from the old, cold war world of the last century to the new world of the next. America used to stand for democracy, against the forces of a collectivized fascism of the left, known for want of a better term as Communism. That battle is over and has been for some time now. And what will take its place? A new world order, in which all men live free and equal lives, out of their mutual respect for each other's opinions? I don't think so, and neither do you.

"What is coming, in our opinion is a world in which the

forces of Islam, and Pan-Arab Nationalism, under the guise of Islamic socialism are in a life and death struggle with the liberal democratic West for control of the world economy and future state of mankind for the next century.

"The reason why you, is that you are by no means alone, on the contrary, you are but one of many people all over the world that the West is contacting, on a grass roots level—community people with something vested in their home towns, that they find far too precious to lose, something that they are willing to fight for.

"In a few months, maybe a year at most there is going to be a revolution in Tanzania, in fact it will be all over this part of the world. The Islamists are going to try to take over what they feel is the soft white underbelly of the West, their former colonies, and the source of their resources. The Armies of many of these countries are now controlled by Muslim forces, who are steadfast in their support for an Islamist World Government.

"They will come down that road, and not politely asking if you would like to make a deal. They will come in Chinese tanks and airplanes and wipe out or subjugate you and your people, beneath the sword of Islam.

"They will want your Uranium, much as we do, Sir, but they won't pay you a nickel for it. In fact they will probably make you slaves to dig it out of the ground for them, so that they can use it. It is very isotopic, and therefore easily separated into weapons grade metal. They will use it to make atomic weapons to fight the West and all its freedoms they so despise."

He pointed to the road.

"I can no more go back down that road and forget about this, than you can stop the rain. There is a storm coming, Mr. Kabingga and you must pick your shelter, or you will be swept away by the flood."

Joshua looked down at Snellville the Lesser. There was a rumble in the distance and the first raindrops started making the hood of the car drum a rhythm. A drop hit him on the face, and then another and another.

"We shall see," he said.

-<>-

...UBSa ^2 4/8 UtTce v1 3/8 URPa ^6 7/8 VLAe v3 2/8 VOLe v2 1/8...

-<>-

On the first day there was only a handful of people outside the Senate. In fact, if you stood there looking out at them, you probably wouldn't pay them much attention, taking them for tourists, like the guards did.

Andy Nickson looked out at the people there and almost didn't see them. They were just another bunch of gawkers, standing around in front of his machine gun taking pictures. As long as they didn't step over the red line they weren't his concern anyway[40], so he thought about other things.

Like, his gun. He dug it a lot. It would put out 300 rounds a minute and was made of high carbon steel and had a molybdenum greased slip and slide action that would blur to invisibility as it spewed righteous, red hot death out the barrel, at 16 inch intervals. He liked the tripod too, with the adjustable legs that he could tune to fit his body swing, just so, and the *Softgrips*™, that molded themselves to his hands like putty.

All day long he sat there, day after day, and just about all he had to distract him were thoughts of his machine gun, and pretty women that walked by. He and Jones, the other gunner, on the other side of the Senate steps would call each other's attention to women that passed, by saying things into their com. mics like, "Legs, four o'clock", or, "Ass, comin' your way!" There would always be an appropriate response from the headphones, and then a bit of babble about how she likes it.

They whiled away the time at their posts like that, and when Andy's relief came at 17:00 he handed over, not thinking much about the few people that had been out in front of him all day, other than to sort of note it down in a corner of his mind, along with a thousand other little things.

The next day there were more people there and in that group were the same faces as the day before. Now he noticed a little bit. He did all the usual things but he kept a fraction of an eye peeled, just in case they were significant. At about lunchtime he said to Jones, "Hey, you notice anything significant about that group by the garbage can?"

He bit into his chicken sandwich.

Jones looked at the group for a while munching his Snakos. Tourists passed by stopping to look and take pictures and point up at the Senate. The group that Nickson had mentioned didn't do anything suspicious necessarily. They just sat on or stood by a set of benches that flanked the garbage can on the other side of

---

[40] Naive as it may sound to you now, there was a time, before the First American Race War, when there were no machine guns guarding the Senate at all. This utopian nonsense came to an end after August 2031.

117

the sidewalk. "No, not really. Why?" he asked.

Andy looked at them. "It's not that they are doing anything wrong, it's just that they were there all day yesterday and now they are there again today. They aren't taking pictures or anything. They're just sitting there, like they're waiting for something."

"Hmm" crackled Jones's tiny voice in his ear-jack. "I'll keep an eye on..."

"Major tits! Three o'clock!" interrupted Andy.

A congressional assistant with huge breasts walked past Jones' position and up the steps. His eyes tracked her like a radar dish. She smiled at him and he flushed a bit. Andy started laughing in his ear.

"Twenty pounds each," he said.

"She smiled at me!"

The day went on like this, and more people started to gather by the benches. At about three o'clock Andy called Sergeant Stegelmier and brought the gathering crowd to his attention. The sergeant said that he would find out about it and signed off. He was gone a long time and that worried Nickson, but eventually his voice came back on the com.

"It's a rally!" he said.

"A rally?!" said Andy. "There was nothing on the day sheet about this."

"No, it's unauthorized. This thing was apparently called by that guy, Veets, on his radio show yesterday. They will be here in a couple of hours."

"Should we disperse the crowd?" asked Jones.

"No, we can't. There is enough tension around here now without a constitutional beef in front of the press too."

Andy chimed in, in his high pitched, wise-guy voice. "The people of the United States shall have the right to peaceably assemble. So far these people are peaceable. They have to cause trouble before we can mow them down like wheat. You know that."

"That's very funny, Nickson," said Stegelmier, "I'll keep you posted."

There were people starting to arrive now in busses, some of them had signs with them, and other paraphernalia that Andy couldn't make out exactly. They lined the sidewalk and spilled out into the street. As more and more arrived they started to crowd over the red line. Once inside that line they were the responsibility of Senate Security, namely gunners Nickson and

118

Jones. The two men looked at each other and a silent 'Oh shit' passed between them.

Andy checked stock on his ammo.

"I've got five thousand rounds," he said.

Jones looked around him, estimating. "I have about sixty-five-hundred."

The police started working crowd control—trying to keep the street clear. They moved people along the sidewalk and tried to get them to disperse, but they had come for a purpose and weren't going to just be moved along like that. The police looked worried, Andy could see it in their faces. That was a very bad sign, he thought.

A line of busses made its way through the increasingly crowded street. They pulled up and disgorged their passengers three at a time. These people had signs too. Andy could read them, they seemed to be professionally printed, with slogans like 'Hands Off Our Money!' and 'Fuck The Pony'. There was one that he liked that said 'We Won't Be Swindled', but that was as much for the woman that was carrying it as for the quality of the slogan.

"Blond babe, 'we won't be swindled', one o'clock" he said.

Jones looked that way for a few seconds. "Where? I don't... Oh! Very nice. What do you think? Doable?"

"They're all doable."

Jones put on a rather good French accent. "'Ello baby, I 'ave a littel sompzing for you!"

Steglmier came on the com. "Gentlemen, we have back up for you on the roof. If this turns into a mess I will cover you into the building, but do not move until I give you the word, otherwise you are on standard orders."

"Roger," said Andy and Jones in unison.

Jones looked at Andy. "I'll bet you a week's pay that we make it into the building alive."

Andy smiled sarcastically. "Yeah, right."

Jones shot him a big white grin that stood out against his black face. "You' gotta try!"

An hour later when the cameras were set up and the crowd was spread out for a quarter mile. Veets arrived. Andy heard the helicopter and squinted up into the sky, looking for it. Where was it?

The chopper came from around Jones's side at a hundred feet. It came in a fast curve and flared to a stop on top of the last bus that had arrived, and parked directly in front of the steps. The pilot kept it light on the skids as Veets clambered out then up he popped and was away, all in one smooth move.

Veets pawed at his thin crew cut, trying to get it to lie flat on his head as the chopper receded. Its noise fell away and he could hear the crowd. They were cheering him.

The top of the bus was a platform from which he could speak. An assistant came up out of a hatch with a cluster of microphones on a stand and set it before him. Veets tugged at his clothing trying to make his rumpled suit look presentable, while the man adjusted the mics to his height. After a bit they were set and somewhere inside the bus Philus threw a switch, waking the PA system. There was a loud pop followed by an ear splitting squeal that slowly died away.

Veets looked out at the audience. They had come from all over the Eastern Seaboard, and some, he could see by their signs, from even farther away. Most importantly, they had come to see <u>him</u>. He waved a big folksy wave, with his whole upper body and smiled big and confident. After what seemed like a long time he spoke.

"Hello Ameri**SQUEEEEEE'WHEEPST!!!**"

Veets smiled hard and tried again. "Hello America**HOOP!** It's great to…"

"Psst, shut off the blue one," said the tech from the hatch in the top of the bus.

"What**POP?**"

"The blue mic. Shut it off!"

Veets looked around at the cluster and finally found the blue mic. He flicked it off with his thumb, and the Tech gave him the okay sign.

Veets smiled, and marshaled himself again.

"I say it again, hello America. It's great to see you all here today. This is a great occasion and it warms my heart to see that so many of you have the depth of feeling to join in our little rally."

There were a few cheers from the crowd, Dagmar normally spoke into a single mic in a darkened booth or at most into the dead glass lens of the TV camera, this was different, these were real people out there, lots of them. His voice didn't sound as booming to him as it usually did, in fact it sounded to his ear like a kitten meowing in a quarry, lost in the immense space.

"We are here today to talk to Congress, America, and it's about damn time too. They have been saying plenty of late and none of it too pretty. So, I say it's time to give them an earful back. How about you?"

There was a slight lag as his words washed over the vast crowd all the way to the outermost edges, and then their answer came rolling back like a tsunami. It was the loudest, angriest, most inarticulate and ugly sound that he had ever heard.

They kind of went,

"YEAHAAAUUNCH!"

It sounded at the end like an axe cutting off somebody's leg. Dagmar felt powerful and frightened, all at the same time. He looked back over his shoulder at Andy. The gunner rather nonchalantly swiveled the barrel up his way, saying in no uncertain terms that <u>he</u> would be the fist casualty in the event of trouble. Andy smiled a friendly, sarcastic smile up at the talk show host.

Dagmar swallowed hard. It was far too late to turn back.

"Well America," he began, "what's it going to be? Are we going to just sit by and let this bunch of second story men take our money without saying a word? Without saying BOO!? Well, are we? I think not!

"In fact I'd wager that we would no more do that than we would let that man loving nincompoop in the White House squander our hard earned money on ponies for his special friends.

"I say, we say no! That's what I say! I say we say NO!! What do <u>you</u> say!?"

The "No" that came back was so deep that the end of it rolled off into the subsonic and he only felt it in his stomach, rather than heard it.

He cupped his hand to his ear. "Hows'at America?"

Now it was twice as loud, **"NOOOO!!!"**

He smiled down into the cameras.

"Well America, I think they should have heard that! The only question is, are Failsworthy and his cronies listening!"

Veets turned and looked up at the Senate, then he thought to grab the mic stand and swung it around so he could speak into it as he shook his fist at the cold stone edifice.

"What about it Failsworthy, are you listening? I <u>say</u> ARE, YOU, LISTENING!? I hope you are boy, because Mr. and Mrs. America, I <u>say</u> <u>MR</u>. <u>AND</u> <u>MRS</u>. <u>AMERICA</u>!, and all their little Americans are talking to you!!! Can you hear them!? Are you <u>Listening!?</u>

"Failsworthy hear me," he said, in mocking imitation of the Senator's own oratorical style. "These people have found their voice! At last, and just at the brink of death's door, they have at last found their magnificent voice, and they have something to share with you, you carpet-bagging brigand! And that is this—NO!

"No you are not going to Shanghai their funds to line your grubby pockets, and those of your fat assed, fat cat friends! It is their money and you can't have it. No, they are not going to sit by and let you reissue the dollar to swindle them out of their political rights, and grab it all back with your pudgy little piggy hands. They categorically, I say CAT-I-GOR-I-CAL-LY, are not, going to let you get away with it!!

"Well, Senator Failsworthy, don't you want to come out and address your constituents? Don't you want to talk to these people!? Come on Senator, come on out and talk to us. You don't just work for the corporations in district twenty-nine. Do you? There are a lot of plain old American folks that live there too, and we have brought them with us to see you"

He turned back to the crowd and started chanting "Failsworthy, Failsworthy, Failsworthy, Failsworthy," emphasizing each word with his fist like he was conducting a symphony. The crowd joined him in wave after wave of the name like an angry ocean crashing against the shore of the island Senate. Veets looked over his shoulder and winked at Andy.

Andy cocked the slide, smiling.

Veets leaned away from the mics. "Go ahead, Corporal," he said, gesturing at the crowd with a sweep of his hand, "but they'll have you."

The sergeant spoke in his ear. "Well, Nickson, how's it going down there?" he asked sardonically.

Andy looked around at his ammo and loosened the strap on his side arm. "Things are a little tense right now Sarg, but nobody has physically threatened the building yet. I'll tell you this though, that guy up on the bus is going to be the first one to go. Jones and I might not be too far behind, but he is definitely getting taken out first."

"I'm sure that Senator Failsworthy would concur. Just sit tight, we have you covered."

"That's very comforting," said Jones.

Veets had turned back to the crowd now and was looking at them like a Cæsar.

"Americans," he said, "you are the luckiest people in the

whole world. You see, you are lucky, because you live in a democracy, and in a democracy, we the people—do you hear me Failsworthy?—I say We The People, call the shots! We the people elect to have certain of those among us come here to the nations capitol to enact laws on our behalf. On Our Behalf. For us. Not for them! Not to benefit them, but to benefit us." He pointed at himself with all his fingers. "We the people." There were cheers.

"Well ladies and gentlemen, Mr. and Mrs. America, it looks like one or two or maybe three or four or five or all the whole damn lot of them have stepped way, I say WAY out of line. And we are lucky because—because we live in a de-mo-cra-cy, we don't have to just sit here and take it from them! We have certain inalienable rights, and one of those inalienable rights is to stand up and be heard! It's called the freedom of speech and I say we use it, I say we tell Failsworthy, and Faircloth, and Simington, and Tinedail and all the rest of 'em, and I don't need to tell you the list just goes on and on and on, to step down! That's what I say, I say Failsworthy out, NOW! I say Senators out NOW!!!"

The crowd started chanting in time to his lead.

"Senators out now! Senators out now! Senators out now! Senators out now!"

It was so loud! Veets had a little trouble thinking what to say next, it was so powerful and wonderful. He felt exalted. The crowd chanted on, and on and on. He let it ride, looking out over the sea of angry people. It was magnificent.

He noticed a commotion out at the far edge of the crowd that started to make its way toward him. It was a group coming his way, pushing through the people, in fact, now that they were getting a little closer he could see that it was a Rolls Royce surrounded by Black Militia.

Harvey's bodyguards, actually they were hired thugs, moved through the throng opening a passage for his car, firmly but politely. Their black barrettes and sunglasses let everyone know that they were members in full standing of the outlawed Black Cells of Afrimerica. And, although they had lost the First American Race War, and been forced to the bargaining table at gunpoint, they had never surrendered, and never given up their brothers to the law. They told you to move, you moved. These men were killers.

The people pushed back letting the Rolls through and in a little less than three minutes, Washington's driver was pulling to a halt in front of Veets' bus. Four guards stood point at the corners of the car while the rest had a word with the bus driver. There was a bit of arguing, but not a hell of a lot, considering. And that was that, Harvey was shown to the entrance of the bus and a few second later he was standing next to Veets looking out over the crowd.

Jones said in Andy's ear, "Here we go, he's mine."

Veets made a slitting motion under his chin to his sound guy.

"Is there something I can do for you Mr. Washington?" asked Veets acridly, as he leaned his hand on the now dead mics like a good old boy.

"Yes. If you would be so kind, I would like to talk to my people," said Washington haughtily. "I have come to address them."

Veets laughed a sarcastic little sneer at Washington.

"No. Harvey. This isn't your show, we aren't loaning out any free airtime. Maybe you could pan handle some spare change out at the back of the audience and buy some of your own like anybody else."

Washington stared at Veets with his yellow-whited, slightly blood shot eyes, sweating. He had hated this man for years, but this blatant disrespect of the rightful representative of the urban black man was more than he could stand. Normally his stony stare was sufficient to cause a guilt reaction in the heart of the hateful white bigots that sought to repress him in his sacred quest to free the urban Afro-American man from the chains of their slavery, but this guy was a real fuckhead and his stare was having no effect.

"I said," he said, "that I have come to speak unto my people! Now please, if you will, step aside or destiny will sweep you asunder!"

Dagmar looked at Washington, an inarticulate scuzzball if ever there was one, in his opinion. He shook his head.

"Destiny will <u>sweep</u> me <u>asunder</u>? What is that supposed to mean? Do you know what asunder means?"

Harvey looked at him coldly, saying nothing and sneering.

"Well, do you!? It means to chop in half, you know, like 'split that bottle o'wine asunder an' gi'<u>me</u> half d'sucker, soz I can get all stoned like!'"

Veins started to bulge out on Harvey's forehead now. "You will not nigger-bate me, Veets." He spat his name like a mouth full of duck shit. "I will keep my dignity even if you will not, for the African man does not rise to such poultry insults from a piece of honky shit like you. Now step aside and let me speak!"

"You mean paltry, don't you, or do you mean comestible birds insults? And, no, I won't step aside and let you Shanghai this gathering for your own nefarious ends. These people came to listen to me, and to speak to the members of the Senate, who are trying to swindle them..."

"And swindle them out of the money that should rightfully go to new entitlements in the depressed inner cities!"

"Enough!" said Veets pushing past Washington and grabbing the mic stand. He nodded to his soundman and the PA barked into life.

The crowd cheered him.

"Hello Americans!..."

"Bullshit, give me that thing!"

Harvey tried to grab the mic stand away from him, but Veets was too fast for him. He turned away and hunched over the mics, trying to continue.

"Listen to me, this man is trying to abscon..."

Harvey leaned over him.

"No, listen to me! These moneys are the rightful property of the Black African man! We are entitled to'oof!"

His words were cut short by Veets' elbow slamming him in the gut. This was a mistake by the smarmy, self-assured talk-show host, as although he had the massive advantages of a college education, years of experience as an orator, and millions of hard swindled dollars of his very own, he had never had to claw his way out of a street fight, or fend off an angry mob with little more than a 2x4 and no wits at all, things that Harvey had done a dozen times[41].

Harvey swung his arm in a great arch up over his head and down onto Veets' back, like hammering a fat obnoxious cockroach. He had beaten people to death before, most of them in the battle of Detroit and the Dearborn campaign, but that had all been years ago. It felt good again. The crowd cheered as Veets went down onto his hand and knees with an "oof!" of his own.

---

[41] All through RWI Dagmar Veets had sat placidly, inside secured buildings and yammered his messages of hate and lies at his angry manipulated public, encouraging them to commit the most horrendous acts of treason against their fellow countrymen in the name of 'the restoration of order', including, incidentally the burning of the Detroit ghetto, but he would never have dreamed of risking his own skin by taking up arms against those he counted as his enemies.

Harvey balled up his fist and swung it down at Veets head thinking to crack it open like a ripe melon, but Dagmar rolled to the side trying to escape. Harvey's fist slammed down instead, into the reinforced top of the bus splintering the metacarpals of his right hand like matchsticks.

"Owooo!!" he screamed, as the mob cheered on.

For a fat guy Veets proved to be pretty fast. He scrambled to his feet and seeing his opponent cupping his twisted bloody hand, he stomped down on it with all his formidable weight.

"AHHHHH!!!" screamed the Right Reverend Washington.

"YAAAAAAAY!!" screamed the crowd.

Veets had the blood lust now and he waited not a moment. He took a little step back to position himself and swung his leg as if to kick a field goal from the fifty yard line, right through Harvey's face. The evangelist/shit-disturber, fat tub of goo that he was did not shoot off into the sky as Veets had imagined he would from the thrust of his mighty and righteous kick, but rather just sort of bucked a little and slid off the bus's edge and down onto the head of his security chief Nathan Mornette.

Mornette, a trained killer and dedicated Afrimerican Separatist, who had survived the entire war in uniform, collapsed under Harvey's unconscious weight onto his back, where he lay pinned like a back flopped turtle. He could see the edge of the bus from whence Harvey had come.

Veets peered over the edge holding the mic stand like a weapon. He frowned down at Mornette like a just and vengeful God.

"And keep that knuckle dragger off my bus!" he said.

Nathan managed to snake his arm under his back and pulled his UZI out of its holster. He heaved as hard as he could to get the gun out to the point where he could wave it in Veets general direction and emptied the clip at him.

Rounds went everywhere, as the gun jumped around in his pinned hand. One of the first rounds glanced off Veets head knocking him back out of the line of fire, and, unfortunately, he sustained relatively minor injuries. But as the rest of Harvey's guard opened up on the top of the bus, the police responded, cutting them down, along with several innocent bystanders where they stood. People, needless to say, panicked and started running in all directions, some of them toward Andy.

The sergeant was asking in one ear for information on the situation on the ground and Jones was offering him additional cover in the other, as about ten people ran straight for him.

126

For all his sarcastic bravado and snippy comments Nickson was a very calm, level headed guy, capable of clear thinking under extreme pressure. He didn't scream for backup. He didn't open up on the running people, though no tribunal would have convicted him for such action. He also didn't just duck and let them storm past his position up the steps of the Senate, and hope for the best. What he did do, was stand up, draw his side arm and fire a couple of rounds into the sand bag wall of his gun emplacement, yelling, "STOP!" in a loud, authoritative voice.

He pointed to his left. "Go that way, it is safe there!"

The people, like the scared sheep they were, stopped and stared at him wide eyed for a moment then the first one broke and ran in the direction he was pointing.

The rest followed immediately behind and complete disaster was narrowly avoided. Nickson never received any commendation for his quick thinking besides a beer from Jones. It was a Budweiser.

The police finally dispersed the frenzied mass after twenty-five minutes, with otherwise minimal injuries, much to the disappointment of many of the assembled Senators who watched the whole thing from the safety of their office buildings on closed circuit TV, Failsworthy not least among them.

He shook his head in disbelief at the inability of the civil authorities in Washington to turn the situation into the wholesale massacre that was clearly needed to cow the population into submission. Opportunities like this didn't present themselves everyday, and to just throw it all away for the sake of a few lives seemed senseless to him.

Support for his currency reissue scheme was growing, albeit secretly, amongst his supporters in both houses and even the far out democratic fringe, like the creeping fingers of a sarcoma. If the people could just be beaten into submission, his plan would go ahead without significant opposition and the country could get on with business as usual. And after all wasn't that what this was all about really, business?

The Hold and its subsequent fall out was starting to bite that top 1% of American corporate society that was the particular lap to which he was dog. This was a threat in no uncertain terms to the American way of life and his personal income. Why couldn't the police see that and act accordingly!? Why didn't they slaughter a few dozen 'citizens' to intimidate the rest? Surely that was a small price to pay for the greater good.

He opened the phone, fuming. There was a soft purring as he

scowled at the screen, and finally Tiendale came on.

"Can you believe it? This is an outrage!" bellowed Failsworthy.

Tiendale mistook his meaning entirely. "Indefensible is what it is!" he said. "Who do these people think they are, telling us what to do? We <u>are</u> Congress after all."

"Eh? Oh, yes, yes of course. But—what about the police and Senate security? Why aren't they doing something about it, is what I'd like to know!"

Tiendail scratched the ragged fringe of hair that ringed his skull, looking just off eye line with Failsworthy as he watched the fracas outside on his screen. He shrugged a little.

"Well, they're breaking it up now it looks like. They do have to cause trouble before the police can step in."

"Exactly," interjected Failsworthy. "And what damn good do they do? They're just letting them get away with it!"

"What did you have in mind, Dan? Mass arrests?"

"Arrests!? Fuck no I don't want arrests! I want a blood bath! I want corpses littering the streets, and crying women screaming for mercy! What I want!? What I want——is something that will break the will of these ungrateful bastard that have my money!"

Failsworthy was unusually angry, thought Tiendale. He was going nuts. He tried smoothing him.

"Oh come on, Dan. You can't mean that! These are Americans we are talking about here, not Chinese people." He smiled and said jocularly. "You can't just bump them off like they were the Sino-Siberian army[42]. These people have some rights."

"Bullshit, they are a threat to the American Government, and that means they are a threat to the American way of life. They should be eliminated. If the police are too squeamish to act then maybe we should call in the Army."

"The Army!? I don't think that is the way you want to go with this one, do you Dan? I mean what about the next elections? They're just twenty months off, you know. Think of your career. They'll call you the butcher of Washington!"

---

[42] At that time it was perfectly all right to make Chinese people the butt of the most horrendous jokes and always to paint them with the brush of the villain owing to the cannibalism and other such outrageous behavior of the Chinese Army during the Sino-European War. Much as it had been perfectly okay to denigrate Jews in the Nazi controlled media of the 3rd. Reich and Germans, particularly in the 'Jewish controlled' media in the decades after World War II.

Faircloth looked at him levelly, his eyebrows creased in mild disdain, like he shouldn't have to explain himself. "Fuck the electorate. The corporations will support me. They owe me, and besides I don't intend to run for another senatorial term."

Tiendail looked at his 'friend'. "Mr. President," he said.

"If there's a country left to rule by '52!"

-<>-

"...of course any military support that we receive will be re-compensated handsomely, once we have secured the Umbutu River system, along with Greater Burundi and the enclave of Snellville the Lesser.

"Of course," said Ziow. "Tea, Mr. McDermott? Snakos?"

"Ah Snakos! I've heard of them. Hard to get aren't they?"

Ziow smiled. "Supplies are limited, but we have our ways of getting them."

-<>-

Bill sat in the hot tub surrounded by beautiful young women, his stockinged feet propped on the edge. They cooed to him and poured champagne into his glass, giggling. Bill smiled and had a satisfying sip.

"It's all about the socks," he said.

"Smartwalk with Spanlon™, only from Continental."

A Bit of Trouble

"What I am saying is that the product is, exactly as we have always claimed, a 100% <u>recycled</u> food product. Our packaging is in scrupulous compliance with all the applicable laws in each country that we sell it."

Joji Kakamatsu, attorney for Tokugowa foods, Floatkyo Japan

-<>-

As with anyone, a thousand things had gone to make Dwayne Swindel what he was as a person. There had been beatings and love, both given and taken, and there had been 46 Thanksgivings, and as many Christmases, and days in the park without a care in the world. There had also been nights shivering in the rain, watching the bright line of fire marching across the plains of Richmond, driving the Black Cells before it. They had all done terrible things then.

He was a complex thing, in the way of most flesh, a stingy matrix of meat and soul wrapped up in fatty layers of vindictive fear, like a malignant dim-sum, staring out at a largely incomprehensible world, with wide distrustful eyes and a response set uniquely tailored to protect him from things he didn't exactly get.

He was a hypocrite too. He hated cowards like himself. He feared the touch of others. He feared that he might let slip his impenetrable shield for long enough that someone would peek inside and see the vulnerable child crouching inside. And he feared, that the light from the crack would first blind and then kill that retched child, leaving only a hollow shell behind. That was why he so strenuously defended himself against the bright cold universe around him, with the bludgeon of silence and scalpels of well-chosen words. He was a chicken shit.

It was the silence that Michael hated most. The words he had learned to turn aside like an aikido master, using their own force against them as a great sarcastic lever. The words were only for other, more distant people's pain.

But when Dwayne turned his silence on him, when he wouldn't budge and he wouldn't say, so that the still air hung between them like a corps, then the silence was something awful.

This fucked with his head, in a seething kind of way, that he resented all the more for its deliberate and pointed effect.

Dwayne was like that now, quiet, unyielding, hard. He had

130

been like this for days now, ever since Nathan came for him in the night and they had sat up talking into the dawn, quietly. Michael knew it was bad then, when Dwayne came back to bed and didn't speak a word to him. He just laid there with his eyes open, lost in thought.

Dwayne now sat in the rattan chair with those same distant eyes looking out at the garden beyond. The Kauai retreat was always beautiful, and peaceful, not to mention easily defended, that was why they had chosen it in the first place, but now it seemed like a prison to Michael.

He got up to get another cup of tea from the samovar.

"Would you like some tea?"

Dwayne didn't answer. This wound Michael's crank another notch. He stood there waiting for a reply as he poured the tea, his back to Dwayne. None came, and he turned around to face him.

"Excuse me Mr. President, I said, would you like some tea?"

Dwayne still didn't answer, but he shifted in his chair indicating that he had heard him. That little shove was it.

"Okay, asshole, just what is your fucking problem anyway!? What do you think you are, the only person in the world with problems? Or just the only person in the world?"

Dwayne just sat there for a moment and then he looked up at him, with his dead face, silently.

Michael looked back at him for the same moment and then bitch slapped him across the head with an open hand.

"Hey you fuckin' ugly piece of shit, I'm talking to you!! Answer Me!! NOW!!!"

He smacked him again and again and again. "Now!! Now!! Now!!"

Dwayne caught his hand and held it firmly.

"Hey, fuck you man," He said with quiet menace. "I'm the president of the United States of America. I don't have to take that kind of shit from anyone, not even you, my dear!"

"Oh don't give me that, 'my dear' crap. You have been asking for exactly that kind of treatment since Nathan came and pissed in your oatmeal last week!

"Now that I have your attention, you listen to me, Mr. Asshole."

Michael pulled his hand away and paced in front of Dwayne, holding his eye.

"Okay, so here you are, the president of the whole United States of America, and your vice comes to you and tells you that your Machiavellian little plans aren't going to just spring into

131

action like so many Chinese acrobats at your beck and call. Shall we cry? I don't think so!

"Oh sure, you wanted the American people to go along with you to bolster Kabingga and his, what is it, 'Brave Freedom Fighters', and well, they basically told you to go take a flying fuck at a rolling doughnut, boo-hoo! Figure some shit out!!"

"But!..."

"No!! You sit there and you shut up. You don't want to talk, fine! Don't talk! Listen!

"I have been patiently coddling you along since this thing began. Nurturing you, looking after you, through the caucuses, through the primaries, through the big one. And when Alpha came up and you decided to support it, in spite of your critics screaming for your blood and the press calling you a frivolous queen and a techno-thug, I was there—always there for you. And you haven't even had the decency to actually break down and talk to me about one God damned bit of it, much less thank me for my contribution!

"Oh, Mr. I'm the fucking president, I don't need anyone, I made myself without the help of anyone! What the fuck did you do, fuck your own zygote? Your dick's about the right size.

"And now that your plans for Africa haven't exactly come off like clockwork you are just going to sit there in your little chair and sulk till the American people say, 'okay we give, just have all our money, fuck the kids education and the house in Vermont'. Right?"

Swindel looked at him for a long while before he spoke. Michael was panting.

"Well?!" asked Michael.

"You done?"

"Fuck you."

"Clever retort." He paused. "In any case, I think you have missed a few essential points in your little diatribe. For example, when you point out that my plans aren't coming off like clock work in Africa, you neglect the fact that they are still going forward, at a slower pace than I would like—but they are proceeding. Also, I am not merely sulking about it. I have taken, and am continuing to take action to facilitate my program.

"In fact, I am not sulking about that at all, though I might well do so, for all the courage of the American Congress. I am however frustrated, I will admit, about the inability of the combined forces of the FBI, CIA, NSA and Navel Intelligence to find the key organizers of the tax revolt and eliminate them so I can get on with the inevitable.

"As for thanking you for your contribution to this Presidency, for your support, and, aid, well what can I say?"

He paused again, pretending to search for just the right word.

"Thanks, Mike, I thank you, and my little dick thanks you. Speaking of which, no actually, I didn't make myself in a vacuum. I am, as you so rightly point out, merely a synthesis of the accidents that went to make me. I came unbidden and undirected, except of course by chance, but in that, I have made what I could of what the world handed me. Not you.

"I have taken the initiative to get off my ass and get an education, to argue longer and louder and with more vitriol than my opponents. I read all the hard books that no one else wanted to read. Not you.

"I have taken that lump of goo that squirted out from between my mother's legs and molded it the best I could, while you! — What the fuck did you ever do? — Have sat around 'supporting' me?! I beg your fucking pardon?!! Thank you? Ask your opinion?!! Oh, maybe I should cut you a check!"

Michael cringed from his acid attack, just as Dwayne knew he would. Now was when a more compassionate, less selfish, less damaged man would have reached out to touch his mate and explain himself at least a little, but Dwayne was not that kind of guy at all. No, this was exactly where his reflexes kicked in, and followed the scent of blood.

He stood and reshuffled his armadillo plates, feeling the warm sadistic glow of the kill. It filled him to his utmost corners.

"So tell me, Michael," he said, staring right down him. "Just exactly what have you done for me? You know, that was any use I mean. Precisely what service have you rendered, that I couldn't have bought for chump change? Eh? I can't hear you!!"

Michael turned away from him. Dwayne smacked Michael across he back of the head once sharply, just to emphasize his point and his position.

"What have you done? Straightened my tie?! Organized a few dinner parties?!"

His voice got very quiet now, making it all the more cutting.

"Let me watch you masturbate while I let you watch me masturbate? There are videos, honey."

"You know," he said. "I have a lot on my mind these days, what with trying to define a policy for Africa that will at once secure for the United States a supply of strategic minerals for the next half century and stop the spread of radical Islam. While at the same time, appeasing both the knee-jerk liberal press, and that pandering bunch of pussies in Congress, not to mention the taxpayers! Oh the <u>fucking</u> <u>taxpayers</u>!!

"So you will maybe display a little more understanding about the fact that I perhaps have very little time to bring you into the discussion. If I don't get this just right Joshua and his people will die at the hands of McDermott and his bloody mob, and along with them Alpha 1, and along with <u>that</u> the hopes of the human race! Surely you don't think that the world, shaking like a dog shitting worms, can possibly stand for more than a few more years at most! This shit is important! Now, if you will, kindly fuck off and leave me alone, dude, I have a chunk on my head at the moment."

He pointed at the door. Michael walked from the room. He stopped in the door and said without turning, "You really are a small man."

"Get the fuck out!"

In minor defense of Swindel, not that I like to defend such ugliness, he had discovered what every other American president since about Woodrow Wilson has—that once having attained the office, it was a bucket of greased cobras and not the garden party it was made out to be, on the way up.

Also there is this, Michael <u>was</u> a bit of a self-sorry little do-nothing but he was right when he said Swindel was a very narrow man.

This narrowness was what made him such an effective politician. He was un-swayed by tangential arguments and the concerns of others. They were only things to be gotten around by whatever means necessary. If he had to lie, that was fine, after all people could only see <u>their</u> issue, the same as him. If they couldn't appreciate his angle then why should he do them the favor? And, ultimately he was right in that cynicism, everyone has their drum to beat and they will say anything, glom on to any sub-clause in an argument, in order to twist the issue onto their particular track and railroad the discussion their way. The only major difference is that most people aren't honest enough to admit it to themselves, much less anyone else, that that is what they are in fact doing. Swindel was, at least give him that, up front about it.

This was why he and Kabingga got along so famously. Joshua Kabingga had become a pragmatist through the years. He was willing to say whatever was needed at the time to appease his critics while at the same time issuing orders for their secret execution out the other side of his face. He and Swindel were one person in that, as are most leaders.

Hitler was a two faced prick, but then so were Churchill, and Reagan and Julius Caesar and Chairman Mao. Contrary to what you were told in school, it pays in spades to fuck the innocent, put a bullet in their head and charge the family for the round.

Let's not forget to vote!

-<>-

In fact that was Kabingga's cynical slogan every eight years or so when he came up for 're-election', "Let's not forget to vote!" It even said it on the sides of the stuffed ballot boxes!

His pragmatic duplicity was exactly that, pragmatic. He was up against the arrayed forces of Sub-Saharan-African, Pan-Arab-Nationalism, under the leadership of Mingetsu McDermott and his Islamic Fundamentalist Insurgents[43]. They were capable of anything. Including but by no means limited to, the slaughter of children and the elderly and the holding of hostages in unspeakable conditions with demands like, "The withdrawal of all infidels from Africa and Asia Minor"!

For them, lying was about as serious a transgression as taking the name of Elvis Presley in vain. So he fought fire with fire, and explosives, and whenever possible, anti-tank rounds and the like.

All that Day had told him had come true. The world <u>had</u> come down around his ears, and he <u>had</u> had to decide between letting the looters steal his fillings and sell his carcass as cold cuts, or take up arms against them wearing a funny looking cap and ridiculously ornate epaulets, covered with stars and fight for his life.

He had chosen the latter, and with the help of Day and his colleagues had been transformed almost over night from Joshua Kabingga, the mayor of a very small and secretly rich town, into General Kabingga, the 'President Damn Near for Life', of the rather largish, and publicly somewhat poor country of Greater Burundi[44].

This is an interesting point here, the speed and manner in which his transformation took place. Often, people's stories are told in big hairy mats made up of millions of self-flattering little lie-strands. They lie that the people involved were always

---

[43] Known popularly as IFI, pronounced iffy.
[44] Greater Burundi, because his patch also included parts of what had previously been Tanzania, Burundi, Uganda and The Congo, also the enclave of Snellville the Lesser.

focused, with a single passion and purpose, and that when the time came they were ready to attain their destiny. They tell you that they were overnight successes that justly deserved to be.

In fact this is almost never the case. People usually spend their lives fucking around watching TV and then have a destiny thrust upon them, for which they are totally unprepared and just manage to squeak by at best. Or, they are born wealthy, and so can scheme freely, knowing that all their dreams and ideas, no matter how puerile and pedestrian, will be received as fundamental works of genius.

Kabingga's rise, (or descent depending on how you look at it), on the other hand, was something to see. In a little under six months he was faced with hundreds of the sorts of choices that leaders dream of never having to make. Like, which group of your close friends would you like to betray. Or, do we stand and fight for this village, knowing we will probably be wiped out, or turn our backs and run, saving our forces for a battle we know we can win next week, and maybe win this damned war, at the expense of the civilians that we are supposed to be defending.

He came up to every challenge, met it like a mensch, and got onto the next, without ever feeling sorry for himself or getting an inflated ego behind it either. Full marks!

Of course this could never last. But he did hold out for six months, before he caved in and started arbitrarily slaughtering people that were inconvenient to him, like an inexorable machine. When he did, it was with a zeal that shocked even Day, who knew all along that the day would surely come.

When he looked back on it all, about 90% of him had no regrets whatsoever. His kids <u>were</u> going to ivy league schools and he was more or less in control of his own destiny. He could even say that, all things being equal, he would do it all again. But there was that one little bit, down in the core of him, that still looked out through his old eyes and was absolutely amazed at all the outrageous lies he told. It honestly remembered all the hateful things he had had to do to wind up where he was, at any given moment. His homunculus[45], if you like, was still the guy under the banyan tree, who worked on his own car between being the mayor and the fire chief of Snellville the Lesser. He didn't hate that man, as so many people from small places that get famous

---

[45] The homunculus is the imaginary 'little person' that most people think is standing inside their head looking out through their eyes.

do. But he did on occasion have to shout down his objections to be effective on TV.

For 20 years the imbalance of power in the region that he had helped strike as a younger man had remained, more or less in his favor. IFI ranted and raved and rattled its saber, but for the most part, kept to the one true path of loud-mouthed mediocrity.

Oh sure, they could do the evil monkey thing. They did manage to kill a few thousand, mostly innocent, people. A car bomb here, an assassination there—even a few spectacular hijackings, but by the standards of world domination, their stated goal[46], it was paltry at best.

This suited everybody fine, providing work for otherwise useless zealots, and forming a thick, free flowing conduit for American tax dollars to gush into his country. Not that Kabingga absolutely had to have the cash, at least at first. They had their mineral wealth, and that would buy a lot of groceries, but it was very nice to have all that mad money around for building pet projects, like the Snellville-Burundi Super Highway, and the Army.

The Army, now there was a Jones. Kabingga had started off small, using the local talent and a trickle of Israeli and American arms. This was fine for a while. And then later, when he had to have a few tanks to counter the threat of the surplus T-90s coming in from Iran and Egypt why they had come just like that, with technical advisors and spare parts and all, it was so easy. IFI was no problem—nothing he couldn't handle—especially with the twenty A10 tank busters the British were getting rid of at a fraction of their original cost. Of course, the maintenance was expensive, but there was a lot of money around to be spent, and so it went, and went, and went. IFI got a little, so he got a little, and a little bit more just to make sure.

By 2045 he had the biggest, best equipped Army in the region, so naturally there was a real war.

It started as a few minor skirmishes along the Congolese border. Nothing extraordinary, and he sent a few truckloads of men to take care of it. They would be back in a week at most. IFI were always doing this sort of thing to tease him— to test his resolve. They would pop a few villagers and then melt back into the bush to see what happened. When a response came it would be a measured one, reflecting his cool head and ability to divorce

---

[46] Only in Arabic, and only in the mosques to the ready ears of the already converted.

his emotions from the particular provocation and act instead of react. This was good, this was right, this was the way the Americans and British did it, like soulless machines.

The three trucks rolled into Polombogo at around sun set under the command of a young captain named Nigel Shumba. Shumba deployed his men and swept the village looking for bad guys and securing a perimeter as they went, this only took about an hour and turned up nothing unusual. Having done with that chore, he had the sergeant billet the men in the church at the south end of town, and he retired to the bar for a glass of peanut beer, a local delicacy.

The beer was lovely, cool and nutty, with a clean finish. The bar man, carefully placed a small bowl of fried yam chips down in front of him on the bar. He smiled, but not with his eyes.

"On the house," he said.

Nigel tried one. They were a little strange, with a fibrous sort of crunch and a bland salty flavor. The bar was empty, except for the barman and himself. Nigel looked around. The place was a bit messy, as if people had left in a hurry.

"Pretty quiet tonight," he said.

The barman smiled with his mouth again, "It won't be later."

There was a long silence then, that served to emphasize to Nigel how alone he was, sitting there in the bar. He raised his glass to the barman.

"It's good beer."

"Thank you," said the barman. "We make it ourselves."

He nodded, drained the last of it and went outside to pee.

Nigel stepped behind the bar and started urinating on the back of the building. He could see the lights glowing in the church windows where his men were bedding down for the night, there was a guard out front, just as there should be, he could see that it was private Encomo, the new guy.

There was a whistling sound up in the sky. Encomo looked up trying to find the source even as it dawned on Shumba what the sound was. He opened his mouth to yell something and the church exploded with a bright flash, sending Encomo in a flat arch away from it. A heartbeat later there was a loud bang. Then it was quiet again.

Nigel forgot all about peeing, and started for the church with his dick still hanging out of his pants. There were people, civilians, running away from the church end of town. He walked over to where Encomo had landed. The man was still alive.

"What happened?" he asked, his broken body lying twisted in

the street.

Shumba looked at the smoking rubble where his men had been.

He nodded sagely, "The church has blown up."

He walked on, to look at the damage. Where the church had been there was a smoking hole full of stones and broken timbers and pieces of people, some of them still dying. He looked around at them, bewildered.

There was a burring noise on the right, he realized he was blind, and a loud WHACK to the left, as the bullet that had just gone through his head lodged in a tree trunk some fifty feet away. He became confused, fell down, and died.

Kabingga's response was swift and again measured and passionless. That was the thing about being an inexorable machine; you had to keep it up all the time. You had to be consistent.

He sent in a regiment to crush the uprising, as it was being called and they chased around the rift valleys for a while, raising holy hell with the villagers and slaughtering Muslims of whatever stripe they might come across. They were very fastidious about one thing, though. They took great care to butcher people of all tribes equally. The last thing that Kabingga wanted was to start a tribal conflict inside his own country.

As they prosecuted their campaign against the IFI insurgents they succeeded in unifying the rural population against the Army and failed to do much against the guerrilla tactics, or 'shameful cowardice', as Kabingga insisted it be referred to, of their enemies. The thing was this, like so many others before him, Kabingga failed to grasp the basic idea that a conventional army fighting a conventional war stands little chance against a popular guerrilla movement fighting a guerrilla war against it. The guerrillas leave them almost nothing to shoot at, besides the innocent bystanders that they hide behind and on behalf of which the Army is supposedly fighting. This in spite of the fact of Snellville the Lesser's very guerrilla past. How could he forget?

IFI would hit a camp with rockets or mortars, and then just fade away into the jungle like a whisper. And he would respond in kind with tanks and APCs that went thundering around the countryside running over people's livestock and demolishing their houses, in an attempt to win friends and influence people!

Kabingga lost fast and furiously, and would have gone down hard in just a few months if it hadn't been for the aid now pouring into Greater Burundi from Washington. What started as a mere torrent, quickly swelled to the proportion of a vast ocean of flaming, unaccountable cash. So he had a bankroll, but that didn't guarantee to save his ass, not that that was what the State Department, necessarily wanted.

He could go hang, quite frankly, as far as they were concerned, but they did expect a return on their investment, beyond the minerals that he continued to supply to them and deny to IFI. They wanted to stop the creep of Islam, just as they had sought to stop the spread of Communism a hundred years earlier. If he could not come up with the goods, sooner or later, they would abandon him for some more likely stooge. He knew this and fought all the harder for the knowledge.

So the map changed, but only slowly. Greater Burundi gradually eroded away along the western frontier, first back to the edge of Lake Tanganyika. There he stopped them for a year or so, using the natural barrier of the lake as a shield. This allowed his men a rest and gave him time to re-think their strategy. Of course McDermott was no slacker himself and started to nibble away at the North, all the while trying to get around the lake.

By the spring of '48 Kabingga had laid a daring plan along the lines at the north and south extremities of the lake. He would allow a weakness to be detected and let McDermott push in along the near shore forming two pockets. Then he would close them and encircle his advanced guard in a ring of cold steel. This was a great plan if you were fighting a conventional tank battle in 1942.

The day came and his men pulled back after lobbing a few coercing rounds into the small fishing villages at either end of the lake. When his response was unanswered, McDermott's scouts reported back to their commanders that there was an opening. The commanders followed the plan exactly, which was to send in a few small teams to mine the roads and test the limits of the enemy. At the same time they called McDermott to let him know that Kabingga was springing a clever trap on them, and that things were well in hand.

Knowing Kabingga's exact strength and the whereabouts of his troops from reading Jane's Defense Weekly and buying satellite reconnaissance from the Chinese, McDermott sent 10,000 soldiers against Kabingga's relatively undefended southern and eastern flanks. It took Kabingga three days to understand what was going on and another two to act on the knowledge. He shifted 80% of his forces over to defend what was now about half of Greater Burundi, and that was when

McDermott took him up on his offer by walking over the remaining garrisons along the lake.

They pushed on and at years end what had been a pretty good-sized piece of real estate was shrunk down to a little barbell shaped patch of ground. This consisted of half of the former Burundi and the enclave of Snellville the Lesser, connected by a ten mile wide strip of land that ran along either side of the Snellville-Burundi Super Highway. This, he could defend. This, the girl scouts could just about defend.

Mingetsu McDermott's advancing troops, many of whom were soulless homicidal monsters themselves, were appalled by the level of sheer brutality and wastage that Kabingga's Army left in its wake. They came upon town after town of poisoned wells, slaughtered livestock and the flayed corpses of suspected collaborators hung from the trees like grisly offerings. The first one they tried to cut down and bury, but it was a counter weight to the trigger of an anti-personnel mine. One killed and two wounded, after that they left them hanging till the buzzards set them off.

In view of this sort of behavior, it was little wonder that the American people, as well as the Senate, had fallen out of love with Kabingga. Okay, so maybe he was their last best hope of stopping the Islamic take over of Africa. You still couldn't go around showing this sort of thing on the news every night and expect the people bank-rolling it to look at each other across the dinner table and not feel like shit. What do you say to your teenaged children, "Oh no you don't understand, honey, it was precisely to save those people from themselves that we had to flay them alive and hang them from trees! Why can't you see that?

"Geez, Agnes, kids these days!"

Joshua Kabingga could just see the hills of Burundi at the far side of the plains that separated them from Snellville. The Presidential mansion—the aggrandized farmhouse that Van Hool had built there for Sarah Otaro—looked out from the small rise at what was still the edge of town, more or less.

From his dining room he could see the airport that ran along side the Snellville-Burundi Super Highway for a couple of miles. It made a bright trapezoid vanishing into the distance, lined along the left side with rows of hangars and the tower. It and the highway were great swathes of the first world that ran through the African veldt. They were foreign. They were his. To him they were much more than the structures themselves—they were the symbols of his success, and his failure.

They represented his amazing success at creating a small piece of the free world there, like an island in a furious sea of fundamental Islam. They meant that free people could come and go and importantly, say, anything they pleased. They were twenty-five years of hard work that you could reach out and touch with your hand.

They were also a reminder that for all his effort, he was still a man under siege. He was surrounded by enemies and the runway was the only way in or out and the highway was the only secure way to move things around his odd looking little country.

He could see a line of smudge in the air above the distant plains to the east and another up against the mountains to the west. This was the smoke from the fires of the IFI insurgents that surrounded him. It was like a dull gray wall encircling his bright little patch of the West. And at night, he could see their glow like a beautiful noose around his neck. Every month it got a little tighter. Every month it was a little harder to breathe.

The airport was also his escape hatch. He knew, because he had timed it, that he could have the family into a Hercules, Pablo and all, and up into the air, bound for Europe, in just under an hour if the need arose. This thought was like a big soft pillow to him. He had told that dude Swarthmore that if Swindel didn't do something and soon it was an option he was going to have to use.

-<>-

Tomlinson checked the partial pressure of oxygen in the 'bedroom'—.15 bar, normal. In there were a thousand sleepy people that were his responsibility. He noted the figure in the log and checked the power draw. He found it a little hard to concentrate with Knute there but he re-marshaled his thoughts and pressed on with his checks. Their heading was correct, the radiation count was normal, the water purity was good and the temperature was a balmy 20°, all absolutely as they should be.

He looked at the board for a moment longer as he began to speak.

"Can't you do that some place else?"

He looked Snortom in the eyes.

Knute continued what he was doing for a while before he spoke.

"Why," he asked, continuing. "There some law against it?"

"No. No law against it, but I find it a bit distracting."

"Me to. That's why I do it! It's so fucking boring out here!"

He paused for a moment to squeeze some more lotion into his hand and then resumed masturbating, matter-of-factly.

142

"You should try it. It might relax you."

"I'd think that you'd be sore by now. You've been at it for weeks like this."

"Come on, fuck you man. Let's beat off!"

Dave shook his head. "I have work to do, the same as you."

He turned around and set his log down.

"Computer, mail, Tomlinson."

The nearest screen showed a picture of a postman smiling at him.

"You have one item," it said.

"Computer, read it to me."

There was a pause and then this, in a deep African voice.

"Hello Alpha One! This is Joshua Kabingga. On behalf of the people of Greater Burundi I send you greetings. We are all very pleased with your progress."

Knute broke his rhythm for a moment. "What an asshole," he said.

"I am delighted to inform you that the people of Greater Burundi have asked me to bestow upon you a small token of our gratitude for your continuing sacrifice. So—

"On behalf of the People of Greater Burundi I hereby grant to each of you one thousand shares in the Umbutu River Project. Congratulations and welcome to the company!

I will let you know of any stockholders meetings. And remember, let's not forget to vote!"

Snortom started laughing.

"Jesus Christ, what a <u>total</u> asshole!" he said. "I'm gonna go thaw a melon and try fucking that!"

Tomlinson looked at him.

"You interested?" asked Snortom.

Here We Go

If you had been walking through the great central mezzanine of the Deerfield Mall that day like Mort Kohut, you might have been similarly surprised to see, none other than, Bill Crenshaw smiling out of the newly installed Deluxe MegaVision® video wall, that had been put there to replace the very one that Bill had destroyed by urinating on it. His fifty-foot face smiled out at the passers by, none of whom found much irony in this situation. Mort thought that was funny and stopped to watch for a moment and see what the old guy had to say.

Since his horrific injury, and subsequent appearance on the Veets show Bill had become quite a celebrity. He was much in demand for product endorsements as the wizened voice of pissed off Americans everywhere.

Bill grinned a big bogus grin. It was all the rage then to do that among public figures—to grin like the Cheshire cat and give a jaunty salute—like you were selling cars. In fact that was what Mort expected him to do up there, sell product, as he had been for the last couple of months, so he was surprised when he didn't.

Bill's now perfectly modulated voice that had been remade for him by the toerags and professional image men that had oozed from the walls at the first whiff of money, washed out across the crowds there, like a wave of wheezy old corn syrup.

"Hello America," he said heartily. "I'd like a moment of your time, if I may, to talk to you, about a shameful, and needless tragedy that is about to over take this great nation of ours." He was wearing a sport coat and slacks.

"Now, I'm a simple man and I don't go for a lot of that malarkey that has been spewing out of the White House lately, but I do know this—this country of ours was built one brick at a time, by hard working, honest people. People like you and me. People with a future, that they wouldn't trust to a single individual."

A crown appeared on his head.

"Those brave men and women knew what perils lay waiting for them as they conquered a wild continent inhabited by savage Indians. And what did they do about it? Eh? Well, I'll tell you, they fought back with guts and gristle and guns."

His clothes morphed into colonial garb.

"In fact they started militias, groups of people to, in the

words of the constitution, provide for the common defense. They knew what they were up against, and they knew what it took to win, so those militias, those first primitive defenses evolved and adapted to become a standing Army."

As he said 'Army' his clothes changed into a doughboy uniform.

"And that Army went out into battle against the most formidable enemies in the world and won. They defended this country again and again against a world full of evil."

Now his clothes morphed onto a Waffen SS captain's Uniform complete with death-skull cap and a monocle that lent a haughty air.

"The world hasn't changed all that much in the last century. Has it?"

Now his clothes changed again, this time into the NATO-Sino conflict gear of a decade earlier with its gray-green drabness and disheveled techno kit all hung about him like lethal Spanish moss. Past him charged waves of computer generated Chinese soldiers dragging body part with them as they poured through the scene.

"Now is the time that we need the Armed Forces the most. Now is when they are vital to us, to provide for the common defense. But that man's man in Washington wants to throw it all away."

The scene changed again and now he was back in the sport coat, standing on the flight deck of the Ronald Reagan as she coursed through Indian Ocean.

"He wants to give all this up so he can hand the money out to welfare bums and his fat cat friends in Washington while we, the hard working people of America, hang our butts out over the abyss without a net.

"Do we want to just sit here and take this from him? I don't think so! Our security is just too damn dear to us. Please, won't you help?"

An F 45 shot from its catapult behind him, enveloping him in steam. The screen faded to black and the White House feed back number came up to fill the screen for several seconds before it was replaced by a Leonardo's birthday ad for fertilizer at Walmart.

Mort looked around at the crowd of people that had stopped to watch Bill's speech. There were a lot of them and many were writing down the number. Louis was getting heavy and he shifted the dead weight of his sleeping son onto his other shoulder as he started to walk across the gallery to the drug store. The rhythm of his walk sort of swanned along to the Mantovani.

He didn't know that Worthy had gotten Bill for a spot. That wasn't surprising, he had barely seen Anna for the past month. She was working flat out and spending a lot of time in Washington at The Lie, the new name of P. Worthington Yeates & Associates Inc.

Come to that, she might not have known that he was in the ads herself. She had to place content for eight creative teams on three floors, putting out everything from direct mail shots, can you believe it, to full-blown TV campaigns, with one assistant.

He suspected that she could still remember him and Louis if she concentrated.

The ads were everywhere. On the public transit network, radio, phones—they were even buying things like cereal box backs and skywriting.

Igor and Stan had a bet going for how long before one of them slipped a condom on and the words 'Army yes, Swindel no!' were written on the shaft. The disturbing part was, Anna had suggested it to Worthy and he was giving it some thought. If he went for it the two Russians wanted a cut.

Mort got to the Drug Emporium at the far side of the gallery, swiped the five-dollar fee, and entered through the security door after only a small wait for identity confirmation.

He entered the store and walked down the isle toward the back, where the high security pharmaceutical section was.

There was a line—he took a number and waited. It was nice to have a rest actually, after all the hubbub of the mall. He sat down into a chair slinging Louis around onto his lap. He was sleeping. Mort let him slump against his chest, drooling, as he waited. Since Anna had dived into this hell of work that she was insisting on surviving, he had had to basically give up pushing chips and take care of Louis full time.

When they met in college, she worked in an ad firm at night while she wrote her Ph.D. on neurophysiology and the effects of psychosis on brain chemistry. This was pretty impressive as it was, but now on natal hiatus from Cornell, she was handling twice as much work at what was supposed to be a part time job, to keep her sane till the new term.

He wondered if she slept at night, or just pretended till he dozed off and then swapped out a fusion pack when he couldn't hear the couplings hiss apart.

They called his number and he entered the drug section.

His order arrived quickly. The assistant put the aspirin and other drugs in a bag and handed it to him after he swiped his card. On the bag was the now familiar picture of the hapless Uncle Sam with his pants down around his ankles. Mort smiled at the woman.

"I see you are taking a stand on this issue."

She shrugged. "They pay us a dollar a bag, that's about as political as it gets around here. It does sum up nicely."

"Yes, very elegant."

Mort turned to go.

"Thank you," she said. "Keep the hold."

"Keep the hold," he said.

-<>-

"In the upper Rusizi River valley, there is no trust between the civilians and the soldiers that are supposed to protect them from the IFI rebels' attacks.

"The people here say that the soldiers themselves have chased them into the bush time and again, looking for McDermott's men. It is they, they say, that have been responsible for the slaughter, that they say, has happened here, and it is they, that they say—know where the bodies are buried.

"For Africa Today, I'm Bob Ryan."

-<>-

All over the country Worthy's ads were running. There were dozens of them, tailored to specific markets. He had a team that specialized in gay advertising, and another one that just handled red neck men in the South and West. Their rodeo ads were polling well in the Sun Belt. They were all under his direction, but after he gave them a broad brief, they had room to create the campaigns. This was the only way to go about it—the job was huge.

The defense department seemed to like what he was producing. At least the polls they had taken were reporting good results. There were people at the pentagon that hated his direct, humorous, style, but as long as Baisch liked it there was really not much they could do about it. He even had someone working on some pedestrian crap in case they got the upper hand.

Monday mornings Mr. Green would show up looking bewildered and staring again and again at his piece of paper. He would confirm Worthy's identity several times and hand over a suitcase, then turn and walk away seeming distracted and suspicious. When Worthy would open the suitcase it would be full of money.

The Lie Inc. had clocked up 35 million dollars in profits in the last month, on a 19% margin and he was loath to pooch that any time soon. Whatever he had to do for that kind of money was okay. Principles were one thing, principal was quite another.

The change in him was almost imperceptible. He certainly hadn't noticed it himself. When he got the phone call that day from the Pentagon he was an artist poking fun at a stupid world that conspired against him. He did whatever and damn the consequences.

But now—now that he was a millionaire, with stuff to protect and money to hide—he suddenly found himself justifying things that he would have regarded as selling out to public taste. Now he didn't want to piss off certain people too much. Now he wanted their money, and an absolutely huge wad it was, a little more than he wanted to be a highly original and creative kook.

Cassandra had noticed. She found it amusing and a little sad, to think that even Worthy had his price. She knew, of course, that everyone in the world has their price, most deny it, but really, it's true. She had always thought the rules just left off when it came to him. He would never have said that anyone, including himself, was incorruptible for something. But still she had not really believed it.

His price was high anyway, and he was not selling out very much for the loads of money that he was getting. He wasn't changing the campaign ideas to be less confrontational and wacky so much as bending over a little bit here and there to not anger certain people in the course of his work. She would call this, publicly, professionalism, but in her heart she knew it for what it was—he was becoming a butt-boy.

The new ads in the Mid-West and South were going over particularly well. They had pictures of piles of bodies taken at Auschwitz and Chang Mai with captions tailored to individual areas.

The Iowa billboard carried the line, 'Des Moines 2051?' This sort of scare tactic was really hitting a chord with the people there, who had witnessed similar things, a little over a decade earlier. And polls taken in metropolitan centers the week before had an 88% rating for the Army and only 15% for Swindel. The Hold was still on, but this was way up from a month earlier. The national TV and radio spots were doing almost as well and the last set of gay ads for the top cities were hitting their mark too. Now that they had Bill Crenshaw on the pay roll, things would get really good.

Knute floated at the neutral core of Alpha, sort of curled up on himself. He seemed to be rocking there in the fetal position.

Tomlinson couldn't really see him too well from the catwalk at the front of the ship. He called to his Lieutenant.

"Hey, Snortom!" he said.

Knute didn't pay him any attention.

Tomlinson shook his head. He put his binoculars to his eyes and pushed the focus bar. Snortom's image became sharp. He was... He was blowing himself.

Tomlinson zoomed in.

'Most amazing,' he thought. 'What the hell am I going to do now?'

He went to the bridge and got the video camera and a megaphone.

"Hey, Snortom! Stop blowing yourself, will ya'?" he said into the megaphone, taping. "We've got a burn to make!"

Knute's concentration broke and the blond dominatrix with the strap on vanished. He did as Tomlinson asked. The Commander was really starting to irritate him.

The camera flew over a black and white desert toward a tall narrow mesa. The eerie choral hum mounted louder as the mesa grew in frame, till the view arrived at the top. There was a man there in an arcane, spring-hung, spider chair-thing, looking on into the arid country beyond. The sound changed, re-modulating, more open and pointed now. He leaned back, arching, craning his neck. It was Bill. He stared with stern paranoia out of the video screen and yelled.

"You! —————Eat!!! —————" The choral music resolved into "Snakossss".

Mingetsu's men had been sweeping the area for the last three months. It was hard work slogging through the jungle killing people, work that many leaders in his position would have left to underlings while they farted around base camp grab-assing with the chore women but not him. McDermott was a hands-on guy. Short and thick necked, with light coffee skin and receding hair. He liked being a soldier. He liked the physical act of killing another person with his bare hands, particularly bayonet stabbing, that was his fave. He liked the way they wiggled when you stuck 'em.

They had just finished a large settlement in the Qu'ue River valley, a place called Farthingdale. Farthingdale had been a substantial place as jungle villages go. It had some brick buildings and a clean well, even a power generating station at the eastern end of the main street. Unfortunately the inhabitants were all quite devoutly catholic, they had to go.

Now he had the same old logistical problem as always—what to do with the bodies. There were a lot of them too, many hundreds. They couldn't just leave them rotting in the sun like that monster Kabingga. They had to find some place out of the way of the press to bury them, so that they could get on with their holy war, and that was just what Abdahla had found. It was a secluded clearing surrounded by dense forest about a kilometer from town.

The troops had been digging all day and now there was a problem of some kind that he had to sort out.

The driver pulled to a stop at a wide place in the road and pointed.

"In there, Commander."

Mingetsu walked down the narrow path between the trees. They were closely packed and he couldn't see very far through the shaded greenery.

'Allah be praised,' he thought. The spot was perfect.

The path made several twists around the tree roots and eventually he saw the jungle brightening before him. There was a death stink there. He could hear his soldiers working with the backhoe.

McDermott came out of the jungle into the clearing. It was bright and hot there, and the flies buzzed around like crazy.

"Where is Abdahla?" he asked.

One of the soldiers pointed and then whistled. Abdahla looked up and Mengetsu waved him over. He came around the edge of the hole that they were digging at a trot. He threw his Commander a loose salute.

"Sir, we have a problem."

"And what is the nature of our problem, Abdahla?"

Abdahla pointed to the hole. "This hole is full," he said.

"Yes, that is why we have the back hoe, to make the hole empty."

He waxed aphoristic. "Every hole is full, until you empty it."

Abdahla shook his head and led McDermott to the edge of the hole. He pointed.

"No, this hole is already full of bodies."

The Commander looked down into the hole. It was the size

of a small parking lot. The earth at the bottom was full of bones and clothing, and in some places, still some flesh, crawling with flies.

"They're about three meters deep down there."

The two men looked at each other.

"I see we are not the first," said McDermott.

His phone rang. He answered.

"Hello?"

It was Ziow.

-<>-

Bill got out of the limo and made his cantankerous way up the steps of the studio. The guard nodded to him smiling.

"Hello Mr. Crenshaw," he said.

"Hi, Frank. How's the family?"

"I don't have one, Sir."

Bill smiled and winked.

"That's what I like to hear. You take care now."

Frank winked back as the old man passed him and entered the elevator.

"Veets show," he said to the panel. There was a short pause and the car started to climb. It was fifteen weeks since Bill had decided that it would be a pretty good idea to show his derision for the president and his policies by urinating on his giant, million volt video face at the Deerfield Mall. In that time he had healed up pretty well. He could get around more or less normally, and while it was true that his stream was more like a little irregular trickle running down a very big drainage ditch, it didn't hurt at all. Also there was this, he was a millionaire now and the money helped him heal in ways he could not have imagined.

Now, even as a wizened old man with mutilated genitals, he could get 'laid' by pretty, young, ambitious women, he met at the Deerfield Country Club, that he now frequented. People recognized him in the street and stepped out of his way, now, the way they never had before. It was miraculous what the great gray green grease could do. He didn't just feel well again, he felt absolutely great.

The lift stopped, the doors opened and he stepped out into the studio, whistling softly.

Technicians moved around, setting up lights and so on. They paid him no notice at all. Bill liked that, in a way. Here in a television studio he was just another guy, kind of in the way of the vaguely grumpy people that worked there. It was a sort of tacit

151

acceptance of him into their club.

A huge grip came up behind him with a light the size of a garbage can.

"Behind you pal."

Bill scooted to one side. "Sorry."

The grip stepped through saying, "That's a bad place to stand."

There were cables snaking all over the ground through the forest of lighting stands. He went toward the lights and bustle in the center of the room.

As he made his way, people shuffled past him with radios squawking on their belts. He came out into the clearing, where the cameras were set up. It was about the size of a small parking lot. Veets was there talking to a woman. Bill didn't recognize her at first.

Bill came up to Veets and caught his eye. The younger man turned and put out his hand, precisely.

"Hi, Bill," he said warmly. "Thanks for coming to the show today."

"Hello, Dag."

They shook hands. Bill smiled to the woman a bit blankly. She smiled back and shook his hand too.

"Hi, Philus Wagstaff. We met the last time you were on the show. I'm Dag's producer."

"Oh yes, of course, how are you?" Bill scratched his head. "I guess I'm gettin' a bit forgetful in my old age."

She smiled. "Oh that's all right. How's your...ah, health?"

Bill looked down at his crotch and smiled a bit ruefully. "Oh it's doing about as well as can be expected. I've got no pain or anything like that. In fact you could stick a mouse trap down my pants and I'd probably be completely unaware of it.[47]"

She laughed a little.

"Thanks, I'll remember that. Can you come this way to makeup please?"

Veets waved to him. "See you in a while, Bill."

Philus led the sloppy old coot away as Veets rubbed at the graze mark the late Nathan Mornette's bullet had left on his forehead. There was a definite scabbed furrow there, surrounded by a bruise. It was a habit he had developed lately—he rubbed at it five times.

---

[47] This was because the lightning bolt that had shot up Bill's penis that fateful day had fried the nerves that led to his glans.

He sat down in his host's chair and looked at his notes. He was having a little trouble concentrating on things lately. It was no big deal—he could handle it. He was organized. And after all what did people expect, he had nearly been shot through the head with a 9mm slug that was doing the better part of the speed of sound only three weeks earlier. He was lucky to be alive!

His manner had changed a little since the incident atop the bus. He had become, if you can imagine such a thing, even more grumpy and smarmy and bellicose than he had been before. Philus had mentioned it to him in passing, that he was seeming a little on edge lately, and he had duly pointed out to her that there was a hierarchy here, and she was by no means irreplaceable, and that she had better just try to keep her mind on her job if she wanted to have it next year.

She smiled and said, "Yes of course." CBS was looking for good people, she knew.

It bewildered him that so many people around him, people that he had trusted for years, all of a sudden seemed like such a bunch of flaky, deceitful cretins, bent on their own ends. They were ceasing to be team players. He made a mental note to review his staff requirements for the coming year[48].

It would later become clear that his staffing requirements for the next season would be quite minimal.

He read on, trying hard to remember what he was supposed to talk about and in what order. That was very important, the order in which things happened. In fact since the shooting incident, the concept of order had weighed on his mind like a stone. He found himself obsessing about order and the classification of things. This had never been a part of his personality before and he had observed it in himself, almost as another person—as if his homunculus suddenly had very anal company. This had bugged him a lot at first, but after a while, after he got himself squared away, he was all right with it.

Dagmar took out a black, medium ball, ballpoint pen, and made very square boxes around all the topic headings that he had already bolded. This stood them out and drew attention to them in a way that made him feel more comfortable.

_____

[48] In fact Mornette's bullet had caused a cone shaped shock wave to propagate through the gray fatty Jell-O ™ of Veets' cerebral cortex displacing and/or damaging several thousand neurons. This is but a teardrop in the vast ocean of the brain, but would nonetheless prove significant.

He reassembled his notes, shuffling them into their original order, taking great care to make sure that all the sheets of paper lined up squarely at the edges. He tamped the bottom and left edges against the table, three times.

They were on in twenty-one-minutes and thirty-eight seconds.

-<>-

"Hey lady! Watch where you're goin'! Mommy! Mommy! Mommy! June, where are my orange striped socks!? 'Pan Pon, Pan Pon. And remember shoppers, there's just 200 more shopping days left till Christmas! Why don't you call your Mother?"

"Stop!!!"

"Sometimes the world and you just don't get along.
"Sometimes there's nowhere to hide.
"Sometimes you just want to kill someone.
"Sometimes, there's CONFORM™"
"For those days that you just don't seem to fit.™"

-<>-

"...at's right Mr. and Mrs. America, you heard me right when I said it and I mean to tell you that it is the God's own truth when I say it that this is the single most amazing product ever devised by mankind after the Bible. You can not find, no matter how hard you look and no matter how many countries you search, a better way," he paused for effect, "I said a better way to clean your drapes than to use the services of a certified, I say a CERTIFIED American Acme drapery cleaner.

"They are the best, the best, the best, and if you don't believe me then you can go and try someone else. But don't come crying to me when those Satanist, baby eating monsters blow the job and bring back your curtains, or drapes or even your beloved Venetian blinds in tattered shards. And there's no guaranty with those other guys. No, no guaranty at all, not like the one you get with a certified, I say a CERTIFIED American Acme drapery cleaner. They give you peace of mind.

"And, America, speaking of peace of mind, we are lucky enough today to have with us someone who is becoming quite well known for giving everybody a piece of his mind. Ladies and gentlemen, please won't you give a big apple hand to the Deerfield Dribbler, Mr. Bill Crenshaw!"

Philus brought up an orchestral version of the 1970s hit, 'Yellow River', as Bill's intro music.

He came striding out from behind the curtain in a very nice

Shikashi suit, his white hair made a perfect ring around his bald dome of a head. He stepped up onto the podium and shook Veets' hand with practiced theatrical gusto. They smiled at each other, amid applause from the studio audience.

"Sit down, Bill," said Veets. "Relax, you're at home with us here."

Bill pulled up the knees of his trousers as he sat.

"Thanks, Dag, it's great to be here on your <u>new show</u>."

Veets feigned modesty, as Bill beamed and the audience crackled applause. "Yes, well, we <u>are</u> quite proud."

"Hi everybody!" said Bill waving to the hundred or so people that filled the seats before him.

They yelled and applauded loudly. There were a few friendly hoots and yells. One guy cupped his hands to his mouth and asked in a shout, "Yo Bill, how's yer wang?!" This got a laugh out of the audience.

"Huge!" said Bill. This really got a laugh, even from Veets.

As this died down Dagmar smiled for the cameras and turned his chair a bit to face Bill a little.

"So, Bill," he said, "first things first—what's your favorite flavor at he moment?"

Bill smiled self-assuredly. "Onion! Onion Snakos, Dag. I've been working my way through the flavors but that's what's workin' for me at the moment."

Veets presented him with an open hand.

"There it is."

The audience applauded.

"So tell us what you've been up to the past few weeks. Recuperating?" This got a laugh. "Working hard?"

"I don't think it'll ever work to get hard again, Dag." More laughs. Bill shrugged sardonically.

"But seriously, Dag, I have to say that I have been working my tail off, ever since you had me on your radio show. Here I thought I was retired for good, with my pension from the bartenders union and my little place up town, and lo and behold I got a whole new career to do. And you know what Dag? You know what? It's great!"

There was a round of enthusiastic applause, just as the prompter said there should be. Veets gave a big thumbs-up to the audience smiling wide.

"So maybe, Bill, it wasn't such a bad idea to pee all over the electronics after all!"

"Well I'll tell ya', Dag, I have very few regrets."

155

Veets raised an eyebrow.

"I didn't say, none, Dag. I did <u>not</u> say, <u>none</u>! But I will say this—In spite of my injury, this being a media celebrity is just the cats. I don't know why I didn't go for it years ago."

"Maybe you weren't called yet, Bill, that's all. Some of us get the call earlier than others do, and that's just the way it goes. Now's your time, so go boy, GO!"

More applause and then Dagmar continued with evangelical fervor.

"Bill, tell us please. <u>You</u> are a man with his finger on the pulse. The pulse of <u>America</u>! What do you think is going to happen next? I mean—and you can bet your bottom dollar that it will—what will it be?!"

"Well, Dag, now that you ask, I have to tell you. I think, that the Hold will hold, for a while anyway.

"Oh, at first I know there were a lot folks that spoke out loud and long about how the Hold was just a little flash in the pan. That it would not, could not, hold. But it <u>held</u>. And I'll tell you why it held, too, because ordinary American citizens like our audience tonight have still not seen the result that they want.

"You know it would be the easiest thing in the world to go around patting ourselves on the back over this." He looked pointedly at Veets. "And say that we did it and will continue to do it because we are brave, or noble, or worse yet to say that we somehow deserve to pull it off, just because we are Americans. Americans do not have and have never had a corner on the market when it comes to bravery and honor.

"We have not done this thing with pit bull tenacity, just because we are good people and our cause is right. We have done it, and will continue to do it, right or wrong, because we haven't got what we want yet. And when we <u>get</u> what we want— when we get a coherent policy out of those ass-licking thugs in Washington—then we will relent. We will pull the cork and the money will flow like milk and honey."

Veets turned solemnly to the camera.

"Do you hear that, Swindel? Do you? A coherent policy. That's what these people want and it is damn well what they deserve, so if I was you, I'd just go ahead and give it to them. There are a lot of federal employees that are sick and tired of getting IOUs in their pay slips. What are <u>you</u> going to do about it?"

He turned back to Bill.

"Bill, what's up with all this nonsense about ditching the

156

Military for a welfare state? How do average Americans feel about that?"

"Just one thing I want to add about the point you just made there, Dag. I have personally seen letters from federal workers in several areas, and they have all expressed support for our cause. They all put the Hold on too."

"Thanks for that, Bill, Swindel, take note."

Bill shook his head and paused momentarily, finding his words.

"Dag, I can assure you that I don't speak for everybody in the country, but I have asked that question of people from San Diego to Bangor and I have yet to meet one that thinks it is anything other than the most utter folly. They are not going to let their money be handed out to slum dwelling welfare bums while they stand there with their pants down, asking for it. It just isn't in our nature as a nation to do something that dumb. Everybody I've spoken to has mentioned that they feel they owe their freedom to the fact that this country has never been afraid to fight. We have a Military that is the envy of the world and they like it that way."

Applause.

"Now, we put the Hold on to stop the president from sending in troops to prop up that nincompoop Kabingga, and incidentally, to show that we don't give two fucks in a cat's ass about ponies. But it is quite another thing to extrapolate that to dismantling the armed forces of the United States of America and giving the money out to the lazy bums that Washington has created with the misguided industrial and educational policies of the past six decades.

"It was Swindel that made that extrapolation. I am calling here and now for his resignation, or frankly, Dag, I say we impeach the queer!"

The studio audience was on its feet, thundering its applause at him for five minutes. Dagmar joined them. After a long time he looked into the cameras and said, "We'll be right back after this."

Philus ran the commercial card. There were the usual ads for Snakos and so on and then she gave Dagmar a ten count on her fingers to come into the paid political announcement.

3...2...1 and she pointed at him.

"America, hear me! What you are about to hear is the sound of a pony. A wild American pony, thundering across the plains of a free America."

As he spoke Philus faded up the archive clip of a mustang

galloping across the desert[49].

"That is the sound of freedom. That is the sound of an animal roaming the great plains of this country with its mane flowing in the wind and of free air being pulled in and out of its powerful lungs. Or, there may be an alternative."

She cut to a clip of some Chinese soldiers in chef's hats barbequing a nag. They poked at it with forks and poured sauce all over it, all the time babbling in Mandarin. The fire popped and crackled loudly on the studio monitor.

"Lets help keep America free."

She gave him another count on her fingers and right on the cut Veets smiled for the cameras.

"We're back, America, and welcome if you just joined us, or welcome back if you've been here all along. We are lucky to have with us an American of heroic proportions, ladies and gentlemen, the electrifying Bill Crenshaw!"

He presented Bill with an open palm.

"Bill, tell us won't you, what do you think that we should do about General Kabingga and his pony loving children? I mean Kabingga, now there is a piece of work for you. This guy comes along and tries to take over the richest chunk of Africa and make it into Miami Beach with the aid of the US taxpayer's money. He gets his ass handed to him by the Arabs and then he comes crying to us for more help. What should we do? Eh? Let 'em hang? Kill him ourselves and have done with it? Do we cut a separate deal with the Arabs? What? What are we to DO!?"

Bill looked thoughtful for a few seconds.

"You know, Dag, I'm no international statesman, I'm just a retired bar tender that's gotten the chance to shoot off his mouth for a change, but I'll tell you what. I think that we certainly should not—either spend American lives and dollars propping up his failing regime—or let those valuable minerals fall into the wrong people's hands.

"It is my stupid opinion, that we should tell Kabingga to pack up his people and get the hell out, chickens, children, ponies and all and move to someplace that they will be happy."

"Like?"

---

[49] The last wild mustang in the contiguous United States was hunted down and killed to make dog food and glue in 2028 by a man named Randy Mills. Mr. Mills was drunk at the time, and couldn't manage to successfully shoot the poor animal, so he sufficed to run over it with a borrowed pick up truck that he destroyed in the process. He got $25.68 for the carcass.

"Like oh I don't know, maybe Utah or Saskatchewan, or some place over there, like the remains of Kazakhstan or Macedonia. That's it, maybe Macedonia. They could live there for a while, and the US could cut a deal with NATO and the Russians and Japanese to swap out troops on a rota basis, sharing out the minerals that we are all paying Snellville Mining and Minerals for anyway. That way we get the stuff we want, at, oh I don't know, maybe a little more than we are paying right now, but nothing like what it would cost to prop up Kabingga and buy his minerals.

"Now this deal wouldn't have to last forever either. I mean, I know that it's not very polite to talk about it, but this is supposed to be an open forum and all. Right Dag?

"You bet, Bill."

"So look, Dag, Africa is going to be an empty place, as far as humans are concerned, in the next ten or fifteen years, right? I mean, am I the only one who can do simple arithmetic. AIDS has infected 98% of the population south of the Sahara desert, and already half of the deaths there from it, are to children below breading age. Not to mention the recurring outbreaks of Ebola Zaire that seem to come along with the rains. Now you tell me, Dag, how much longer can they go on like this? Five years? Ten at most! Those poor devils are going to be being born dead to dying mothers in not too long!

"Now God knows that we, the Western world, have tried to help those people. We have showered them with condoms, flooded them with health workers and done everything short of threatening them at gun point to try to get them to get their breeding practices under control, but they will not have it!

"When all is said and done, and the place is just empty ground heaped with dead bodies and the occasional zebra, I say that is the time to move in and take what we like. Not now, not at such a great cost, when a little patience will do the job just fine."

"But surely we can't let the Arab Nationalists just walk in and take it over. They want us bad, Bill!"

"No, no, no, I didn't say that, Dag. That's where our NATO, Russian and Japanese allies can be so valuable. They can hold the fort against the onslaught from the north. They use these minerals too you know, and they want to keep the supply flowing the same as us. If we just keep the mines open and the airstrip and adjoining highway, that shouldn't be that big a deal. Like, when the US Marines kept Guantánamo Bay open all through the Castro regimes, last century. It cost relatively little and yet, and

159

yet, it did the trick!"

"So you figure then that we can afford to wait a bit, is that it Bill?"

The old coot nodded his head emphatically, spreading his bony hands to emphasize.

"Look, the Alpha 1 project, the main reason for all of this has already gone. The first phase anyway, and the follow ships, if they ever go at all, will not even be built till we get word back. Alpha won't get to Alpha Centauri for another six years. Besides we have enough material stockpiled to get a pretty good start, on the main structures anyway. I say we have plenty of time to put things right. Why rush when we don't have to?"

Veets nodded sagely.

"Swindel, what are we going to do with you, boy?"

He signaled Philus for a close up just off screen.

"Dwayne Swindel, I hope by God that you are watching this broadcast, boy. Your resignation has been called for. The nation has put you on notice, once and for all. Your dumb plans will not go through, you have lost. It is time to walk away Mr. President."

She cut back to the wide shot as Dagmar turned back to Bill.

"So tell us, Bill, any plans to run for office yourself? After all, a lot of Americans agree with what you have to say."

Bill shook his head modestly.

"You know, Dag, I actually thought about that a little when this thing broke. I said to myself, Bill, you can do that, get on out there and give it the old college try, but you know, that was just a lot of publicity drunk nonsense. I am not and have never been a guy with what it takes to get elected. I think that I will stay doing what I do best. I kind of like being a thorn in the side of Government, I couldn't stand to be a part of it!"

Veets laughed along with everybody else.

"Thanks for your time, Bill, and keep up the good work!"

The two men shook hands while the audience applauded loudly. Philus went to the break, giving them a big okay sign...

-<>-

Aluwishus Faircloth smiled to himself as he watched Veets' show in the corner of his monitor. He had a lot to smile about. What Crenshaw had said was right. There was widespread support for the Army among ordinary Americans. Not that it mattered much, with both houses securely in the pocket, but still it made good press. And that in turn, generated further support, that bolstered the nerve of the Senate, and around and around it went. He figured he couldn't lose.

The president had his back to the wall, there was nothing left for him to do, but cave in and abandon Kabingga to end the Hold.

If he did, that would cause a crisis in Central Africa that required the Military to sort out—money for him. Or else the Arabs would take over, get cocky and try to dominate Europe, again requiring the Military to sort it out in a larger theater roll— even better.

If Swindel didn't cave in to the Hold, then Failsworthy would reissue the dollar. This sheer idiocy would cause riots, again needing the Army to stop it short of another civil war.

Or he wouldn't have the nerve to reissue, and the civilian Government employees would walk off their jobs in about a week, and the Army would have to step in just to keep essential services running.

He was looking forward to the next few weeks, as all around him colleagues would implode, trying to cover their butts as he followed his plan like a great stoic ship of state, unswayed by their fickle lusts and passions. This is where the breading would tell. Those others, with their petty ambitions would go down in flames trying to grab at chump change, while he would fulfill his families destiny as statesmen. It was inevitable.

On his monitor there were several other shows running simultaneously around the edge of the screen like a necklace of information around the main feed from the Senate floor.

He had a row of commercial stations across the top feeding him news and current affairs and down the sides he had sports and weather on the right and stock quotes and financial news on the left. The bottom of the screen was a hodge-podge of shows off the networks interspersed with opinion trend analysis from both houses and live feedback from Arkansas.

This circle of information was how he kept his finger on the pulse of America. It was a formality that very few senators and representatives bothered with anymore. They voted their wallets. He sometimes felt a twinge of—well he didn't really know what to call it. There wasn't exactly a word for it that he knew, but it was a feeling that he sometimes got, that he was just a sad old anachronism bashing his head against a wall while the rest of Washington rushed past him, barely taking time to laugh.

He had a twinge now. He knew it would pass if he just waited it out.

He looked at the bottom of his screen. The graphic displays told the story. The level of the Hold was a red bar with percentage points of the taxpaying population marked out next to it. It stood at a whopping 93% and had barely moved in the past three weeks except during the president's last speech, when it had risen slightly.

There was a screen showing one of the network feeds out of New York with the Phill Dumbrowski show. He paused there for a moment hoping that it would help cheer him up.

Phill stood on stage telling the usual jokes and bantering with the audience. He didn't have the hammer out yet, but still the tone was light and happy. Al watched for a few minutes waiting for the old Slugo, but it was still too early for that, he went on.

Next to Phill's show was a vote projection for reissuing the dollar. It was hovering around 44%, respectable but hardly a threat to the American way of life. Next to it was a confidence rating for the Military taken as a poll in Little Rock last night at 6 pm. It was in the high 80s. That, at least was working out as expected.

He had to hand it to Baisch. He had gone to a professional advertising firm and spent some money[50] and the numbers were looking very good there, not just in the South either, but even out on the wild West Coast where people usually didn't have much time for the Army. He had told Baisch to go ahead and do the do. He would see that it got bankrolled. That took a little finagling, but it was worth it, even if he was going to owe some big favors someday.

At first he didn't want to use the CIA, with all their ghoulish methods. He thought they were a political liability and a personal threat. But when it became clear they were about the only way forward, he contracted them for 'financial and logistic services'. They turned out to be pretty nice guys after all. He was starting to feel more at home with the idea. So maybe they would pick his running mate. So?

He glanced at the center screen. Tiendail was still filibustering. He looked agitated, like he had something important to say.

"Main, sound," he said.

The sound on the main screen came up to an audible level.

"...thing I can tell you is this. If you do decide to, and I can certainly recommend that you do, then there is only one choice left to make in the whole process, which type of grease are you going to use? Lard? Well, now there's a thought, what about lard?

---

[50] So far, just over a half a billion dollars.

It's a damned fine lubricant I'll grant you that, it won't freeze up on you the way graphite will some times when it gets <u>really</u> cold. And it's cheap!"

He paused and slowly took a drink from a glass of water that was in front of him, thinking.

"Lard, however has its drawbacks, and I <u>will</u> enumerate them!

"Firstly,"

"Main sound off."

"There is a disti..."

His nattering faded back down leaving Faircloth in silence again. He was thankful for that.

The man had been at this filibuster for the last week, tag teaming with Failsworthy and others, trying to delay the vote on the president's proposed Social Alternative. To their thinking, every day they delayed the vote, the more damage they did to Swindel and his administration. They figured they could eventually drive him out of office, and still hold onto power, themselves. Faircloth didn't rate their chances. He and the rest of the Military bloc were hanging back and letting them stick their necks out. This would be marvelous.

The thought of Failsworthy shafting himself cheered Faircloth. He looked around at the various commercial stations at the bottom of the screen, there were no less than three commercials running simultaneously for the Military, now that was coverage.

On the feed from the steps of the Senate the crowd was thin and orderly. There had been almost no trouble at all since the incident with Veets and Washington, and crowd control was keeping order among the demonstrators that remained. That was good. It would be very bad press if the Military was called in to maintain order by force, too soon. The American people didn't like the idea that they could be shot down like dogs by their own Army.

He was feeling better by the minute. He checked the Dumbrowski show again. Now the comedian had his trademark hammer out and was wagging it enticingly at the cameras as he told his last joke of the show.

"WTTW, sound."

"...Poodles? I thought you said noodles! Well, excuse the fuck out of me!" He slammed himself in the head with the hammer, knocking himself cold, as always.

Al laughed along with the rest of the country as the credits rolled.

That was all he needed, he was in high spirits again.

-<>-

Hirohito looked at the human. He was doing things with the hard clear sticks again. He was always doing that. They were in a different place than before. It smelled less, and the light was warmer. There weren't any cockroaches to eat.

Hirohito liked the other place better. They always had a lot of things to eat. Interesting things. Now there was just the clear sticks and flat clear bowls, like the one just outside his cage.

He got into the wheel and ran for a while. It squeaked. His ear itched.

Hirohito stopped and sneezed. He scratched his ear. Some little bits of his fur floated down into the flat clear bowl. He ran some more.

The human picked up the flat clear bowl. He put the clear stick in it.

Hirohito was thirsty. He got a drink of water.

Oh Yeah?

It was one of those days in Washington, when the air seems to hang like a smothering blanket over your face and your lungs labor with the thick soup you must breathe. It was July.

Nathan Swarthmore sat outside the oval office, sticking to himself. He was a youngish looking man with just a light dusting of gray in his dread locked black hair. He was the vice president of the United States—an office that at one time had some meaning—now it was only assassination insurance.

For the past fifty years the people who run for president chose their running mates on the basis of having them be inappropriate to hold their office, in case they were taken out. In this Swindel was no exception. He chose someone just this side of a political liability. Nathan Swarthmore, the Surf Nazi mayor of San Diego.

Swarthmore was an intelligent, if deeply agendized man, and a vastly incompetent administrator. He had plunged his city into debt like a red-hot sword into butter, so the citizens could have a generous 'wave allowance'.

The wave allowance made it possible for everyone in town to surf, four days a weak. Young people flocked there by the thousands making it the youngest and least working city in the country. He had a single in the charts for over a year, too.

His attempt at water sports based, slack-assed National Socialism had teetered along sucking up federal money and insurance policies like a black hole for nearly fourteen months before the lynch-mobs could no longer be kept at bay. He was forced to take up residence in a different house each night to avoid being cornered and torn to shreds by the good, hard working, people of San Diego.

Swindel threw him a lifeline and he took it without too much thought.

His youth bloc vote clenched Swindel's victory in the '48 elections, and as a reward, Swarthmore had spent a good portion of the last two years roaming the globe as a sort of 'roving goodwill ambassador' to countries with good waves and white sand beaches. On his own, he had also been developing political strategies and sending back assessments from around the globe.

The president was surprised by his lucidness at first. He didn't know how to take the idea of having a vice president that was actually good for something. Was this a threat? Did he need to *do* something about him?

After a while the idea grew on him and he finally come to like Swarthmore's candor and insight, in spite of their occasional head butting. After all he was a fascist, he couldn't be expected to easily compromise.

He got up and began pacing slowly in front of the door, wishing that Dwayne would get around to him. He had been sitting there for almost a half hour. There was a noise and he looked up. Swindel was sticking his head out the door.

"Hey, dude, come on in," he said.

Nathan smiled and strode over to Swindel. They shook hands a little awkwardly.

"Come in, come in," said Swindel holding the door and gesturing into the office.

"Thanks."

Swarthmore stepped in and took a seat.

"Coffee?"

Swindel spoke to the intercom. "Two coffees, black, one sugar."

He sat down behind his desk and folded his hand comfortably in his lap.

"So, Nate, how's every little thing out in, where the hell were you last?"

"Chile, man, it was bitchen."

"Good surf?"

"Totally, like fifteen footers, man, and they took about sixty seconds to break.

"Most excellent! Cool dope too!"

Swarthmore tossed a small packet across the table at him.

"Stuff that up your amygdala and see if you don't strip a few bolts!"

Dwayne smiled, pocketing it.

"And, uh, the regime? What did you think of that?"

Swarthmore looked a little lost for a moment, trying to remember if he had paid any attention to that. Then it came to him, something that he had thought of while he was sitting on his board.

He had been waiting for the next set of swells and as his board dipped down into a trough he felt this 'thing', wash over his mind. It had been quite striking. How to put it?

"Yeah, man, the regime... Like I was sitting on my board and I like had this, I don't know—feeling I guess. It was like when I went down below the crest of the wave it was just like what's happening down there, politically. You think that you can see what's coming next and then it rises up on you and you get lost in this wall of flowing chaos. If you freak out, man, you're shark food but if you wait it out, then you'll ride up on top of it. It was like a metaphor for the situation."

"I see," said Swindel not really getting it.

"Yeah, so it goes like this, if we react to the situation down in South America, which is, at the moment a humongous wall of chaos looming up on us, with the usual fight or flight mechanism that's everybody's default setting then we are going down hard and fast. Like, total washing machine for sure. I don't have to spell out what the Glowing Barbeque has in mind, if they get the chance.[51] There's a lot of peasant meat down there.

"What we need to do right now is just sit tight and wait them out for a while. If we can keep balanced and stay on top of the Domingues administration, they will ride up over the top of this wave of emotion and we will see farther and find broader alternatives once the crisis down below, has passed."

Swindel smiled with appreciation at his seemingly muddled clarity.

"You spin a mean metaphor."

"You should catch me when I'm stoned."

Swindel laughed. There was a knock at the door and his secretary came in with the coffees.

"Thanks, Billy, you can set them on the desk."

She put the silver tray down and smiled, waiting.

"Thanks, that's all," said Swindel.

She nodded and left after winking at Swarthmore.

Nathan sipped his coffee. It was rich and bitter-smooth.

"How's Michael?"

"Oh he's fine. He's a bitch to live with sometimes, who isn't, but he's fine. You should come for dinner next week."

"Thanks I will. Wednesday?"

Swindel looked at his screen. "Calendar, this week."

He had something Wednesday.

"Thursday okay?"

"Thursday then. Eight?"

---

[51] The Radiant Path was the name of the present incarnation of the radical leftist movement in Chile, Bolivia and Ecuador/upper Amazonia, nick named the Glowing Barbeque because of their dogged allegiance to their Chinese masters, and the open secret of their possession of at least one tactical nuke.

"Eight."

Swindel tapped a few keys and then ignored the thing.

The two men looked at each other for a while in silence that started to stretch a bit. They both knew what was next.

Finally Swarthmore squinted at Swindel, as he did, to preface difficult questions.

"So, Dude, The Hold, what's up with that?"

"Oh, man, it's bogus. As you know, I tried to get support for Joshua against McDermott and his bunch of bloodthirsty throwbacks, and the whole fuckin' country freaked out on me, like frenzied chickens and held back their dough! Shit! It was incredible, almost like they saw it comin'! And like I expected maybe they could just shut up and take it as usual, like they always do, but no they have to go and grow a pair on me. Who knew?!"

"What, you just expected them to roll over and take it?"

Swindel considered for a moment. "Yeah, of course!"

There was silence and then after a second he went on.

"So the next thing is, I say 'okay, you want your dough, you can have it, all of it', who needs a Military anyway, if we aren't going to use the thing like a gold plated 2x4 then why have the ugly expensive bastard hanging around sucking up money anyway!? So I suggested a social program instead, nothing too radical, just, you know, three hots and a cot plus a few goodies like the library and a hospital for when you slam your finger in the door of your Cadillac.

"No big deal, nothing to get all puckered up about! Oh, and of course the reactionary element has to run amuck with it on commuter talk, pouring gasoline on their own goat! I mean I knew where the thing was parked, absolutely, but I didn't, expect them to go lighting it!

"Veets and that crowd are on a jag like a junky with a stolen credit card and as expected, Failsworthy and Co. are on the war path."

Nathan rolled his eyes.

"Expected."

"Yes. So anyway here I am with my shorts down around my ankles and the taxpayers are screaming for my head."

"I saw the ads."

Swindel shook his head.

"What the fuck am I gonna' do, man? There's no money left!! The fucking taxpayers have stashed it under their mattress and are sitting on it with guns. It's a snake pit and half of Washington is trying to push me in!"

There was silence while the VP sipped his coffee considering what to say.

"Good coffee, Dwayne."

"Thanks" said Swindel, smirking bitterly.

Sawrthmore made reasonable, shrugging his lips.

"Right, man, so you tried it on and they puckered. That was a nasty surprise, so let's get ugly about it, right? I mean look, you have some choices here, and dude you better make 'em or you're gonna' be swamped. So let's look at 'em and stop fiddle fuckin' around.

"First off, you could ask for the cooperation of our colleagues in Congress to come to a compromise solution that would not really please anyone and would probably smooth the voters enough to keep you from out right impeachment. That would leave you owing so many favors on the hill that you could pretty much write off the rest of this administration and as for next term, fuck, forget it man, you're foam. Also, I can't recommend it on general principles, not being that kind of gutless putz myself. I mean come on, man, it's my way or the highway, or what are we doin' here in the first place.

"Secondly, you could try to get enough dirt on everyone else involved to force it on them behind closed doors and miraculously the whole problem will dry up and blow away. I expect you have already taken some sort of action on that count. After all this is Dwayne Swindel we're talking about here. The Fumbling Bunch of Idiots come up with much?"

The president opened a drawer and pulled out a folder as thick as his fore arm. He held it up.

"This covers all the majors. I like to do things the old fashioned way," he said explaining the hard copy.

"The only problem is I can't exactly black mail the entire country, and this isn't driven from a central point. After all the hoopla, it's a genuine grass roots movement, propelled by a burning hatred of government in general.

"Still, I have some pressure here."

He dropped the folder back into the drawer.

Nathan smiled. "My point I was coming to. We may need to do that, but maybe not right away.

"Thirdly you could try doing a counter campaign. That will cost a lot and be pretty risky. Also it's still asking permission, and that's not what this is supposed to be about. Is it?"

"No."

"So that brings us to your fourth option, which is bold and devious, and could back fire and kill you politically in about a weekend."

"That is?"

"That is, you could cut Kabingga loose and let McDermott have at him letting everybody know you rolled over for the American people. All they can do then is say 'good boy' and release the Hold."

Swindel looked at Swarthmore in mild disbelief.

"Excuse me? I thought I was talking to the Surf Nazi ex-mayor of San Diego. Who the fuck are you, man?

"What am I supposed to do here? Fold up shop and go home, is that it? Admit defeat?! What have we been saying to each other for the past three years?"

"No, no, no, hear me out, man."

"No! You hear me out, <u>man</u>!

"I did not lynch niggers in Richmond, on Television, and, ick, kiss babies and shake peoples' hands across the whole country, to get this office, just to throw it all away the first time there's a fight!

"Besides Joshua Kabingga's a friend of mine, not just a political acquaintance, we're buds, dude. I am not going to walk away from him like he was asking me for a quarter! That's —— treason.

"Also don't forget there's the little matter of Alpha 1. You remember space travel and all that. What am I going to do, strand a thousand people on Alpha Centauri II and send them a message 'Sorry, best of luck, love Dwayne'?

"It's important. We need the minerals in three years so we can start processing and meet the launch window for the colony ship!"

Swarthmore nodded. "Yeah, right, man, I know all that, so <u>listen</u>! Will ya?"

Swindel made an open gesture to him.

"I'm here!"

"Dude, Kabingga, your 'bud' there, has been sledge-hammering political opponents to death at the stake. He will do or say anything to keep a grip on whatever he has left there in Africa. He's an albatross, man.

"The American people and their Euro-trash allies think he's a scum-bag. Man, they hate his ass big time! And you go and want to send troops to help him out? Of course people are up in arms! Of course they want your head on a platter for supporting him!

"Tell me, Dwayne, do you really think that people, I mean the average Joe, is a morally bankrupt piece of shit like you and me? Do you think they realize that whatever it takes is whatever it takes and the personal tragedies of un-powerful people don't matter anymore than whether you had the fish or the chicken for dinner?

"They think the world is still a fair place, where, if you work hard you'll be cool. They don't want to fucking know that their guys are on their own side and there is nobody on theirs!

"Sure they want Alpha 1 and fusion reactors and all the rest of it. And Kabingga, or someone like him is the price of these luxuries, but, dude, people don't want to be reminded of it! They just want to cruise and think about the weekend.

"You have committed the ultimate sin and called the electorate on their shit, right out in front of God and everybody. Of course they hate you! You need to cut him loose and let McDermott have at him for a while. Let him sting him in the butt like a hornet, just to show that you are above his kind!"

Swindel looked hurt.

"He is my friend, I'm not gonna just drop him. That sucks, and you know it!"

"Dude, dude, absolutely! You won't let him go down! Look, what you need to do is make it *appear* that you have abandoned him. Right? But you don't.

"Look, he can have the whole family out of there in a about an hour, Pablo and all. He's timed it for Christ's sake and there is a plane standing by 24/7."

Swindel looked incredulous.

"Pablo's timed it?"

"No, he's a horse.

"The point is, you get Kabingga out along with the usual few thousand important people and let McDermott take over the place.

"He can't administrate it. He can't even mine the ore. All he can do is deny it to us, Europe and Japan. They need it more than we do right now. Japan's doing Floatkyo, a really light, strong, high-tech thing. They want the titanium—let them fight for it.

"They'll rumble with Islam and probably get a black eye. Especially Europe, they're bigger pussies than the Japanese.

"So Kabingga and Co. take a powder for a while. They go for a vacation in the Alps—they don't surf—and our allies get their tits in a ringer.

"Now we are required by NATO IV to bail them out,

171

Congress has nothing to say about it! The electorate has to take it too, because under the treaty, the Europeans have to pay the bill if they can't cut the mustard and we have to come bail their shit out. Right?

"If we can keep calm for about a year, I figure, then we can walk back into Snellville wearing white gloves for the inspection, with the resurrected Kabingga leading the delegation.

"It's beautiful man, we spend other people's children, not ours. Bobby and Suzy stay at the beach while Klaus and Tatsuro take a bullet that Nigel and Pierre gotta pay for! We can't lose!"

Dwayne sat silently considering this for a while.

"We can always lose."

Swarthmore looked at him evenly.

"You figure?"

Swindel blinked.

"How exactly, did you plan to resurrect Joshua after what will inevitably go down during the fall of Snellville? His people aren't going to just walk away because we tell them to jump. These guys are pit bulls, and they know what happens if they lose to McDermott. He's a fucking Tutsi for Christ's sake! They had a better chance at Shan Shang.

"What do you propose, Dude, a PR campaign? 'Joshua Kabingga, he's our man, if he can't do it no one can', and everybody's just going to forgive him? There will be carnage."

"What I propose, man," said Nathan clearing his throat. "What I propose is that we get the CIA to depose him before the fact, putting some 'expendable' in as the savior of Snellville. We let the schmuck do the dirty and take the hit for it, while Josh and the Misses are shopping in Geneva. He is the democratically elected, and then unjustly deposed leader. We can even get a come back movement going and have a few UN resolutions passed. It'll be great! Even he'll think it's legit. The company's been doing good work since they went freelance[52], sometimes even <u>they</u> believe their own bullshit these days!"

Swindel looked distant. He was thinking. He was elsewhere. Finally, after a while, he focused on Swarthmore.

"Or I can fight."

Swarthmore shrugged.

---

[52] Most people don't realize it but prior to 2033 the CIA was actually, technically, answerable to the Government of the United States by law. The Tiendale administration of course dispensed with such nonsense.

"Or you can fight"

The president nodded.

"Okay. Thanks, Dude. I'll take it under consideration," he said.

Nathan got up. He smiled and walked to the door, the interview was over.

"Sure, man, you do that."

-<>-

The entire Umbutu River system drained down from a metal rich chain of degenerative granite mountains called the East African Rift Massif. That was the problem. Or, it was the opportunity, depending on how you looked at it.

If you were a hippo, or a crocodile, or a reasoning, compassionate, human being then it was indeed a problem. Because it meant that it was 'worth' something to someone.

If, on the other hand, you were a greed-driven narrow-minded prick it was an opportunity. To make a little money you were going to have to placer mine the hills above the rivers and that meant that in a dozen or so years you were going to destroy forever the ecosystem of East Africa.

It was going to be tough work to make that money, but the people with an interest in the Umbutu River Project were willing to pay top dollar to do it. So, they hired Fung Chu Fat.

He set his transom and prepared to take his first measurement. His assistant stood across the small ravine holding the reflector. Fat waved to him, and he waved back. He looked through the eyepiece.

Mr. Fung was a mining engineer, originally from Beijing. He had just been discharged from the 7th Kowloon regiment after their defeat at Shan Shang. They were paying him 9000 Yuan an hour, ($62.58). Waiters in Sao Paulo were making more.

-<>-

A small black child in a dirty frock sat playing on the dirt floor of her hut someplace in the third world.

"Feed the world, or keep it free for democracy?

"Educate her, or give her father a job so she can eat?

"These are tough decisions, tough choices.

"They're the ones we make every day.

"We're the General Dynamics family of companies."

The little girl looked up at the camera and grinned beautifully.

"We're building a better world for all of us."

-<>-

173

Swindel squared his shoulders to the camera and assumed an intent, sincere look. The little red light went on.

"Americans hear me!"

He paused for effect and then continued.

"It has come to the attention of this administration, in a very clear way that you are dissatisfied with the set of choices that you have been presented with thus far. You have made it plain that not only do you not want to help the freedom fighters in East Africa with their brave struggle to keep Burundi and the enclave of Snellville the Lesser free for all men, but also that you chose to reject the notion that we have a social responsibility to our fellow countrymen. What you seem to be saying with this Tax Hold, is that you just want your money for yourselves."

The camera zoomed in till he filled the screen.

"Well, America, I have heard you, loud and clear. You just want your money. So okay, you have your money. You have made your point."

"Shut off that shit, will you? I can't stand listening of him again!"

No one responded so Nadia got up, huffing her exasperation and turned down the volume herself.

Stanislow shook his head.

"What's the big deal, he has important lies to tell us, so maybe we will hear something good for a change. Besides is your ante. You are in, you are out?"

Nadia scowled at the table thinking.

"Throw in me for five. Anybody want a beer?"

Mort and Stan both nodded and Sergei raised a finger. She went into the kitchen still exasperated.

That idiot Swindel was destroying the country to show he was boss. It was ridiculous, by the time he browbeat the American taxpayers into submission there would be only chaos to rule over.

She opened the fridge and grabbed the beers. There was gunplay outside. Someone had to blink pretty soon or she was getting on a plane for the West Coast. Out there all was still pretty normal. Not like here.

Nadia put the beer bottles down in a clump in the middle of the table amongst the pot and sat down on her backwards chair, facing the game. She picked up her cards and looked at them. Garbage. She smiled with her eyes very slightly and only for a second, then folded her cards and raised Mort ten.

He looked at her, but she was staring off into space sipping her beer.

He thought.

"Nah. You got shit, Molotov. What are you doin'?"

She didn't turn her head, but just looked at him askance through her slitty Slavic eyes.

"Poker."

Mort looked at her for a while more.

"In or out," She said.

Mort threw in a ten-dollar coin. "You got a pair of twos."

Sergei looked at Mort, who was straining to hear what Swindel was saying on TV.

"...theless it is not the viewpoint of this administration that that stance .....ceptable. We disagree. I cannot agree. When I ran for this office it was on t... ...atform that I would do what was ordinary and reasonable, remember."

He spread his hands.

"A regular guy, ...ember.

"Well that's what you got, a regular guy. I stand up! If you don't like what I say, if you disagree ... me, then I would like to hear what you have to say about it, b......n't stymie me! Let me do my job!

"You elected me to stand up to Congress and do the <u>right</u> thing, instead of the ...venient thing, or the party thing, or even th....opular thing! Well, this <u>is</u> unpopular! But it's right. It is something that is ...alled for in the normal course of events, just as..."

"Excuse me, Nadia," said Mort. "I'm sorry, but could you turn it up a little, I actually want to hear what the Swindler has to say about this."

She looked at him incredulous.

"Ass-bite?"

"I know, but please, indulge me will ya? He may be going to do something important."

Stan looked at him skeptically. "Like?"

Mort had to admit that they had a point, but still he was curious.

"Let's find out."

Nadia shrugged and turned the volume back up a bit. Now Swindel was plainly audible.

"There are practical and moral reasons why I have done what I have done. These were not rash decisions and they were taken only after thorough examination of the best data available."

Stan raised Nadia another five, looking at her like a lizard.

She stared back at him for a moment.

"What?" She asked.

"First of all there is the practical consideration, that this country needs access to the East African mineral deposits in order to pursue the colonization of the Alpha Centauri star system."

Stan lit a cigarette and regarded his sister through the tendril of rising smoke.

"Five dollars."

"This project is vital to our national interests and those minerals are crucial to the project. They must be secured in order to complete the building of the first colony ship by '26."

"Yes, I know five dollars."

"Five dollars. You have something, you have nothing." He shrugged. "So? Five dollars."

Nadia looked at him coldly for a long moment, then threw in a fiver and followed it with another ten. Stan raised an appreciative eyebrow, like 'okay, it's your funeral.' She smirked and turned to Mort.

"Is too rich for you?"

"Secondly, there is the question of whether this country has an obligation to help others when they are attacked by medieval yahoos like Mingetsu McDermott. I think we do, and so have many other presidents before me. When Adolph Hitler tried to take over Europe and destroy the Jews and Gypsies, the US didn't just sit by and let it happen.

"And when the Chinese Army decided to just walk westward eating everything, goat, rice and peasant alike in their path, we and our Russian allies went and spoiled their little dinner party.

"Where is that resolve now?"

Mort smiled inwardly. Now he was sure that she had nothing. He threw in his ten and winked at her. She smiled back falsely.

"You know," said Sergei, "he has a point. US is always getting involved in other people's problems before. So why not now? Why are American tax payers suddenly giving shit about policy for a change?"

Mort gestured with his beer bottle.

"That's an interesting question."

"Of course. I was not colonel in Russian Army for nothink." Sergei tapped his temple.

Stan blew a smoke ring. "No. It was for thirty seven dollars and fifteen cents a week as I recall."

176

Sergei threw in a ten. "Also food."

"Potatoes," they all said as one.

"Anyway," continued Mort, "this situation isn't so different, just this time the populist opinion is winning out.

"People always want to stay out of it. But the politicians, who don't have to go fight, want to get involved.

"They have the advantage of the long view. Like from a heavily armed bunker in Colorado, while the kids from Kansas or Belarus get their balls blown off first hand.

"He's talking shit too. In both those wars the US Government was motivated by self-interest not altruism."

Stan threw in a last ten. "Call."

"...is now in the hands of the American people. You have the power, but it is up to you to use it. I entreat you, use it wisely and not for a short-term gain. That way lies ruin. Try to look at the big picture. Think about what will be going on in the world five, ten and twenty years from now. Don't be over optimistic either. Ask yourselves if you really think that it's all just going to work itself out for the best.

"I have tried, now it's up to you."

Mort spoke to the Television. "We're doin' it man, just step out of the way!"

Nadia pointed at Swindel.

"This man is idiot! And he thinks that I am too!"

Stan tapped her cards on the table.

"Earth to Nadia, I have call you."

His sister scowled at him, smirked and tossed her cards into the pot admitting defeat.

"Fuck off little brother, take my money. You would take the bread from your own nephews' mouths!"

He looked at her matter-of-factly. "You have no children."

"Not yet!"

Sergei's eyes opened wider. "You are pregnant?! I will kill that fucking mail man!"

Mort laughed. "Check please!"

"No, he's Puerto Rican Jew," she assured him, smiling.

"Seriously?" asked Sergei seriously.

"Da."

A twinkle crept into his eye. "You are pregnant?"

She took his hand tenderly and looked at him, her face full of hope and promise.

"No, he is 'Rican Jew."

Her brother mimed playing a fiddle as everyone but Sergei

laughed.

Sergei shoved the pile at his brother-in-law.

"Deal."

Everybody else laughed some more.

"My critics," said the president, "have been quite outspoken in their condemnation of my programs, especially in Congress.

"They have said Alpha 1 is and I quote, 'a vast pork barrel project intended to rob the taxpayers and throw the money away on a frivolous adventure'. They, and their lackeys in the media, have stood around criticizing me while I have gotten on with the complex business of government.

"They have condemned our efforts to support the cause of freedom in Africa without taking sufficient time to understand the intricacies of the situation. They have said that 'the problem is simple'. I can assure you, that is not the case. The world is about as simple as protein synthesis."

Stan finished shuffling and passed the deck to Sergei to cut. He tapped the deck and drank his beer brooding.

"You know," he said. "The world is not simple place, but I think that the problem before our valiant leader is not so complex as he makes out. Why he has to make fine distinction like is microsurgery?

"His critics are right, he is asshole."

Stan started dealing.

"Okay, five card draw. Ante up, if you think you can afford to risk your unborn children's future."

He laid down the cards.

"Maybe, dear brother-in-law," said Stan, "he has information that you don't."

Sergei looked at him a bit blankly.

"That you don't know," explained Mort.

He turned back to Stan.

"Da da da. He is president of United States, so maybe he has a spy or something. Still, direct action will win the day."

Stan gave himself the last card.

"Yes, well, you were not colonel for nuthink."

Stan's mocking of his accent was not lost on him.

"No Private Sterabinski, not for nuthink."

"I'm in for twenty," said Mort, tossing a couple of coins into the pot.

"...course those members of Congress that have been the most vocal are beyond criticism themselves. Why, Senator Failsworthy, my esteemed colleague, would never in his wildest dreams think of using his position in Government to increase his own personal wealth. I'm sure there must some mistake with this tax statement and these records that I have right here."

He held up a thick sheaf of dog-eared papers and leafed through them as he spoke.

"Oh, heavens to Betsy, I know that this 12 million dollar campaign contribution from Interglobal Cyanamid must have been put on this tax return someplace! I wonder who could have erased it?!

"And this one from Boeing for 18 million, it doesn't seem to be listed either! I wonder why?"

He stopped, pulled out a small piece of paper and held it up.

"Oh boy, this is a really cool one! It's a receipt that Senator Tiendale put through his petty cash fund last year for 197,000 dollars and 69 cents, for miscellaneous erotic consultations! Wow Senator your consultant must be really sore!"

Sergei had a straight going. He matched Nadia and took a card, laughing at Swindel's bitter joke.

"He's right," said Mort. "He's not alone in Washington. There's plenty of dirt to go around."

Nadia was looking intently now at the screen.

"Is he doing what I think he is doing, committing act of total war on legislature?"

They all turned to look at Swindel.

"...is little gem here is a picture of the private island in the South Pacific where they and several others, I'll read you the list in a moment, did some of that consulting. I'll bet you didn't know that the US Congress had its own island. Did you? You can't go there, but you paid for it, every last dollar of it. That was part of the Park Land Acquisition Act..."

They all nodded their heads.

"Yes," said Mort. "Absolutely. He can't possibly survive this. Ladies and gentlemen, we are witnessing the president of the United States of America go down in flames."

There was a long burst of gunfire down in the street, and then a loud BANG. It sounded close. Sergei got up and stepped to the window. He had a gimbaled mirror hung outside on a post. He swiveled it around so he could see down into the street. There was someone crouching behind some garbage cans trying to hide.

"It is abuses like this by the Senate and House members that have run up the staggering tax bills in this country. And it's these special privileges they seek to protect in their attacks of my

179

policies. They are the problem. They are the pigs at the trough!

"I have worked to give you good, responsible government. You will never get a straighter deal than that as long as you live. While they are trying to assassinate my character, destroy my administration and steal your money, I am trying to get on with running the country. But there is a limit, and we have passed it. I need your help.

"Only the American people can save this country now. It is in your hands. You must release the Hold immediately. It is vital to the security of the United States, that we pay our bills. We must have the tax dollars that you legally owe.

"As your president I order you to release the Hold. If you do not comply immediately measures will have to be taken."

The three at the table laughed.

Sergei came back into the room and sat down.

"It was nothink much," he said.

He looked at his card. It was the six he was looking for. He raised Stan ten.

"What was funny that I missed?"

Stan lit another cigarette.

"It was nothing much, now he has <u>ordered</u> us to release the Hold."

Sergei opened another beer and had some Snakos.

"Mr. President?"

"Excuse me, Mr. President?"

Dwayne turned away from the reporters. There was another one there, it was Dave Emery form TBS. He stuck a microphone in his face.

"Mr. President, your critics are saying that you have over stepped your Presidential authority, and they are starting to call for your resignation. They also point to a conflict of interest in your holding certain stocks in your portfolio. How do you respond?"

Dwayne smiled genuinely.

"I'm glad you asked me that question, Dave.

"We in the administration, and I mean the whole team, and not just myself, are working everyday to boost public confidence in our governmental institutions, as well as our industrial output to well above our third quarter expectations. And by the way, Dave, that's a nice tie."

-<>-

Virally Delivered Genetic Tagging & Beautification System
Inventor: Tokugowa Industries
US Patent # 835,980,052

-<>-

He was a tall thin man with a prominent forehead and jet-black hair that he kept cropped short to match his neatly trimmed beard. There was a certain dignity about the way he carried himself, his stance and the way his shoulders seemed to move smoothly along their own line when he walked. He was upper class, even in his class, and let you know it without having to address you. He was dangerous.

Yasad Al Hazier started out life as the son of a wealthy Iranian merchant-cleric, Farzad Al Hazier. A man of considerable position, he was going to have a son to succeed him as the monopoly holder for cigarette import to Iran, no matter how many daughters he had to smother.

As a boy Yasad grew up in the family compound, in the outskirts of Teheran, where the sun was warm in the courtyard and he never had want of anything.

There were fig trees there that hung heavy with delicious fruit in the summer and fragrant jasmine that climbed the walls. Birds would come to eat the fruit that fell to the ground and he would play games with them. He would try to catch them with a little net his mother made for him. He almost always missed the fast little animals as they flitted away to perch in the branches above and scold him with their tiny voices. One day though, he was luckier, and he caught one of the fleeting jewels in his net.

It struggled to free its tiny wings from the encumbering threads, but it was stuck fast. He looked at it there as it fought to escape and worked out how to untangle it. This he did very carefully, taking great pains not to hurt it. At last he had the bird free of the net and he cupped it gently in his hands, not letting it go, but making sure that it had enough room to breath. He could feel its little heart pounding in its chest like a tiny jackhammer. He looked into the bird's eye. It looked back at him coldly. Yasad opened his hands as he raised them over his head, and the bird flew away. He watched it climb into the blue dome of the sky, and disappear over the garden wall. He looked at his hand. There was a little piece of pooh in it.

He went to a private school along with a few other wealthy children from his neighborhood. They were children much like himself, coddled and privileged. Life was great.

Once when he was about twelve the family housekeeper took him to the souk with her to buy cloth for making drapes. The souk was an adventure that would change his life. It was an amazing place full of color and noise and the strong smells of spice and petrol and dung. By the time they left, his neck was sore from snapping his head around to look at wonders and his face ached from smiling.

After that all he wanted to do was go back there, and he ever connived to find excuses to go. He eventually found that he could skip school in his teens and go there on the flimsiest excuses, and no one seemed to mind. He was doing well academically, even in difficult subjects like English and math, so what was the harm. He met interesting people there, dealers, prostitutes, ideologues and thieves. They liked him—he always had pocket money and wanted to have fun. Life was grand, and it could have just gone on like that forever as far as he was concerned, but that was not to be.

This cozy deal all came unraveled early one morning when there was a knock at the door. The houseboy opened it to find the political police standing there with a writ demanding to see Farzad and to search the premises, for 'security' reasons. He let them in, and they proceeded to tear the house apart.

Eventually they found a stash of liquor, including a case of

Glenmorangie single malt scotch, and another of Moët et Chandon champagne. Farzad had apparently either crossed somebody above him, or simply was in a position that someone else wanted, Yasad was never sure which, so Farzad had to go. And go he did, off to a labor camp in the Elburz Mountains, where he worked breaking stones out of a rock face for the last few months of his life[53]. He died of pneumonia.

The police watched Yasad after that and refused him admission to university. They hounded him wherever he went as the son of a traitor and a heretic, two things his father had never been. Even at the souk, he was shunned, because of his constant tail by the police.

Eventually he joined the Army and the curse of his father that had dogged him for over five years seemed to disappear. He went for every opportunity to show himself to be a good Iranian soldier. He attended commando school and jump-school and attended extensive study courses in the intricacies of the Koran and its effect on policy.

When he was a sergeant he signed up to fly helicopters. They turned him down, but he was allowed to drive tanks and eventually to command them. One day, he was a twenty-eight year old Lieutenant at the time, the commandant called him into his office on the far side of the blazing parade ground for an interview.

He walked across the baking plain in stiff military fashion and when he got to the office he took time to dust off his boots before he entered and then stood around for a few minutes with his arms held out from his body to let the sweat evaporate under his armpits. The Army had made him a fastidious man. The Army liked that in a man, and he wanted to be liked by the Army.

He knocked and entered, saluting crisply to his superior. The commandant was there along with several other people that he didn't know. They were plain-looking men in ordinary clothes. Except, he noticed, they all had on new white running shoes.

"Sit down, Lieutenant Al Hazier, please."

The commandant motioned to a chair across the room from the others. Yasad sat down stiffly.

---

[53] Farzad never new it, and it probably would have meant nothing to him had he known, but the rock face he was excavating was eventually to become the hiding place of the top secret Quak Al Hooqume nuclear complex, a place that would eventually kill his son Yasad, along with several others.

"Lieutenant Al Hazier," said the commandant, "these men are from the ministry of external security, they have come here today to talk to you about a matter of great importance, I suggest that you listen with your fullest attention."

"Yes, Sir."

There were three of them and the one on the left spoke first.

"Tell us, Lieutenant, your father was a merchant, was he not?"

"Yes, Sir, and a cleric, an assistant Mullah."

"Ah, I see, an assistant Mullah, very interesting. And when you were growing up did you meet any of his business associates, foreign business associates for example?"

"Yes, Sir," said Yasad, wondering what all this was about. "Often my father would bring them home and my mother would cook them a beautiful meal, and after we would all eat together they would retire into my father's office to discus business, sometimes late into the night."

"I see, that's very interesting, Lieutenant. And, did these people speak Farsi or perhaps Arabic?"

"Well, Sir, as I recall some may have spoken in Farsi but most people spoke about business in English."

"Ah, I see, and did you understand their English that they spoke in your family home?"

"Yes." He paused wearily. "My father taught me the tongue of the great Satan from an early age, he had intended that I follow him into business, it is the language of world trade as you know."

"Yes, yes, quite," said the man on the left. "And tell me, Lieutenant Al Hazier, do you ever speak English now? For instance to your friends and associates."

Yasad thought about that for a moment before he spoke. This was sounding dangerous.

"No," he said at last. "I haven't spoken English in a few years as far as I can remember. I don't have any foreign friends. But I do read it occasionally, some of the manuals for our older equipment are written in it."

The three men all looked at each other for a moment, then the man in the middle spoke to him in flawless Midwestern English.

"So," he said. "You decided not to follow your Dad into the family business. How come?"

"Well," said Yasad in less perfect accent. "Father was thought to be a heretic by the holy authorities and so he lost his monopoly. There was nothing left to follow. I chose instead to

184

serve my country."

"Yeah, I see. And what about you? Do you think he was a heretic?"

Yasad shrugged. "Sir, he was my father. I recognize the divine authority of the Ayatollah and his sacred mission, but I can't believe that my father was an infidel. He never drank liquor himself, of that I am sure, though he may have had it in the house to offer to foreign guests, he was a very gracious man, and quite successful.

"The holy Koran says that a good Muslim doesn't drink, it does not say that he is a bad host."

"Are you a good Muslim then, Lieutenant?"

"I try, Sir. I study the Koran in my spare time, though I was refused a place at university for that purpose. I am prepared to die in the holy jihad, if that's what you're asking."

Now the third man spoke, also in English.

"Tell me, Lieutenant, how would you like to go to the Mullahs school and serve your country too?"

Yasad looked at them for a moment. He gauged them to be sincere.

"I would welcome the opportunity, Sir."

The third man nodded. "All right, thank you for your frankness, Lieutenant," he said in Farsi. "You may go."

A month passed and he hadn't thought anymore about the odd interview, he was busy trying to improve his crew's kill ratio against the US/ NATO Schwarzkopf II on the simulator range out in Qum. There was a knock on the door of the simulator and a captain stuck his head in.

"Lieutenant Al Hazier?" He said.

Yasad took off his headphones. "Here."

"You've been relieved, Lieutenant," he said, handing him a thick envelope. "I'm Bozoglean, your replacement."

Yasad looked at the envelope and then back at Bozoglean.

"We are in the middle of training!"

"Sorry," said Bozoglian. "Orders."

Yasad handed him his headphones.

"You are surrounded at a thousand meters. Your driver is Rafsanjani, and the gunner's name is Farouque. He leads a little bit too much, good luck, Captain."

He hit the intercom switch.

"This is Al Hazier, I've been relieved. Good luck, it's been fun."

He stepped out the door past Bozoglean, into the hallway

185

and opened the envelope. It said to report to the Defense Ideological College at Isfahan immediately. He would never drive a tank again.

At the DIC he underwent three years of intensive mixed training in Advanced Covert Operations, Islam Abroad and Ideological Purity, along with refresher English and US Pop Culture. When he graduated he was a captain in the Iranian Secret Service and a cleric/covert operative. His assignment, Los Angeles, California.

Yasad moved first to Switzerland, where he established a web site called The Mosque, along with several bogus mail order businesses selling Islamic religious paraphernalia and disseminating anti-Iranian literature. He waited a year and then made a phone call from a pay phone outside Montreux, to the Iranian embassy in Madrid, and said this word 'Niloufar', which means water lily.

Three weeks later there was a 'bungled attempt' on his life. His car blew up in the underground parking lot at the Balexert shopping mall in Geneva. He was having a crepe at the time, up stairs in Migros.

He heightened his rhetoric on the Internet and two weeks later, while he was paragliding in Villars, his house was bombed, killing Mr. Schiengarten, his neighbor.

He now called for an all out jihad against the "Satanic Charlatan in Iran", the Ayatollah Fotouhi, his boss. The internet was alive with chatter about this—they even noticed in Larchmont Virginia, at the Defense Intelligence Center, just as they should.

This really pissed off his hated enemies in the Near East and this time they sent the real heavies. Two Syrians and an Egyptian with orders to fuck his shit up bad.

They cornered him in an alleyway leading onto Place Molard in Geneva and broke his legs with baseball bats and shot him through the shoulders with a very loud but not very powerful handgun in front of dozens of horrified witnesses. This part hurt a lot. They stuffed an Iranian flag in his mouth and put the now empty gun to his head. The crowd's hearts raced like mice, they were going to do him right there in front of the tourists! In Geneva!!

The Egyptian pulled the trigger, but of course nothing happened. He pulled it again, and again the gun misfired. He swore loudly in Farsi. "You mother-fucking traitor! The Ayatollah says hello!"

He was about to beat him to death with the pistol, when a siren was heard far away, right on time and the three assailants fled in a stolen Mercedes, with French plates.

His asylum application to the US was accepted without question, and he moved to Venice Beach, California, where he lived for over ten years, keeping pretty much to himself.

Yasad liked it down at the beach, even if it was a hot bed of iniquity. His neighbors were mostly peaceful people, a little unstable to be sure, but that was to be expected in such a degenerate society. They were, of course, doomed to burn in hell for eternity as all infidels are, but they didn't seem to mind, and he was not going to bring up the subject.

The weekends were a bit of a bore, sometimes. The beach was very popular in the summer with loud, inconsiderate, young people from the inner city, especially on Saturdays. They would parade around like strange violent peacocks, throwing garbage in his yard, and trying to pickup on each other. He hated the weekends with their people, but the rest of the week was fine and in the winter he could walk on the beach any day he liked and see almost no one.

He loved it then, in the winter, just after the sun came up, when the sea was a steel gray sheet stretching clear to the horizon, and the sand pipers scurried before the gentle waves. He would walk along the tide line with his pants rolled up looking at what the sea had left.

He had a mail order business much like the one in Geneva, but this one was pro-Iranian. He disseminated Islamic literature, and established a small mosque in an old hardware store. There he gave lectures and led prayers, and celebrated Ramadan and other Islamic high holy days. He sold tee shirts and coffee mugs and base ball caps imprinted with the Iranian flag, or likenesses of the Ayatollah, and other Islamica, like pictures of the Blue Mosque in Istanbul. They kept him in reasonable style, nothing too showy, but a nice little bungalow in the canals.

He passed information on social trends and the comings and goings of important people back to his Government by way of encrypted messages over the Internet and sent out secret orders to their covert Hezbollah operatives throughout the US by way of his column The Voice of Allah, that he ran every week in, Islam Black Africa's, or as he knew him, Dave Smith's paper the Voice of Black Islam.

Usually the message was the same one, roughly speaking, to stay put and bide our time. Allah is patient. We will win in the fullness of time. He would send this out each week tangled up in the Arabic text of his column, along with a reference to the Koran giving the key for next week's message.

He had been doing this a long time. He knew it served God to wait but there were times he just wanted to take a sniper rifle, pop the president and leave it at that. Allah was patient—he was not always. He had begun to feel a bit like a forgotten man.

A few weeks ago, though, everything changed. The world changed. It just didn't know it yet. It would find out soon enough.

A letter had come in the mail advertising aluminum steak knives. This is how his orders came, as advertisements for aluminum steak knives.

He opened up the amazing offer and looked at it. It was the usual sort of thing you would expect to find in such a mailer, except there was a typo. The typo was a period in place of a comma. He tore the top and bottom panels off, leaving only the center section. He slid this into the media slot on his phone. He punched in a code and a voice spoke from the screen.

"Authenticate Yasad Al Hazier, mother's maiden name Ramazani. Message follows. Commence Harissa. Repeat, commence Harissa. This is not a drill."

There was a little trail of smoke from the slot as the laser burned the dot.

'!' thought Yasad.

He phoned Dave Smith immediately.

-<>-

"I'm Hillman Fienbladt. What's in that snack you're eating? We'll have the whole story, pictures and all the vital details on prime news time at eleven."

-<>-

Bill looked into the camera practicing his sour expression. He was about to do an ad for something. He wasn't sure what exactly, some kind of financial product he thought. He tried to flex his sincerity muscles.

There was a twinge there, an uncertainty spasm. He suddenly hated himself for a fleeting second. What the fuck was he doing!? He didn't even know what he was endorsing! This was ludicrous!

The director looked up from his notes.

"You about ready there, Bill?"

Bill looked at him. He was a young guy wearing a baseball cap. Bill squinted a little.

"What's my motivation here?" he asked.

The director looked at him for a long time. He blinked once.
"Fifty thousand bucks."
Bill nodded. "Okay, I'm ready."
He got it in one take.

-<>-

Yasad moved through the concourse like a shark amongst sheep. He made his own line through the crowd as though they were a diffuse, irrelevant fog. He was looking for one man, Dave Smith, and none of them were him. He had on a green jacket with a gardenia in the lapel, just as he had said he would and he had a briefcase with him. Other than that he had no luggage. As he walked, he scanned the vast room for trouble. There was nothing to speak of, other than the few security guards at the doors. 'Americans are like little kids' he thought.

Suddenly out of the crowd stepped a skinny black man with Afro-Sheened hair sticking out from under one of Yasad's own Islamic baseball caps in a tweed jacket. He had a paunch under his UCLA sweatshirt that only served to accentuate his thin frame. He stuck out his hand.

"Mr. Al Hazier?"

Yasad shook his hand as the American expected. "Mr. Dave Smith. How do you do?"

"As well as can be expected, considering our struggle," he said in a pleasant but serious way. "How was your flight?"

"Not bad, lots of little kids with nothing to do, but other than that it was pretty quiet. I did some reading."

"Good, very good."

Dave released his hand and gestured toward the exit.

"Come this way please, I have a car waiting. Do you like sushi?"

They went through town by minor streets and came through the park to a little place that Dave knew tucked away in a residential neighborhood. All the way there they talked in pleasant trivialities feeling each other out on various ideological and social points. Until now they had only done business together, though the banter and asides of that business had let them both know that they were of like mind. This was their first opportunity to actually get to know each other. They both took it slowly at first, trying to read the other one's eyes in their answers.

Dave picked the restaurant for its seclusion and privacy. It was worth the little bit extra it cost to dine there for those qualities. They sat in a small room, by themselves, where they could speak freely.

"So," said Dave. "What exactly brings you to New York City all the way from the West Coast?"

Yasad smiled. "Well, it's business actually, though it is also a pleasure to do it."

"I see."

"Yes, by the way, Mr. Smith" ventured Yasad. "You seem to be a man of vision. Tell me please, where would you see the United States in say the year 2100 say, in an ideal world, let's say?"

Dave thought about this for a second before he answered.

"Well, in an ideal world, I think I would see the US as part of a greater world wide country dominated by people of color, who are after all the majority of the human race, as well as being the first people. Don't get me wrong. I think that this country could be a great place if it were ruled justly, instead of under the totalitarian regimes of the white Caucasian man.

"And maybe this dream can come true sooner than I would have thought possible. After all that is what the Hold is all about isn't it? Calling an end to the status quo? Saying enough is enough?! That's what it's all about, Sir. The people have at long last said no!"

"Yes, yes I agree," said Yasad. "I think that the American people have at last realized that all their institutions, their Churches, their Government, the stratification of their society, even their own family values are corrupt at their heart. It is time that they were offered a real alternative to all of these. It is my hope that they will turn to Islam for guidance.

"It is interesting what you say about the US taking something other than a dominant roll in the world theater. Most Americans are not comfortable with the idea of their country being something other than the dominant power it has been these last hundred and fifty years or so."

Dave shrugged.

"Well I am, after all, a Black Muslim. I have no trouble with the idea of submission, as long as it is to the justice and wisdom of Allah.

"What this country needs is to turn over a new leaf. And when it does, I will be there to help guide it. That is my duty both as a Black Muslim and as an American. If our role in the coming world will be one that is less arrogant and more just, how could that be bad?

"The miso is very good here, and the sashimi is out of this world. I recommend them both.

"Tell me please, Yasad, where do you see Islam in fifty years?

I mean is your vision one of dominance by Islam over the Western paradigm?"

Yasad poured himself some green tea and considered what to say next. He took a little bit bigger chance now. He could feel his pulse in his neck as he spoke.

"I do not see Islam as dominant over the Western model, so much as I see it replacing it all together. The system is wholly bankrupt, and it is the accepted opinion that Islam is the way forward.

"I see a world in which Muslims lead and Christians, such as there still are, follow the wise teachings of their Islamic mentors. I have to say though, I don't see a world that has properly prepared itself for the peaceful acceptance of Islam that we would all like to see. It is most unfortunate that some blood will probably have to be shed for the great change to occur, but if it must, it is His will."

"Yes," said Dave. "I agree with you there, wholeheartedly. The world is not yet ready for the change though the time is certainly well past. People are afraid of change, blindly afraid. They see only bad things in it so they resist the inevitable course of history. That is why blood must be shed, not because of the change, because of the resistance to it.

"There will come a day when the Black African man will rise up and take back from the white devils what they have stolen from him. I pray for that day to come soon. The longer the wait the worse the conflict will be. We were the first people and we will be the last, of this I am sure. We will be big about it when we are returned to our rightful place, but there are many injustices that must be redressed along the way."

A waitress knocked and opened the door.

"Hello, I'm Miki, can I take your order?"

They both had the miso soup for a starter and the sushi selection. Dave ordered a yakitori for them to split. She left them alone again.

Yasad tried to figure out his chopsticks as he continued.

"The world is a complex and difficult place. It is a place that has been ready for a long time for the great change, but as you say, it is people's resistance that causes the majority of the problems. Many of us have been working on our preparations for a long time now and though there have been the occasional upstart society that shines for a short time like a young light, they fade, and the old peoples prevail. The United States is such a young country, and the old peoples who were here before it will be here when it is gone. The human race is at long last ready, now we must remove the only obstacle that remains."

"Yes," said Dave. "The West. Hopefully our society will either step aside for the human race's good, or else, as seems eminent, perhaps it will fold up under its own weight and things may then proceed.

"There are those among us, myself and others that I know, that have been working toward that goal for a long time. We wake up thinking about it and it is the last thing that we know before we doze off at night. The ground has been prepared and now when the time is right we will be ready to pull out the last wedge that supports the vast tower of hateful racist babble that lords itself over us."

Miki brought their soup and some shredded daikon as a freebie.

"Sushi coming up next," she said.

Yasad looked around for the spoon that wasn't supposed to be there, and then followed Dave's lead in drinking directly from the bowl.

"Ah," he said. "This is good. Rich and subtle."

"Yes, and very good for you too. The tofu, the little cubes have almost no fat and are high in protein. You can put soya in it if you like."

Yasad put a few tentative drops of soy sauce into his bowl.

"You know, my friend, you may not have to wait much longer for your dream to come true. There may be a way for the great change to come sooner than any of us could have ever expected."

"I hope so. I assume that you are referring to the Hold. It may have a good affect on this country. Hell it could even bring down the present Government if it stays much longer! Wouldn't that be something to see! The president ousted and all his wasteful programs shelved so that the moneys could be redistributed to the deserving under-classes. I can't wait!"

"Yes, well you may not have to, in fact there may well be a way that events could be rushed along at an even faster pace than by this Hold alone. What I am talking about is direct action—action that would be decisive and final—action that would cause a fundamental change. Action to accomplish in a few short years what would otherwise take many lifetimes!

"What would you say to that, my friend?"

Dave looked at him very seriously across his soup bowl. He set it down and a twinkle of understanding glinted in his eye.

192

"I would say, that would be a truly great day for the world, Sir. If such direct action is to take place, you can count on me and my associates, to be there, ready to lend whatever help we can. Whatever help.

"I know a lot of like-minded people too. Actually, I am quite familiar with direct action."

"Oh?"

"Yes, in the Race War I was involved to some degree with the Black Cells."

"I see," said Yasad. "Very interesting. What exactly did you do?"

Dave looked around conspiratorially.

"I killed people," he whispered, his heart racing a bit.

Yasad smiled.

"Don't worry, my friend. Your secret is safe with me."

There was a knock at the door and Miki brought their sushi in.

"Everything okay here?" she asked.

The two men looked at her and then at each other.

"Yes, everything's fine," said Dave.

"Good."

"And we have a Yakitori coming," said Yasad.

"Right," she said clearing the bowls as she exited.

Yasad looked at his plate. Dave poured a little soy sauce onto both their plates and mixed some wasabi paste into his.

"Horse radish, very hot. You dip your fish in it."

Yasad mixed a bit in his as well. He picked up a piece of tuna copying Dave, dipped it and put it in his mouth. The coldness of it shocked him at first but it was quickly replaced by a rich luscious complexity of flavors. It was strange and wonderful.

"Excellent."

"I told you. I love this place."

"You know," said Yasad, "many people here did what they had to in the war, and great things very nearly happened then. If only there had been allies from outside to help, you might have won the day in spite of the odds.

"Next time it won't be the same. Next time there will be help there when you need it. I feel certain. In fact I can see the day approaching when Islam and Black Islam will join together in one unified world Government, free of the petty squabbles that so easily separate people in today's unfocused world. When that day comes, and I can assure you that it will be very soon, then all your hard work and waiting will pay off. It is His will. Then the

Holy Koran will be the whole of the law. It will be glorious."

Dave smiled broadly.

"Then the Black African man will play golf while his inferior white servants toil in the fields, and mines and factories. It <u>will</u> be glorious.

"It is inevitable!"

"Precisely," said Yasad. "I will call you next week with some details of how we may proceed."

"I look forward to it."

They shook hands across the table.

"What's this one?" asked Yasad, pointing with his chopsticks.

Dave looked. "Octopus. It's octopus."

-<>-

"What exactly is your problem, Snortom?"

Snortom looked at him.

"I'm bored, Dave. Duuuh!"

"Well, I think you better try to cope, Mister, We still have six years to go."

"Bite me!"

Grumblings

It has been said more than once, that if the American people had known what Failsworthy and his pals were up to in the Senate—if they had any idea how conniving a bastard he was—they would have hanged him long before they actually ever did. This is, of course, just romantic nonsense, because, ultimately, they did, and they didn't.

What they knew, as certainly as the taste of their tongues, was that he was a scoundrel of the first order. One colleague actually suggested that his face be used in the Congressional record in place of the word criminal. What they must have known too was that he was scooping out of the public trough in great pudgy handfuls for years. They couldn't not know this about their representatives, him especially, if only they read the newspaper, or even watch TV, which is just about the only thing they ever really did do.

The self-apologetic notion that the electorate were hapless dupes of this fat assed putz and his cronies is utterly laughable. It was as plain as day that they were being shafted, and still they didn't do anything about it for ages, but grumble.

There is this though, while the American people were as guilty as Failsworthy, for all their sloth and negligence, he _was_ hiding his activities concerning the reissue of the dollar.

He was not stupid enough to resort to a simple scam. No, his artifice was subtle and obsequious, and not wholly ham-fisted.

He had bribed elaborately, and not just with cash, either. He offered favors and political leg-ups and blind eyes by the dozen. And he did it in the broadest possible way, spreading his river of corporate cash and vouch-safes into a vast deltaic sewer of you-owe-me-ness.

The net result of all his grueling graft was that by the time the word got out that he was trying to Shanghai the nation's bank account, it was too late.

He had the votes and then some to carry his motion easily. What he should have known if he had been slightly less arrogant, was that having the votes on the floor and having the will of the people were two entirely different things.

What he and the rest of the joint session of Congress that he was addressing that day should have realized and did not, was that the American people were pissed off like horny tomcats and that the country had virtually ground to a halt. This left people plenty time to talk, and plan, and get to Washington.

Our legislators were surrounded by savage enemies thirsting for their blood, and they were completely unaware of it. Had Congress known, they probably would not have had the brains to give a tinker's damn.

If he had not given his speech, but just let there be a quiet vote about it, he would have been spared a great deal of indignity later. But he felt compelled by standard practice, and so went on with it.

He sweated of course, as he stood there looking out from the podium at his, for the most part, bought and paid for colleagues. This speech was nothing more than a formality. He was going to get away with this stunt, and he knew it. But it showed good form to stand up and deliver the sound bites and seem to be convincing people with the strength of his ideas.

He cleared his throat, signaling that the circus was about to begin. He marshaled his timbre and then started.

"Americans, legislators, friends, hear me! For what I am about to say will change the course of the history of this great nation of ours. I suggest you listen. For, there is a huge cry outside the gate. A cry by the American people for change, and change now.

"They are through with supporting meaningless programs and have said so with their wallets. They are through with false democracy, and they are through with waiting. The time has come to answer them.

"They have said that they want a change, by refusing to support the policies of their renegade president with their money. I say we give them back the country they own. I say it is well past time to stand up and say that they are right in the greatest possible way.

"So it falls to us to stand up and do the right thing and exercise the Constitution of the United States of America to the letter of the law and that letter says this. The Congress of the United State shall have the sole right to raise taxes, levy duties and coin money. Coin, Money.

"Well, that's what we're going to do. We are going to coin some money. In fact, what we are going to do is coin quite a lot of it, all of it in fact! We are going to re-issue the dollar as a financial instrument!

"Now I know that there have been some pretty strong reservations about the logistics of this thing, but I just want to reassure you all before you vote on this, that we have the infrastructure in place to make it come off without a significant hitch.

"I know that it has been predicted by some that this is impossible, that there is no way that we can reissue a currency of this size, fast enough to accomplish our goal. That is not the case.

"What we will do is to credit any bank account with funds in equal amount old dollar for new as held at the moment twenty-four hours from the instant the president's gavel marks the bill passed. This will be done electronically, and any moneys held outside the banking system will become null and void at that time.

"Funds held in dollars over seas will need to show a valid export document dated before the Hold went into place and will only be redeemable on reentry to the contiguous United States, Hawaii and Alaska.

"Ladies and gentleman, the fate of the United States is in your hands. Vote well. Vote yes."

There was applause from the floor as he stepped down from the podium. He went back to his seat and sat down to await the vote.

There was nothing to do now till the roll was called. He looked at his notes for the committee appointments.

He was setting up one committee specifically to investigate the allegations which Failsworthy himself had started, that there were gross irregularities in the president's campaign funding, and conflicts of interest regarding the stock market. He was setting up another to look into the suspected instigators of the Hold, professional shit disturbers and the like. And yet a third one to investigate some members of Congress that had proven to be too troublesome in trying to bring about this landmark legislation, they were about to pass.

He knew actual convictions would be hard to get. But right now it was enough to keep people off balance.

This muscle flexing was only made possible by the huge influx of corporate cash that was pouring through his hands. It felt great to be powerful. It felt like he had at long last come to his natural state, in control and confident. He could push a hand this way and gush money over an ally, or that way and drown an opponent like it was nothing. It made him buzz just to think about it.

Al Faircloth looked at Failsworthy, and after a moment caught his eye. Neither man made any kind of acknowledging sign to the other, except to hold their gaze for a while. Then, Faircloth smiled a tiny sardonic bit, and looked away, before the other could respond.

'Revolting little man,' he thought. 'He hasn't the faintest idea of what he's getting into.'

The words squirted through his mind unbidden. He could almost hear them. Faircloth found it ironic that they should find themselves allied against the common adversary of the American people, their very constituency. He knew all the reasons for it and had never really questioned the illogic of politics, but this was just plain distasteful. He would do it but he didn't like the taste it left behind.

It also made him a bit nervous to think that they had to do it so publicly—that they had to make such a show of this. His office overlooked the steps of the Senate and he had been watching the crowd slowly gather there for days. He was one of only a handful of people in the room that had any idea that what they were about to do was the least bit cavalier. He wasn't prescient—he couldn't look into the future and know there would be trouble, but he could at least count. Not like the other witless egotistical thieves that surrounded him.

That morning as he drank his coffee he had watched Veets' stage bus pull up through the thin morning crowd and park in front of the Senate steps. Something like this was to be expected he told himself.

By the time he went to lunch they had erected a large display on top of it.

Vice president Swarthmore banged his gavel for attention, turned to the clerk and said, "Call the roll, man."

Veets' producer Philus pulled the image back a bit to isolate the VP and make him seem alone in the vast chamber of the Senate. This had a good feel to it, he looked far enough away to hate. She put this up as a kind of passive background and laid a window over it with a panning close up of the individual legislators as the vote progressed.

"Armstrong," called the clerk.

The camera held on Senator Armstrong. "Armstrong, aye."

Andy Nickson wiped down the barrel of his machine gun with elaborate care, wondering what the day would bring. He looked up at Veets where he stood panting after the short climb to the top of the bus. Veets looked at him.

"Hello, Mr. Veets," said Andy, polishing. "Having a little rally today are we?"

198

Veets sneered at him.

"We are here to practice democracy, direct democracy, of the people for the people and by the people. Today, democracy is a verb."

"Very laudable of you, Sir. You know, Jones here," he pointed with his thumb, "and I are here to back you up." He clicked the receiver shut. "I just though you'd like to know that. Just in case you had any doubts."

Jones gave Veets a big cream of wheat smile. "You can count on us! We never miss."

"Play nice now," said Andy, dismissing him.

Dagmar spat, turned back to the crowd and the cameras and gestured to the giant screen above him.

"Well, America," he said into the microphones. "There they go again! The politicians! Armstrong is the first traitor, but he won't be the last I can assure you that! He is just the first in a long line of scoundrels led by none other than that very same pick pocket that we just watched right here, Senator Daniel Failsworthy. Let me tell you something Senator, we are not going to let you get away with this!"

There was a roar from the crowd. It was not like before when he had stood here, not as deep and focused. In a way it was more threatening than it had been before. It was like the crowd was not there to yell. And, worst of all, they were not all of a single mind and under his control. There were those in his earshot that were not following along with his sermon. They were talking amongst themselves and, he could see, casing the defenses of the building.

The count continued behind him as one after another the Senate voted. Most were yaes.

"Failsworthy," he said, shaking his fist at the screen, "you better be watching this, because this is the American people talking to you! Not your corpulent corporate masters with their phalanxes of bloodless gray lawyers, and not the executive man's man. These are real live American patriots who have come here today to witness your dastardly act of craven theft. We see your hand poised over our wallets. We know what schemes lie festering inside your pustulant black heart! We hear your squeaky shoed little attempt to sneak up on us and steal our money, and we are not, I repeat ARE NOT, going to let you get away with it! We <u>will</u> stop you.

"That's what we have come her for today, to stop you! And, stop you we will!"

"Banning," called the clerk.

"Banning, aye."

"You see?" said Veets. "There goes another one! It's just like we weren't here! Just like foxes in a hen house! I say they're busted! Do you hear me Banning!? I say you are busted you bastards! I don't think that he can quite hear us out here! What do you good people say?!"

The crowd came back with a jumbled cry. It was stronger now, and tailed out only after several seconds. He started to take his stride.

"I said, WHAT DID YOU SAY?"

Now the crowd responded more strongly, in a wave.

"Busted You Bastard!!!," rolled back from the throng. It was rounded out by the crowd into something like 'Bustea yuu Basataaa...' but it was there. It was loud, and unified. Now they were one voice, now they were his.

Andy looked at the sea of people that stretched before him. They looked, well, like a crowd he thought, except different than he expected them to look. Usually people move around a lot at a rally like this one. They jump up and down and wave their arms over their heads, but these people didn't. They stood there yelling, when they were told to by Veets but they didn't hold their hands up much. Also there was this. They were, many of them anyway, wearing coats. That struck him as odd, now that he thought about it. Why would people be wearing coats in the middle of a hot July day in Washington DC? That was crazy, those people must be sweltering.

"Tell me, Jonesy—," he said. "You notice anything funny about this bunch?"

There was a pause and then Jones' little voice spoke in his ear.

"They're holding."

Andy nodded looking over at his gun mate. "Yeah, that's what I think. They have weapons under their coats. Man, they must be sweating their balls off! Hold on a second."

He switched over to the open com. channel.

"Sergeant, we may have a situation down here."

"Oh?" came his response. "What makes you say that?"

Jones cut in. "Stegalmyer, quit fuckin' around, man. We believe these people have weapons. Please advise."

They could hear him trying to figure out what to do.

"Okay," he said at last. "I'll get back to you."

"Yeah," said Andy. "Well don't take too long will ya!"

"Hartung," said the clerk.

"Hartung, ...aye."

Veets shook his head exactly four times listening to the roll.

"Hartung?! That's it, Nebraska. You can kiss democracy goodbye—your favorite son has just stolen the family car! Jim, you son of a bitch! How dare you vote like that?!"

He pointed at the screen. "You are Busted You Bastard!!!"

There was a moment and then, **"Busted You Bastard!"** rolled back across the crowd and washed over him in a baptism of half-assed hatred.

"Kellog," called the clerk.

Senator Kellog looked up straight into the camera.

"Kellog, aye."

"Thanks a lot, Senator Kellog! Maybe we'll get to return the favor sooner than you think!..."

It went on and on like this with Veets lampooning and berating each legislator in turn as they voted. Those that voted no, and there were not all that many who did, received only silence from him and the crowd. And each time there was a yes vote it got a little louder and a little more demonstrative. Even the TV guys were getting nervous.

Andy called for backup several times before he got an answer from Stegalmyer. When he finally did respond it was to say that they had backup standing by, but that the situation was too sensitive to send them out without 'visible just cause'. Nickson and Jones looked at each other across the steps.

"Okay, understood," said Andy. He signed off from the sergeant.

"Well," said Jones, "it's you and me, Nickson. We cover each other."

Andy lit a cigar. "Ah ha. Try not to shoot me. Okay? This is a new shirt."

"I'll do my best work, Corporal Nickson. You do the same."

"Count on it. There will be a slight lag on my coverage, while I 'attend the primary target'.

"No problem."

By the time they were nearing the end of the roll, Veets had his audience whipped up to a pulsing frenzy.

"Willmont," called the clerk.

"Willmont, aye!"

The crowd booed Willmont for her vote. She was the last one in the roll and there was a long pause while the count was double-checked. That done the page handed the counts from both houses to Swarthmore, who considered them for a moment.

He looked out of the screen at the assembled people there and said in a flat emotionless voice, "By a vote of seventy-one to twenty-eight in the Senate with one abstention, and four-hundred-twenty-six to one-hundred and nine in the House of Representatives, I declare the bill totally passed."

Dagmar Veets looked out at the sea of people that filled his view. At first they didn't do a thing. They stood there as the message sunk in that their Government had just conspired to shaft them in a new and extraordinarily underhanded way. Then they started to growl.

It started at the back and swept forward building on itself as the wave of vocal anger propagated forward. It mounted and mounted as it went, till when it reached Veets it was a deafening wail. It sounded like this,

"UURRAAHH!"

Andy cocked his machine gun and swung it up at Veets.

This was magnificent! Veets had never in all his life seen such an out-pouring of emotion as this. It was amazing to him that it could happen. He felt exalted, bathed in their furious noise. He squared his shoulder precisely to the crowd.

"Well Mr. and Mrs. America," he said, looking into the cameras. "I say we go tell it on the mountain!! Come on what are we waiting for?!"

In truth Veets could not have imagined what he had done. What he thought was about to transpire was that the crowd would press their way past the guards and into the Senate, where they would yell a lot and intimidate the legislature into reconsidering. As I said at the start of this narrative the man was a fat idiot.

The crowd surged forward trying to course around the bus. The people at the front got pushed from behind, whether they wanted to go or not, and as they were pressed up against the vehicle they started to die under the weight of the people behind. The bus heaved up and tipped as the first few hundred swarmed around it.

That was it. Andy pressed the trigger trying to kill Veets for his sheer stupidity. But as the bus tipped over, the bloated media personality lost what balance he had and fell back down the sloping roof of it.

Now, Andy Nickson was one of the better shots you were ever likely to meet and he would certainly have hit his mark had it not been for this accident. As it was he tried to follow Veets with the row of FMJs[54] that poured out of his gun, but the blimp rolled too fast and Andy's slugs only ripped into the bus' roof instead. Philus and her engineer were splattered into thick goo as round after round laced through them. Their screams were never heard and in fact the bodies were never fully accounted for due to the ensuing fire.

Veets landed hard on the ground, and Andy would have got him there and then, but for his catching Jones' situation out of the corner of his eye. He swung around and started covering his friend as the crowd rushed his position. Andy managed to cut down enough people to form a sort of meat fence between Jones and the onrushing people. This stopped them for a few seconds and he swung back around to get Veets again. The man was gone.

Andy looked around for his target but he couldn't find him.

Now Andy looked straight in front of him. There was a guy with a cowboy hat leveling a shotgun at his chest. Jones got him and about six other people including part of a news crew, in a short burst.

Andy switched over to com.

"Visible enough for you, Stegalmyer? You fuckin' asshole! Get us some fucking back up! NOW!!!"

He laid a wide swath of fire from in front of Jones' position to about 20° out, back and forth back and forth, slaughtering civilians like ants. Jones reciprocated and it was starting to look like they might just make it out alive. Then Andy's gun jammed. This left Jones open, but he continued to cover Andy as the corporal tried to un-jam his weapon. He got the round out and re-shut the receiver. He cocked and swung back to cover.

Somebody shot Jones in the head with a .45 and his fire abruptly stopped. Andy couldn't see exactly who it was so he just mowed people down like weeds for as far as he could reach.

After a few moments he looked to his left. There was a fifty-year-old housewife, Millicent Henderson, coming over the sand bags armed with a pickaxe. It was too late. He couldn't get his weapon around in time to take her out. She swung down on his head with all her might. The point of the pickaxe, which her son

---

[54] Full metal jacketed rounds.

Filbert had spent almost an entire morning sharpening, went through Andy's Kevlar® helmet like it was a paper plate.

The last thing that Andy ever realized was that he could see up her dress as she raised the pick above her head. She was not wearing panties.

'These people are savages,' he thought.

Then there was a sound like a piece of marble breaking.

Millicent charged on up the steps of the Senate, not even looking at the twitching body of the soldier she had just killed. She didn't care about him. He had just been in her way.

The reason, by the way, that Andy couldn't find Dagmar Veets to shoot him with his machine gun, as he was so intent on doing was this—while Andy was busy murdering civilians, in an attempt to save his friend Jones' life, the bus, pushed by the crowd rolled over on top of the fat moron. He was lying there on his stomach like a beached whale, and the next thing he knew there was a bang and he felt an immense but momentary pressure on his back.

Through sheer luck, when the bus rolled over on top of him, it was a window that tried to squash him and not the sheet metal side panel. The window, which was constructed of tempered safety glass, exploded into a million little irregular peas, that popped up into the air and then rained back down around him like water.

Philus hung above him in her chair with blood pouring out of her.

Meanwhile, back in the Senate, the mob was pouring in through the doors. Stegalmyer's 'back up', ten lightly armed conscripts, fell back like dominoes. They did manage to take a few American lives in the process, but they slowed the inward tide not one bit. And after a few moments they were shoved up against the walls of the corridor and pummeled and shot to death by people not unlike your next-door neighbors.

In the Senate itself, the assembled legislators could hear the ruckus, and the few that had seen action in China recognized the popcorn maker sound of small arms fire. They had enough sense to panic, and either duck beneath their benches, bad move, or run like college track stars for the tunnel[55]. Some even made it!

---

[55] It is not realized by most people, but the US Congress has had a special tunnel to protect them from their own people since as far back as 1970s. It leads from Congress to the congressional office building, and cost over 50 million dollars to build.

The doors burst open and the sea of America flooded in. They did not, as previous visitors to this august institution had, stop and marvel at how ornately beautiful this monument to the ideal of self-rule was. They did not say to themselves, this is what it is all about, a people standing up and saying, 'We choose this course for ourselves and our progeny', and having the moral courage to make it stick against stiff odds. And they did not get misty eyed and have the hair on the back of their necks stand up at the thought of just how much sacrifice and personal bravery, even unto death had gone to make this amazing thing possible.

They did however, rip the ornate decorations off the walls, their walls, and use them as bludgeons to slaughter the first few wide eyed Senators that they encountered, like seal pups, where they sat. They ripped down the curtains and used strips of the material to bind and gag others, and they shot some of them in the head just for the hell of it.

Now the Senate was starting to twig on to the fact that what they had done was not exactly going to go down like a tax cut smothered in butter. Now there was panic! Now there was a wholesale rush for the tunnel! Man was that ugly!

Swarthmore, when he realized what exactly was going down, made no pretense whatsoever about bravely going down at the helm of his rat infested ship. He dove for the tunnel with his secret service guard making a hole for him by whatever means they needed to. They were soulless unemotional pros and didn't blink. They stuck their guns to people's indignant temples and said move. They moved. After he was gone the senators and congressmen swarmed back into the hole. Those at the back were being hacked and shot and bludgeoned, so as you can imagine, they were in quite a hurry. Someone tripped, up at the front and then someone else tripped over them and so on and so on. The tunnel jammed up with people, they were trapped. They were terrified. They were dying.

Millicent Henderson got to the podium now and grabbed the mic.

"Hey listen, listen," she said. "Don't kill 'em all, yet, we need a few to lynch outside for the cameras. Otherwise they will just lie and say they are all still alive and pass more thieving laws! Remember Veets! Remember Dagmar Veets!" She believed that Veets was lying dead, out on the pavement under the bus, remember.

In fact, Veets was staggering to his feet at that moment, inside the over turned bus. He could see people pouring past the windshield armed with every sort of weapon imaginable. They were rocking the bus with their passage and hitting the vehicle with sticks and garden implements. As he staggered toward the front of the vehicle, he could see one guy, a kid really, stop in front of him. He had a sledgehammer and he swung it against the windshield like a golf club. The glass exploded inward filling the air with shrapnel and noise. Their eyes met and the kid smiled. Then pulled a bottle out of his jacket and threw it at Veets. It broke at his feet. It was gasoline.

Veets' eyes got real big and he started scrambling toward the opening as fast as he though he could. The kid laughed and laughed at the funny fat guy tripping over all the stuff inside the bus. He was really comical, he thought. He pulled out one of his flares and sparked it to life. After a few seconds it was burning very brightly and he threw it at him.

Veets dodged the flair, but it went past him and landed in the gasoline. There was a 'Woof' behind him. Now Veets ran as fast as he really could, over and around the jumble of seats and equipment and just got out of the bus in time. His clothes were on fire when he stepped through the front of the bus. The kid stood there laughing at him.

"Why the fuck did you do that?!" Veets demanded, flames peeking over his shoulders.

"Ha ha ha. Why not?! Ha ha. Ha ha, AH ha ha ha!!!"

He pointed. "You're on fire, asshole! Ah ha ha ha!!!"

Veets grabbed for him but the kid was much too fast. He ducked and ran on up the stairs into the Senate.

This exchange was caught by what was left of one of the news crews and went out over the network, so millions of viewers got to see Veets be humiliated by a 15-year-old pyromaniac from the Bronx. They let him burn on camera for a while, until he was screaming for help and rolling around on the ground. And then, when they finally had their footage, the sound guy put him out with his Coke®.

"Thank you, thank you!" blubbered Veets.

They helped him to his feet and he stood there swaying slightly with the back of his coat and trousers gone and his bright red back and buttocks sticking out like some sort of surreal baboon.

Bob Ryan held out a microphone at him and said, "Tell us Mr. Veets, what's it like to be set on fire by the youth that you've come here today to inflame?"

He seemed sad, swaying there, looking like shit. "It really

burns me up!" he said.

Shouting angry people flowed around him like a crazy river running up hill into the Senate.

"My people! They need me!" he said, and staggered up the steps with them.

The news crew watched him go.

"You get that?" asked the assistant producer.

Frank, the cameraman, gave her a big okay sign.

When Veets got into the Senate he was appalled at the level of mayhem he found. There were people pummeling representatives and senators that were pleading for their lives through, bleeding, busted teeth. One guy just kept saying, "I voted no!" over and over again while he was lashed to a pillar and used for target practice.

Veets ran down to the podium and wrestled the mic away from Millicent, who was singing 'We shall overcome'. She tried to brain him with her pickaxe but he saw her coming and ducked in time to see her bury it in the floor. She heaved on it trying to get it out of the planks but it wouldn't budge. Veets cold cocked her with a pudgy fist.

"Hey! People, people please. Listen to me! Stop this! This is not what we came here for! We came here to stop them thieving our money, not to commit murder!"

There was a momentary lull and then someone shouted, "Hey fuck you!" and they started in all over again.

Failsworthy was cornered at the tunnel mouth and dragged kicking and screaming up to the balcony. They wrapped a decorative gold sash rope that had adorned a curtain around his neck and tied it nice and tight. All the time he kept shouting condescending orders at them to stop immediately, he was a US senator! And so on.

"STOP THIS NOW," shouted Veets. "That man has to answer for his crimes in open court! LET HIM DOWN!"

They had Failsworthy up on the rail, ready to push him off. There was a tense second and the whole room seemed to go quiet.

"Let him down," said Veets, staring authoritatively at the rabble in the balcony. "I am in command here and I say to let him down. We want him alive."

They looked disappointed, and they grumbled, but they did as Veets said. They took his hands and started to help him down. His legs were shaky even on solid ground, but the rail was narrow and wobbly. He slipped. He fell forward. The rope took up slack and went taught. His neck strained. He filled his pants. The rope broke, and he landed on three people, killing one and injuring the others.

He was not dead, yet. Veets shouted for order for ten minutes, and finally he got them calmed down enough to talk sense to them. He told them that the Army was on its way and that they had all better clear out or they would be shot down like rabid dogs. He said to let the senators and congressmen go, that their point had been aptly made and that further killings would only diminish their progress.

Most of this was bullshit that he made up as he went along, but he was a trained salesman and he was eventually able to sway them. They filtered out onto the steps and started to disperse.

Outside, the police were swarming in from all sides and they could hear the helicopters coming. The crowd scattered as fast as they could. Most of them got away. Most of them would later deny any involvement in the Sacking of the Senate. They would all have airtight alibis for their whereabouts on that day. But right at that moment they were all filled with a warm sense of glee at having righted a great wrong and done a great favor for themselves and their children. To them America was a beautiful place again. For days after that, there was much camaraderie and lying in bars all over the United States. They were murderers, nonetheless.

The body count that day in the capitol city of the most powerful nation on earth was 1614 dead and 2105 wounded. Of the dead, some 89 were either senators or congressmen, as well as 103 of the wounded[56]. The rest were, in descending order of magnitude, rioters, police and innocent bystanders. Still, the next day the papers carried this headline,

The Slaughter of the Senate!

---

[56] Including representative Irving Seamore, who managed to slip out through the crowd and made it as far as the outskirts of Lexington Virginia, where he was necklaced with a 170-50-R-14 tire manufactured by the Goodyear Tire and Rubber Co. of Dayton Ohio. He later died in Bethesda Naval Hospital.

J'accuse

"Order! I <u>will</u> have order in this house!" drawled Senator Faircloth. He banged his gavel with his good hand.

Actually, he would have been a good deal more accurate to say, 'I <u>will</u> have order in this gymnasium,' as that was were they were holding these hearings while the Senate and various other Government buildings were being rebuilt.

In the first three weeks, after the Sacking of the Senate, there had been many, 'Public manifestations of popular anger,' throughout the US at various Government buildings. On August 13th the federal office buildings in San Francisco, Los Angeles, Dallas and St. Louis were ransacked and burned with considerable loss of life. Three days later there were bombs exploded at some twenty-two IRS buildings, including the Fresno processing center, which held records for the contiguous United States west of the Mississippi, Alaska and Hawaii. No one was hurt in these incidents, but there was some data lost. And on the 20th there was a march on Washington that numbered over five million people. This devastated the city by the sheer bulk of humanity eating, excreting and generally just being there. They trampled the hedges and tore down whole trees to block the roads. They needn't have bothered either. The place was a virtual ghost town by then.

When the tanks came to get them out the next morning the people running before them crushed parked cars in their haste to get out of the way of the flame throwers, and since many of them hid in the deserted buildings, the National Guard had to do considerable damage itself just to get them out. All in all, it was a complete cluster fuck for everyone involved.

Swindel wanted the people to be persuaded to go peaceably home and let he and the rest of what was left of the Government alone to get on and cut some kind of a deal. What he wanted was for everybody to get out of his way, and he fully expected the Senate and House to do so now that they had had their noses bloodied. As far as he could see they had been cowed, and he felt it would be convenient now if everyone would go back home, having accomplished this.

But, he was unable get enough people to go along, so the remaining troublemakers could be singled out and slaughtered where they stood. He had to rely instead on Baisch's abilities to quell the trouble.

Baisch was loath to use too much force against the American populace, but his idea of enough was still a hell of a lot. He sent regular Army units into every city over a quarter million people and imposed martial law. Looters were shot on sight and people gathering in groups of more than 100 were dispersed, in direct contravention of the constitution, by whatever means necessary, including shooting some of them.

The American people did not like this but they took it. In fact, after about the fourth week, the violence and civil disobedience tailed off markedly. There was still the occasional demonstration or bank riot, but even those died away as people got used to the idea that this was not going to be the next American Revolution—that the authorities wouldn't allow it.

That was kind of funny. The authorities never allow revolutions.

King George never *allowed* the American Revolution. He fought it and hated that he lost America. But the people that lived there in 2050 were not made of the same stuff that their forebears were. They were told 'no', in a slightly firm tone of voice and that was it. They did just roll over and take it!

They all had very good excuses for not risking their fat necks for a nebulous ideal like freedom. They had mortgages, and 'the kids' welfare to consider' and 'a responsibility to this community' and so on. It was all very logical and responsible behavior. It was also exactly what you would expect from the gutless bags of shit that the majority of Americans had become.

After a while they started coming into banks and handing over their money without a word said. In went their 'old dollars' or yen or euros or whatever, and their accounts were credited at the going rate. They got their thumbprint scanned. The scanner made a tiny pin prick that they couldn't feel, and they could spend the stuff again. That meant that they could use their credit cards to buy more big-ticket bullshit and so on. It also meant that the Government could get its back taxes during the exchange, and they took all of it that they were owed, and a little bit for a cushion.

The little pinprick gave everybody a cold, and unknown to them, a virus delivered, genetic tag, so they could be checked for 'loyalty and compliance'. 13,275 people's ears would eventually glow.

All of this grief, all the lives lost and all the unrest and upheaval, and all the shit eating capitulation on the part of the American taxpayers—all of it could have been avoided—by abolishing income tax and instituting a sales tax of around 27% on everything. This would have, on the one hand encouraged savings, driving the value of the dollar up and saved billions by eliminating the IRS and on the other, taxed the black economy, which accounted for almost 20% of the US GDP It would also have been a real PR coup for whoever had the guts to institute it. Quite naturally this would never have occurred to anybody in Washington.

Everybody in the gymnasium was still babbling to each other, and the sound echoed, well, pretty much like a gymnasium, into a vast hollow blur. Faircloth felt lost banging away with his pathetic little gavel there in the huge noisy room. He frowned and picked up the bullhorn that he had below his desk for just this situation.

"Hey! Eva'budy shut up! Ya-hea'?"

They shut up and paid attention now.

Faircloth shut off the bullhorn with a loud click.

"Thank you very much ladies and gentlemen, this hearing is about to commence. I would appreciate your attention!"

They saluted the flag, in a motley, plaster sheathed, sort of way.

His long time colleague and adversary, Senator Daniel Failsworthy, was recovering slowly from his injuries at the hands of the mob. The hospital at Bethesda was the best facility with the best doctors that money, the taxpayer's money, could buy. Many Americans, including some of those that had fought in Manchuria, as well as to overthrow the Government still had no health coverage at all, even though they were forced at gunpoint to pay for his care. He liked that. It made him feel special.

He sat there in his hospital bed, in his private room with his head screwed on sideways like a curious dog, watching the hearings on TV. His neck would stay like that for the rest of his life, but at least he was still alive. Not like some.

There was a commercial on at the moment for a stronger America.

Throughout the unrest, The Lie™ had pumped out a steady stream of commercials boosting the Government line. They had carte blanche to say what they liked as long as it was in support of the calm return to legitimacy and order. Worthy made a bundle on it all.

He used his same people and Bill was most popular as the voice of the regular guy, talking straight to Americans as one of them. He was as sour as battery acid, and that was how America was feeling, sour.

Through the magic of television the public had been led to forget, that their comrade and compatriot Bill Crenshaw was a millionaire with as much in common with them now, as they had with fruit bats.

Bill was still his old erasable self, with his penchant for cynical banter and a strong personal dedication to state his point of view come what may, but he now held poor people in outright contempt, whereas before he hadn't. And, he felt that his friends, particularly his new ones, were somehow different than the average Joe. This miraculous transformation from grumpy misanthropic populist to grumpy misanthropic elitist pig had taken all of 4 months and cost around 15 million dollars. Amazing isn't it, what a bit of cash can do!

Of course he was smart enough to keep his patrician opinions to himself, unlike most people with dough. He didn't feel a need to rub his grubby bucks in people's faces just to bolster his minuscule self esteem, not yet. He still played the part perfectly, giving his cantankerous advice and paid for opinions out like they were candy canes. And it must be said that he actually did believe in some of the things he said, or at least that if people did as he advised that it would be best for them.

That was where it got a bit muzzy for him. He had lost track of what he used to think when he was just a retired bar tender, back before he became a celebrity. He was not quite sure either if those had been good opinions to hold, or whether he had just been deluded like the rest of the cattle. He kept saying the words. He kept taking the checks.

"...So just remember everybody," he said looking out of the screen at Failsworthy, tiltedly. "Just keep strong and wait a while. This bullshit will blow over soon enough and the country will be back on its feet in no time. Liberty's got a black eye, but she's all heart. God bless you."

This last bit was particularly hypocritical as Bill was an absolute atheist.

He was replaced by a paid social message from The Right Reverend Harvard Washington Jr. Harvey stared out of the screen like a startled, surly, orangutan. His eyes opened a bit too far and they shifted around distrustfully before he spoke. There was a shock of relaxed hair hanging down in front of his forehead and in spite of the best efforts of his, hired for reasons of color, make up person, there were minute beads of sweat at the edge of his hair line, that caught the light and sparkled. This was a picture of a lying bastard if ever Failsworthy saw one, and he had seen one every morning of his adult life as he shaved.

"Americans of all colors listen to me, now. I have paid for this broadcast time in order to ask you all to please give generously to my new program for disadvantaged intercity children of African origin, America Up. This fund will give these children the opportunities that..."

"Sound off," said Failsworthy.

He couldn't listen to this guy blab about his personal issue while the country was just about going to hold it together by a few stitches. He should be pulling with the rest of them to restore order and decency to the entire nation, not just his little patch. It was an outrage that he could be so selfish at a time like this. Why even his <u>own</u> party had put aside their issues for the moment to pursue the greater goal of rooting out the organizers of the uprising and making examples out of them, not to mention the fact that they had to rebuild a good portion of the federal infrastructure as well as getting on with business as usual. He made a mental note to have Washington investigated. This sort of opportunism could not be tolerated.

Failsworthy was not alone in these feeling either. All over the country people who in gentler times could normally be expected to reach down deep and shower his causes with oodles of cash to alleviate their guilt at being prosperous had been turning their backs on him. This commercial was a move of desperation.

Harvey had spent three weeks in the hospital after he kicked Veets' ass in front of the entire nation. He had shown that the days of a person of color having to take shit off of a honky racist asshole were totally over. Then he had spent another three weeks at a health farm in Palm Springs to get back in fighting trim for the summer fund raising season, and in that short time his lieutenants had managed to lose or steal half his money. It was scandalous that a man of God should have to put up with this sort of opportu-mistic thievery from his own people!

These thoughts lay broadly across his mind as he spoke, like a smothering blanket of resentment. His every word was tinged by them. Harvey shifted his position on his squeaky chair as he spoke causing lots of funky wrinkles to appear across the shoulders of his coat. He was looking through a teleprompter with his speech scrolling up it, but he used that only as a guide, diverging constantly into little finger-like dead end digressions. And of course, he was inarticulate as always.

"...the injustice that ever blights the intercities of this white dominated country of ours, the pilfering opportunists that take what is not theirs, but is the rightful property of the children of the slaves that built this nation. These are the issues that we seek to undress! These are the things that have made the people of color so resentful of their white racist neighbors—the fact that they always have more than them, and indeservedly so.

"I pull it to you then, that it is up to you as a member of what ever race you are, a member of, to give money to the poor and underprivileged people of color of this nation so that they can become what they can become—better off!

"Please, won't you give generously? Visa and MasterCard accepted gladly."

He stared out at 250 million people for the last few seconds of his paid time sweating resentfully. They held his image too long. He looked phony, untrustworthy, bogus. At last he was replaced by Faircloth again. The senator was questioning Paul Schinefeld, an NBC vice president.

"Mr. Sinefield what was the line up for the afternoon broadcast on April 7th of this year for the Eastern Seaboard region?"

Schinefeld adjusted his tie with elaborate care, moved around in his seat and adjusted his papers before he spoke. He looked up at the Senator, who was seated on a dais so that he would seem superior to those he questioned.

"First of all, I would like to point out to the committee that my name is Schinefeld not Sinefield. And second..."

"I beg your pardon Mr. <u>Schinefeld</u>. Will you please answer the question, I remind you that you are under oath."

Schinefeld looked at his lawyer and took a drink of water.

"Thank you for your reminder. It is not my responsibility as a vice president in charge of public relations to keep a log in my head of the show line up for the past year for daytime broadcast over the terrestrial net. I believe that the line up was in no way unusual on that day. It is my belief that our regularly scheduled programming went out that day if that is what you are asking."

"What I am asking, Sir, is what the schedule was for that day. If you can't supply that information we can subpoena it from your company. But since you seem to want to 'cut to the chase' as they say, then I am happy to move along to the issue that you have raised—whether you deviated from the norm on that day.

"Did your company broadcast any announcements that day about groups of people placing a hold on their income tax payments for the year 2049-2050 inclusive, and if so where did you come up with this information?"

Faircloth pointedly looked at his notes and not at Schinefeld as the PR man answered.

"Well that depends how you define the term 'group.'"

The Senator looked up over his reading glasses.

"Did you broadcast an announcement that day to the effect that there was more than one person who had placed a hold on their IRS payments that day, yes or no?"

Schinefeld's lawyer nodded.

Schinefeld said, "Yes, we broadcast an announcement at approximately 12:55 Eastern Standard Time that there seemed to be a trend on the net, of people placing a hold on their IRS debit to their accounts. We got this information from CNN. Our research department checked on this information and it appeared to be correct so we mirrored their broadcast."

"I see." said Faircloth. "And later on in the day, did you make another broadcast concerning this trend?"

"Yes, at 3 o'clock Chicago time we interrupted a soap opera with a bulletin to more or less the same effect but on that occasion we had some fairly reliable numbers to quote.

"This is all a matter of public record, Senator. Why do you ask?"

"Why don't you answer, instead of wasting the taxpayers' money in trying not to answer? I am trying to determine the level of responsibility of your company in this act of treason by certain citizens of this country. This committee is here to ask some difficult questions, and you have to answer them to the best of your abilities.

"Now then. Tell this committee if you will, why you chose to broadcast this information to the American people knowing full well what effect it would have."

Schinefeld looked openly bewildered at this.

"We broadcast it because it was news. That is our business, to broadcast news, in fact it is mandated by the FCC that we do so. As to our 'knowing full well what the effect would be' that is not our bailiwick. We are not here to censor the news stream in order to manipulate the public will. We do not have an agenda[57]

---

[57]This was an outright lie of the first order. NBC was owned by Tokugowa Foods, and was sitting on a story of great interest and

and are not responsible for what happens from our broadcasts. That is the whole point of having a right to free speech. It is free."

"So then you deny that you were in contact with various subversive elements within this country at the time of the broadcast. Is that correct?"

Schinefeld's lawyer stood up.

"Senator, we can not respond to such a nebulous accusation as 'various subversive elements within this country'. Just what exactly, do you mean by that?"

Faircloth banged his gavel to emphasize.

"I will ask the questions here, and your client will answer them!

"Do you deny that you were in contact with a man by the name of Dagmar Veets at the time of the Chicago broadcast? Yes, or no?!"

The two TV men looked at each other for a long moment starting to understand what was really going on here. Then Schinefeld spoke.

"Mr. Veets is a media personality. It is quite normal that he and NBC Television be in contact on a regular basis. At the time he worked for one of our affiliates.

"As to whether Mr. Veets is a subversive, I can't tell you one way or the other, but I do know this. It is not a crime in this country to be 'subversive', whatever that is."

"So then you admit that your company actually paid him to spread the message of anti-Government tax avoidance on that occasion. This committee duly notes that. And do you now deny that you have since that incident continued to pay him to spread such sentiment, and in fact have given this man his own TV slot?"

"Since when is it a crime to give somebody a job in this country?! Yes. Yes, we have paid him in accordance with his legal contract to speak as he so chooses, within the bounds of reasonable taste, on his shows, both radio and television. To do otherwise, without just cause would have been illegal.

"But what bothers me here, is the implication that you are trying to make, that our company somehow is responsible for the American taxpayers stopping you and your fellow legislators from misspending their money by whatever means they felt necessary. We are not!

"All we did was to report the news. If you don't like the news

---

importance to the American people, that would reflect badly on Tokugowa if it got out. Of course it did eventually, anyway.

don't blame us, change events!"

Faircloth looked at him for a long moment. When he spoke his voice was matter of fact.

"This committee is unconcerned with what bothers you Mr. Sinefield. What we are concerned with here is whether there was criminal complicity between your company and Mr. Veets. And it will be the mandate of this committee to determine what guilt lies with his, and possibly your own co-conspirators. His guilt is fairly well established already in the video record, but your company's is yet to be completely determined. I can assure you however that outbursts such as this one will not help your cause."

"Schinefeld" he said. "It's Schinefeld."

And so it went for days and days and days. They hauled all sorts of people before the committee and asked them every manner of leading, outrageous and weasel worded question, so they could twist their answers to use against them. Somewhere along the line they dragged Dagmar Veets in there and grilled him like a pork chop.

"State your full legal name to the committee, please."

"Dagmar Ivan Veets."

Faircloth looked at Veets standing there for a while. Veets had to stand throughout the entire questioning because of his painful back. It was a red roasted mess of welts and scar tissue, interspersed with the occasional suppurating pustule. He was wearing a hospital gown that was specially modified to close only across his ample butt.

"Dagmar. Ivan. Veets. That's an unusual name you have there, Mr. Veets. Where did you get a name like that?"

"From my parents. It's a tradition in my family."

"What I mean is what kind of a name is that—Veets?"

"It's Hungarian."

"I see," said Faircloth. "Ah, so your parents weren't even Americans is that it?"

"My paternal great grand father came from Hungary. Why, there some law against being Hungarian?"

The question was a genuine one, as by this point Veets was an out and out paranoid.

"Hum. No reason really. Now, Hungeria. A lot of anarchists used to come from Hungaria. Didn't they?"

"Hungary. The country is called Hungary, not 'Hungaria'." He paused for emphasis. "The answer to your question is yes and no, not exactly, some rather famous anarchists came from the Austro-Hungarian Empire, notably Gabrielle Princeps the man who shot Arch Duke Ferdinand and started World War I—but he was Serbian. My family isn't Serbian. You had maybe a point to make. Like maybe this particular point about my background is salient in some degree? I take it you know what salient means," he added almost as an aside to himself.

Faircloth smiled.

"Why yes, as a matter of fact I do know what it means. Now the reason I ask about your back ground and particularly about anarchists, the apposite point, is that we have several hours of video and many hundreds of hours of audio of you inciting the American people to overthrow their duly elected Government." Faircloth paused for emphasis. "I was wondering if that sort of thing was congenital in your family. If your parents taught you to disrespect authority, or if you were just an aberration."

Veets didn't like this. He cocked his head slightly, like a kick boxer taking stance.

"Oh, I see. I'm sure that my fellow Hungarian Americans will be very interested in your opinion of them come the next election. Your racist implications have been noted by the electorate, Senator." He shot glances around him.

"What you have recorded are my shows, and they are talk shows in which I and my guests discuss lively topics of the day, as we have every right to do. It is true that I cheered on those patriots that placed the Hold on their accounts and would have succeeded in stopping your sinister attempt to spend 70% of their money without their permission, if you and your thieving colleagues hadn't figured a way out to take *all* of it off of them *illegally*.

"Do not you presume for a moment, not a single instant," he said shaking his finger at Faircloth, "that you are going to get away with this—that it is going to slide by unnoticed. And don't think that your slimy, and may I add pathetic, attempts to assassinate my character are going to go unnoticed or un-prosecuted either for that matter. You…"

"How ironical, Mr. Veets," interrupted Faircloth, "that you should choose that particular word, 'Assassinate'. It is you who has been the assassinator here. It was you who roused the rabble to sack the Senate and murder and attempt to murder myself and my colleagues.

"And, it was you who failed, Sir, in your attempt to assassinate this country's democracy in the name of saving it. That is why you are standing before this committee to answer today, and why we are still alive to hear you."

Another Senator, Handale, leaned over and corrected Faircloth even as Veets spoke. "Assassin," he whispered.

Veets raised his hands for emphasis.

"If you will recall, Senator Faircloth, it was me who saved what lives I could in the Senate that day. It was me who appealed for calm and it was me who dispersed the crowd, and so it is you who sit up there that owe your lives to me. You should be thanking me, not investigating me. Maybe next time I won't bother! Also there is this, the word is assassin, not 'assassinater'!"

"I can assure you, Sir, that there will never be a next time."

There was a silence between the two men for a moment.

Dagmar considered reaching for the bailiff's side arm and just killing this unctuous fuck on the spot but as he glanced that way, he noticed that the bailiff, a younger man was watching his every move.

"Now then," said Faircloth. "It has been pointed out to me that you did in fact come into the Senate chambers and call for calm as you have said but it remains to be proven that you were not at fault in the initial attack. That is a criminal matter and not the purpose of this committee. The justice department will get around to you presently. Of that you can be sure.

"What we are here to determine is whether you and several other people are to be tried for treason, in trying to stop the legitimate Government of the United States from carrying out its lawful policies. I suggest you cooperate, Mr. Veets."

"Yeah, or what? Ha? What are you going to do to me? Incarcerate me without due process of law? Have me marched out and shot?

"Come on, Senator Un-Faircloth, you have made your vague implication, just what in the hell do you plan to do about it? The world is watching, you better make it good. What are you going to do to me, if I don't 'cooperate'? Well?"

Faircloth looked at him smugly.

"Mr. Veets, you are a US citizen. It is your duty to cooperate with a congressional investigation."

"Yeah, says who? The Constitution? I trust you have read the Constitution of the United States of America. Right? Well I have and it doesn't say in there that I have to cooperate with you. It says that you can ask me questions, but it also says that I have certain inalienable rights.

"My public speaking is a matter of record and I stand behind every word of it. So tell us Senator, what are you going to do to me if I don't cooperate? If when you ask me some stupid fucking question like 'don't a lot of anarchists come from <u>Hungaria</u>?' and I can't muster the self-restraint not to answer back that it is irrelevant and obfuscating and just plain fucking idiotic, what the fuck are you going to do to me, asshole?!"

People laughed as Faircloth banged his gavel for order.

"Order! Order! Sir, you will not use such language in this house. Is that clear?"

Veets threw his hands up in the air nodding his head.

"It is a gymnasium!"

"Is That Clear?"

Veets rolled on.

"And this gymnasium is in the United States of America, you know the place with a Constitution and a Bill of Rights, and one of those rights, one of those inalienable rights I was talking about just now, is the right to <u>free</u> speech! I will say what I have to say, and if my words make you uncomfortable so be it. It is my ideas that you should feel threatened by, not my words! Where does it say that I have to make you comfortable, Senator? You seem to have forgotten your place, Sir. You work for me, not the other way around! You will not dictate to me what terms I may use, not in this country! Not in America! I will speak as I please, and if you don't like it you can..."

"Mr. Veets!!!"

"Go fuck yourself!!!"

The gym boomed with laughter.

Faircloth stood up with his bullhorn yelling "Order! Order! Order!" with almost impossible pompousness.

He turned to the bailiff and yelled, "Gag that son of a bitch!" through his horn.

The bailiff collapsed with a perforated eardrum but his assistant went and tried to put a gag on Veets.

"Fuck off, sunny boy! I have committed no crime, now get away from me!" said Veets.

The bailiff grabbed for him and Veets swung a porky fist at him back. He connected with the bailiff's head sending him flying. This was a tactical mistake on Veets' part, as it only brought down excessive force to bear on him for all his rightness and half hard indignation. Six bailiffs jumped him and wrestled him to the floor, where they handcuffed and gagged him. They dragged him to his feet with the crowd yelling encouragement to both sides.

One bailiff spoke close to his ear. "Try that again and we will definitely fuck your shit up. Okay?"

Veets nodded once. The bailiffs stepped away form him. A couple had puss all over their shirts. Veets stood there with his hands behind his back, his eyes moist with the pain. The crowd quieted down a bit now, as Faircloth called for order through his squealing bullhorn.

"Now," said Faircloth at last. "Since you seem to need a little time to think about your responses here today, we will hear from a witness to both the events in the Senate and also to your diatribes against him on the steps there in the days leading up to those events."

He motioned with his gavel. "Turn on the video to Senator Failsworthy."

Behind him the video screen flicked on with a picture of Failsworthy looking out crookedly from his hospital bed.

"Good morning, Senator," said Faircloth. "How are you feeling this morning?"

Failsworthy seemed to consider this question for a bit.

"As well as can be expected I guess," he said.

"Now then, Senator, we would like to ask you some questions regarding this man, Dagmar Ivan Veets, that we are questioning here today, would that be all right?"

"Sure, go ahead."

Failsworthy picked up a glass from the bedside table and drank from the straw.

"Senator Failsworthy, do you recall the events leading up to the attack on you and others in the Senate?"

"Yes, quite clearly."

"And tell us, Senator, do you recall what this man, Veets, had to say regarding the Congress of the United States leading up to that attack? Were there any remarks that you recall in particular that stand out in your mind for instance?"

"Yes, I do recall several remarks that he made in the days and weeks leading up to the attack. In particular I recall him calling me a swine and a thief and I seem to recall that he said several times that, and I quote here, 'that I was not going to get away with it'."

Faircloth nodded.

"And just exactly what do you suppose he meant by the term 'It', Senator?"

"At the time I took it to mean that I would not be permitted to undertake to re-institute the lawfully established tax system after it had been stymied by the unlawful actions of a few self-styled anarchists that we seem ever to be plagued with in this great country of ours..."

They went on and on and on, with Faircloth asking the leading questions and Failsworthy giving the perfect sound bite answers, while Veets had to stand there as a gagged witness to the whole dog and pony show. At one point he was so frustrated by this ridiculous farce that he started jumping up and down and kicking the furniture and so on, until Faircloth interrupted himself to ask the bailiff to take off the gag.

"Did you have something polite that you wanted to share with this committee, Mr. Veets?"

"Look," said Veets. "You guys have been going around and around with this thing recounting what I said about this or what someone else said about that and interspersing all this with party political statements. Why don't you get to the point and save the taxpayers, whether they like it or not, a few million bucks.

"What I said is not in dispute here. In fact no one, so far as I know, has denied a single thing in this entire proceeding.

"Did I accuse you and the other senators and representatives of stealing the taxpayers' money? Yes I did. And did I organize a public demonstration against you? Yes I did. So what? That is all quite legal, and normal, in fact it was what I perceived as my duty at the time, and I still do. We said what we said and what happened, happened. The thing is this—there were people in the crowd that had it in mind to murder you. I did not make them do that.

"You did not provide adequate security for yourselves in the most armed country the world has ever known, when you undertook to go against the popular will. What did you expect to happen, that people would just take it? These are Americans we are talking about here. We are a surly and individualistic people.

"Tell us if you will, Senator Failsworthy, what did I say to the mob when they were about to hang you?"

Failsworthy started blinking a lot as he remembered his terror.

"You, you said to let me down."

Veets looked around at the crowd.

"Well?"

"But you were the one that got them to get me up there in the first place, Mr. Veets! I hope you get the chair for that. Your little group of followers killed eighty-nine of my friends. Don't expect any gratitude from me.

"Furthermore, you tried to stop Congress in the lawful execution of its duties, under the Constitution, I take it that you have read that document. Congress has the right to collect taxes, and coin money. That is what we did, and you have no right to stop us. This is not a direct democracy, Mr. Veets. It is a representative one.

"If the Government sets a policy, it is not your place to circumvent it. You can't just take the law into your own hands and do as you please. I don't care how surly and individualistic you are. We are a country of laws, and we all must follow them. If you don't like the Government's policies, then I suggest you vote them out of office, not kill the individuals that work for it."

Veets shook his head.

"You self-righteous putz. You are not the only one to lose friends in the sacking. I lost two, be that as it may, I can't believe that even you can sit there and defend your actions. The people have spoken and they have said in no uncertain terms that they reject your policies absolutely and without exception. They will be back and finish the job if you do not relent and release their money, or they will strike and this country will come to a screeching halt.

"It is a shame that so many had to die, for the American people to make their point. You might have listened to them decades ago but that's history now. Anyway, if I could have, I would have stopped them, but you made them bananas! It was not my actions or words that aroused their anger. It was yours. You and your fellows are the ones to blame for your butchery at the hands of the electorate! They hated you. They still do.

"I dare you to get elected dog catcher in Billings Montana! Your careers are at an end. At least have the decency to save the taxpayers' dime and nix this ridiculous fiasco before it embarrasses you further! You have nothing to gain!"

Failsworthy stared at him from the screen sternly.

"We have justice to gain. You and your thugs will go down for this, so help me God! Veets, you are a traitor and a bellicose jackass, that this country can ill afford! It is you who is at an end. Enjoy it, you've earned it."

It went on for another hour like this and finally they took Veets back to the hospital and tended to the ripped open sores on his back. At last he could lie down again and after a while a nurse came in and doped him with beautiful morphine. He floated then, watching the distant television. It couldn't touch him anymore.

They questioned dozens and dozens of people, and they got some of the highest ratings in the country for days. People wanted to hear what the people they questioned had to say for themselves. It was like a new kind of Roman circus, with gladiators pared off against each other with rhetoric rather than swords. Many of the fights were blatantly unfair, with heavily armed lawyers pitted against hapless, undefended proles. They hewed into their soft flesh and bled them white with rocket propelled, heat seeking questions, and laser guided accusations that skewered them right through their ignorant, innocent armor. Then it was carnage. Then it was great television. The ad revenues were phenomenal!

Later, they inadvertently brought in a lion. They though that he was on their side now, because they had made him a millionaire, and showered him with gifts and let him shoot off his mouth whenever he liked. They also thought that because he was old he was toothless.

If they had been less arrogant they wouldn't have made these mistakes. They would have realized that just because you think someone owes you a favor and they are jovial toward you, doesn't mean that they are on your side. They also wouldn't have thought that they were special people, blessed with a unique vigor in their later years. Bill was still his own man, even if he was rich. And he was by no means either docile or weak.

He came before the committee there in the gymnasium at their request. He wasn't subpoenaed. This was going to be a friendly little chat with America's favorite personality, who was squarely in the Government camp.

"Hi, Bill," said Faircloth.

Everybody called him Bill now wherever he went. It was like he was their cantankerous old uncle. He was irascible and lovable, in a grating sort of way.

"Hi, Senator Faircloth. How's the arm?" asked Bill, pleasantly.

"Oh, not to bad now, it still pains me a bit, but it's healing up nicely. Thanks. How's ah…?"

"Fine, fine. Price of fame I guess."

They both laughed pleasantly.

"Now tell us, Bill, please, you were one of the first people to put a hold on your account, is that correct?"

"Yes, that is I think so, Senator, I am told that I was among the first people to do that, but that is just what I am told. I didn't see the figures myself."

"I see. And, what happened exactly, I mean did you get a message from someone, to the effect that putting a hold on your account would be a good idea? Did you hear it on the news, or what?"

"Well, Senator, in a way you could say that I did get a message on the television. I got it from President Swindel. I was watching his speech about that monster Kabingga and he said that he wanted to buy his kids a pony.

"Actually, of course, that is not what he said. What he really said was that he wanted to send more money and military aid to him because he felt a kinship between Kabingga and the American people, because his children loved horses just like American kids, and Russian kids and everybody else's kids, so he guessed. But still the message was pretty clear. He wanted more money for his military-political adventures over in Africa, for ill-defined ends and he wanted the American taxpayers to foot the bill. Well, Sir, I didn't feel that that was fair or reasonable, considering all the taxes we pay already, so I just went ahead and put a hold on my account, like I guess a lot of folks did that day. We felt we had to take direct action, on our own behalf.

"You know, I figured that probably he would get the massage and change his mind about Kabingga when he saw how we all felt, but he didn't. Instead the president came up with this crazy idea to dismantle the Military and give their budget away to a bunch of bums. After that I think people just dug in their heels."

Faircloth nodded.

"Bill, was Mr. Dagmar Veets any influence on your decision to place and keep the hold on your account?"

"Veets? No, certainly not. In fact, as you well know that is how I received my injury, in a show of disdain for him. He tried to make political hay out of the situation, but he wasn't responsible for the Hold being placed.

"You know, it's funny that this committee should want to punish him for standing up and doing what every American should have been doing all along—speaking his mind. There are a lot of people in the world who would be willing to fight for that right, if someone like the United States would go give 'em a little help. The people that founded this country were such people, but their descendants kind of went to sleep for a while. So instead of us supporting the good guys we always seem to come to the aid of despots and criminals."

"Surely, Bill," said Faircloth, "you aren't suggesting that it is a good idea to preach violence against your own Government. This is a democracy—change should come peacefully, and according to the public will. Not at the call of an anarchist!"

Bill shook his head emphatically.

"No, you miss my point. I am not saying that people should be, or for that matter <u>were</u> led to precipitous action, to violence, by Veets or anyone else. I am saying that in a democracy, people have a <u>responsibility</u> to each other, to state their clear opinion, and if necessary, fight and sometimes die defending the rights of others to state <u>theirs</u>, whether they agree with those opinions or not. That seems to be what this country and most especially Congress have forgotten. That it doesn't matter one whit if you don't like what's being said, even if what is being said is that you are all a load of thieving jackasses who need desperately to be hung by your balls and burned to white ash. You have no right to even question us, <u>your bosses</u>, in fact your only reason to be at all, politically speaking, about what we chose to say or to whom we chose to say it. It is not your place! It is also not your place as a legislature to just do whatever the hell you want with our money. The Constitution gives Congress certain rights, so that it can carry out the will of the American people. Those rights are entrusted to you on <u>our</u> behalf, not yours. When you and the president and your IRS pit bulls forgot that and decided that you knew what was best for <u>us</u>—one of the best-informed electorates in the history of the world—we had to stop you. We should have stopped you ages ago. Your actions are proof that you cannot be trusted.

"How dare you guys reissue the dollar?! That right that is entrusted to you for us and by us, to coin money, is there so that we can do commerce. But you have used the letter of the law to slit our throats! If we wanted you to have our money we would give it to you, you fucking bandit!"

Faircloth had had enough of this.

"Mr. Crenshaw, thank you for your testimony."

"I am not finished yet. You see—you're doing it again. You don't hear what you want, so you try to shut me up! Well I won't shut up! I have a right to free speech and you are no one to stop me! Who the fuck are you to tell me that I'm finished?!"

"Thank you."

They actually had to drag Bill from the room. He clung to people and tried to hold onto the door, protesting. The bailiffs were younger and stronger than he was and eventually they managed to peel him away from the doorjamb and expel him from the gym. The last thing he said to Faircloth was this, "I'd start looking for another job if I was you, sonny boy!"

Faircloth and his committee dragged on for days,

questioning people at great length about the Hold and the events surrounding it. Many of those questioned had eloquent arguments to make about why the Hold was necessary and why Congress was out of line on the dollar issue, but their words fell on deaf ears. In the end the committee came to no hard conclusions about what had happened or just exactly who was to blame, neither did they recommend any action. This is not too surprising as it was not really their aim. In truth all they wanted to do, was to postpone the debate about what they were up to with the public money while they distracted everybody with their little diversion on TV, which was this.

The day after the reissue, when people started coming into the banks with their money in their hat in their hands, a select group of senators and representatives met with Swindel. They went into the oval office and had sandwiches and beer, and talked about things. They said to him in no uncertain terms that he had a choice to make. It was a simple choice, and not one that he had to think about for very long—it was this.

Did he want to, abandon his plan to disassemble the Military, keep Alpha 1 and send troops to help Kabingga, or did he want to continue with his program of demilitarization, abandon a spaceship full of people half way to Alpha Centauri, and let Kabingga go down the tubes, pony, minerals and all.

Swindel chewed his chicken salad sandwich thoughtfully. The men in front of him were quite serious about their threats and were now capable of carrying them out. He took a swig of beer.

"Okay," he said, "but no half measures. I get Alpha 2, Joshua gets planes, advisers, the works, and you get to build the Military up into a monster."

A couple of powerful people nodded, and that was that.

Worthy received another visit from Mr. Green.

-<>-

"It was reported today by our correspondent in Flotkyo, that there was no denial by their spokesman, Joji Kakamatsu, of the accusations against Tokugowa Foods, that their very popular product sold under the brand name Snakos™, was in fact made from 100% reprocessed human feces. The company denied misleading the public in any of its campaigns, saying that they had always said from the start that the product was '100% recycled'. The company spokesman went on to say, that the product is not only nutritionally complete, and perfectly safe to eat, but also that they are tasty crunchy good!

"In other news, the Chinese led vote for sanctions against the Kabingga regime in Greater Burundi, and the enclave of Snellville the Lesser, went down to defeat on the floor of the UN today, with Japan, the US, and EU countries all rejecting the proposed sanctions.

And now on to sports..."

-<>-

Faizel Malowi wasn't too bright. He lacked imagination, and that was a good thing, actually, because he had a weird job that would have made an imagination a down right liability. He had to deliver an H-bomb that had been manufactured at the Quak Al Hooqume nuclear complex to a couple of fictitious Jewish Queers, in New York City, without anybody finding out about it. If he had started thinking about the ramifications of this, things would have gotten complex.

He rented a U-Haul in Barstow as he was instructed, lugged the thing in the back, and started driving eastward. It was August 6th.

Up Up and Away

You could tell just by looking at her, by the torn gown and the bruises around her pretty face, by the battered crown of rays, that she had been through one hell of a fight. She was beaten but not bowed. There was a quiet bravery in her that left you touched and breathless. She was every teenaged boy's wet dream, sexual, martial, elegant. She was Liberty.

There was the sound of gunfire and bombardment outside, and the sound of people dying. There was a baby crying somewhere off in the distance, just at the edge of hearing. And as she moved in shadows, with quiet confident stealth, you could see that she was an island in the sea of chaos.

Liberty stepped forward. She stopped for a second, listening with her whole lithe body, becoming the night. She heard a shell pass overhead, it kept going and then there was a boof far, far away. She continued on until she came at last to her place of safety. It was warm here and the light was friendly and yellow, not like the hostile blue shadow land beyond.

She took off her dusty, tarnished crown, and gave it an absent polish with her thumb as she looked into the middle distance remembering. Horrible things. They filled her eyes.

She was brought back by the sound of the child crying for its mother amid the rat tat tat tat of small weapons fire. Liberty's eyes came to a new and deadly resolve. She hung her crown on a nail, peeled off her torn gown and stepped toward the beckoning light.

Now she stepped into the shower. It was glossy and technical and as the steaming, sexy water gushed against her perfect skin a wind started to blow, teasing her hair. It flicked and danced about her face. She was angry. She was beautiful. She was coming back to life. Somewhere in the background there was a sax playing a slow sultry rendition of the star spangled banner. She looked at us, dangerous and beckoning. She cut the shower.

Now she slipped on a fresh gown over the tailored Kevlar® vest that just missed covering the pert cheeks of her ass. She put on her low cut flack jacket and tossed her hair nonchalantly over her shoulder. With bandoleers of fifty caliber tracers slung over her shoulders that accentuated her cleavage, she bent down exposing that tantalizing little bit more. Liberty came up with her new crown. It was shiny, and the spikes were needle sharp, around them was wrapped a single elegant strand of spiraling concertina wire. It sparkled in the glancing light. This was a tiara of death. Her skin was slightly mottled by her camouflage makeup and now she put double lines of flat black war paint on each cheek and down her chin. She was ready.

Liberty grabbed an enormous assault riffle off the rack, checked its action, with loud purposeful clicks, slotted in a fresh clip and drove it home with the butt of her hand. She picked up a bag of grenades and slung it over her shoulder like a fashion accessory.

She cocked and locked her piece, and set stance, ready to kick open the door. She breathed hard pumping herself for the fight. It was time. She crossed herself, and went for it with a deep ballsy war cry. AAHHHH!!!

BOSH! The door flew open and she charged outside, laying down a cordon of fire before her.

Standing there was a man. He looked vaguely Arabic, African, Hispanic and Chinese all at the same time. He was dirty, fat and sweaty. He looked dumb and evil, and capable of anything. He was holding a small white girl as a human shield and shooting past her at a company of UN troops. They were pinned down and helpless.

He turned his head to face Liberty. Seeing her, he spun her way holding the girl before him, and leveled his cheesy machine gun, right past the cheek of the crying child. He smirked mirthlessly. The little girl was terrified. She screamed. We could hear Liberty's heart pounding.

In slow motion he squeezed the trigger and the hammer started to draw back. Liberty smiled like an angel, and ripped a burst of three from the hip. The shell casings arched up past her pretty face, singing hollowly.

His frightened, unbelieving face grimaced as the three slugs obliterated it, with exquisite thudding splatters. He dropped the child as he arched back in visual echo of Liberty's brass, leaving his blood soaked fez tumbling toward us.

The girl landed on her feet and ran to Liberty, who picked her up gently and turned to camera before she spoke.

"I'm back," she said. "Don't you want a piece of me?"

The screen went black and a man with a deep voice spoke.

"This time she's playing for keeps. US Rearmament Bonds, they're not just a great investment, they're your duty."

Mort looked at Anna for a long few seconds before she took his eye.

"Nice campaign, honey. You must be very proud."

Anna shrugged. She was amoral about it.

"Thanks, we are happy with the numbers so far. I know that it's a pain for me to be gone so much, but I did bring home thirty grand on that spot. Worthy's got a few more in the pipeline, but they're not due to start for another couple of weeks, maybe we could take Louis out to Cape Cod for a few days."

"It doesn't bother you to be part and parcel of the lie?"

"Honey, I placed the air time. Don't blame the teller when the bank president refuses your loan. Besides, you don't think that anybody's going to actually buy this crap do you?"

"In Kansas..."

"In Kansas," she interrupted, "they get what they deserve when their babies come home in a body bag. On the coasts, where it matters, people are not going to believe a word of this bullshit, so we get a little rich, and maybe Louis gets to have a good education."

Mort nodded. "Yes, there is every good excuse in the world, and nothing is of any importance. It's all just a game. Right?"

"Well, now that you mention it, and you seem to go out of your way to mention it, yeah. It _is_ just a game. And it <u>doesn't</u> really matter whether we make the ads or somebody else does. And it <u>doesn't</u> really matter if the people out in the hinterland buy rearmament bonds instead of investing in farm equipment. And above all else it doesn't matter <u>at</u> <u>all</u> if you disapprove of me for placing the airtime for the campaign. People have the information to hand and the intellectual ability to decide for themselves whether they want to buy bombs or seed. It is not my deal to look out for their morals.

"And just while we are on the subject, let's not forget to mention the fact that each and every weapon in the arsenal, every commercial on TV, and every tax form processed depends on computer chips. How many did you sell last year? 14 some-odd million, or so? I think there is as much blood on your hand as there is on mine."

She stopped him there. After a moment, Mort shrugged. "Guilty."

"Well?"

"A'wright, a'wright already. I just hate the blatant manipulation in these ads, that's all. It's so creepy and insidious. 'Liberty's on her way back!' It's like living in Hitler happy land! It's like a Capra movie, or what was that show—Leave Me a Beaver? Something. I just want to mangle someone for it!

"I'm sorry. I'm sorry I brought it up."

Anna smiled.

"Don't worry about it. You're right too. Probably something stupider will happen next, and the lie will out no matter what, why we chose the name. Like maybe we can change that? I say we take the money and run."

"Where did you have in mind?" he asked jokingly.

"California."

"California?"

"California. I applied for the job at UCLA."

"Dude! Like totally! Ya! You know."

Mort jumped up and started surfing on the coffee table. From where she sat it looked to Anna like he was surfing on the nuclear submarine that was on the TV behind him. The table held for a few seconds till the glue joints popped. It skewed and sent him tumbling into the potted palm, where his head made a noise like 'Dink!' against the ceramic flowerpot. Anna laughed.

Mort didn't, he was unconscious.

The sub dove beneath the waves with a final spray from her tanks and was gone, leaving only the deep blue water with a trail of foam behind.

The foam dissipated and suddenly it was the sky we were looking at, high and cold, at the edge of space. The camera tilted down and revealed a distant, curving horizon, across it moved small specks that left behind them, sparkling exhaust trails. They were missiles, in-bound from China. Some were starting to break up, to 'MIRV'.

Now over camera shot an F 164, bristling armaments. The plane rolled once and we cut to the cockpit. There was radio chatter here and blinking lights and on the head up display there were multiple target reticles swimming over the scene. The pilot pushed some buttons in quick succession and the reticles locked on. His thumb depressed a big red button and he rolled away, into the roar of the rocket exhaust. There was a deadly pause and then his visor lit up with a blinding white flair as the warheads were taken out.

The white flair filled the screen, and resolved into a refrigerator door. Mom opened it and got out some milk for the kids. She was pretty and thin and perfect. The kids were perfect too. Tommy was square and good-naturedly mischievous, and Suzy, his little sister, was pink and round and petite. They were having cookies.

"Don't eat too much, kids," said Mom. "Your Dad will be

232

home soon for dinner."

She looked out the window into the night, lost in thought. There were flashes on the purple horizon. We pulled back from Mom, safe at home and the GD logo faded up.

A warm friendly woman's voice said, "General Dynamics. We keep America safe. To find out how to invest with us in America's future, ask your phone for GD stocks. You'll be glad you did."

Dwayne pushed the slogan back in his mind along with the rest of the chatter in the room. He found it hard to concentrate when there were people around talking and even more so when the TV was going. He was trying to write a speech and attend a cocktail party at the same time. The speech was about the advisors he was preparing to send at long last to help out Joshua. He wanted to make it clear how important it was that these troops be sent, how strategic Snellville's minerals were, and how all this fit into the greater plan of things. At the same time he wanted to win the American people back over to his side and have their support, even if he was already going to get their money. This was tough, as he was roundly hated both as a politician and a statesman.

The cocktail party was a necessary triviality. It was a reception for Baisch and his team, to thank them for doing such a great job of selling the American people on the idea that freedom was worth fighting for. This they had done very well indeed.

Defense stocks were up by a whopping 70% over a year earlier. Everybody was 'buying a piece of Liberty'. People were giving FMC stocks as birthday presents and there were contests to win a hundred shares of preferred Boeing and the like going at burger chains. Baisch had even gotten his ad man, 'Worthy' to come up with DTV, the war channel, and a defense stock lottery in twenty states! Now that was initiative. He wanted to throw this party for them, but he would rather have not attended.

Phrases kept passing through his mind for the speech, mixed with things that people were saying around him, and the clink of cocktail glasses. There was a woman laughing too loudly someplace.

"Clachink!...and so anyway this guy comes into Bob's office and he has this bright orange dildo stuck on his head. See? And...the necessary needs of the moment...Diz puts the Jazz in your Clothes...That our, That all our endeavors shall, should not go awry for the sake of short-sightedness. Astray?! Awry? Astray...tinkle, cla-clink...A ha ha ha ha," she laughed. "Drink,

Sir? Hey what's up with the snorkel? What about the Groucho nose?! A HA HA HA HA...Drink, Sir? We can not, must not allow this opportunity to slip through our fingers...Drink, Sir?"

He was brought back by a young man with a tray of drinks held in white-gloved hands. Dwayne looked at him for a long moment, trying to focus on what this person wanted.

"Would you like a drink, Mr. President?"

Dwayne looked down at his hand. There was an empty glass in it, with a stupid flamingo swizzle stick jutting out of it. He set it on the try and took another one.

"Thank you," said Dwayne automatically. He always said it. It was a reflex stored in his spine.

The young man smiled and gave a courteous but restrained little nod. Perfect. Dwayne took a drink, it was a scotch rocks, full of smoke and ether.

He thought about the crew out on Alpha 1. There had been reports of trouble, and a rather amusing video clip. They were starting to go a little mad out there, crawling through the endless night, and they still had another five and a half years to go before they would be able to get mud on their shoes, or feel the wind on their faces, and a thousand other things that he did every day. He savored his scotch.

There was a man standing with a woman across the room, they were talking together and looking around. They didn't fit here. As he watched, Baisch came over to them and spoke. Then he led them over.

"Mr. President, I'd like you to meet somebody. This is P. Worthington Yeates." They shook hands, and Swindel noticed that his grip was a little too tight, he was nervous.

"Oh yes, The Lie," said Swindel. "How do you do?"

"And this is Cassandra Robertson. Together they are responsible for our PR campaign. They are in large part what this party is all about."

"I'm very pleased to meet you both," said Swindel. "Your work has been a great help to us in our efforts to bring the voters around to see our point of view. I am glad to have this opportunity to thank you personally for your help."

Of course, two months earlier, Worthy and Cassandra had been the spear point of a campaign to hack Swindel at the knees and pin him to the ground for the pentagon, but now that things had changed, well, all was forgiven. They were on the same side now.

"Thank you, Sir," said Worthy. "I've had a lot of fun doing the job, and it's nice for a change not to have the financial constraints that usually hamper my creativity. We hope to continue to build on our success with The Lie."

Cassy smiled. "Look, sorry about the early stuff, we were just doing our job."

Worthy looked horrified. What was she saying?! That was a dead issue!

Swindel looked a little puzzled.

"You know, the baboons and all," she clarified.

Worthy wanted to shrivel up and die. Now that he was a millionaire he shouldn't have to put up with this kind of thing, especially from an employee. Baisch looked around paranoidly, trying to smile through the pain.

Swindel couldn't help noticing Yeates' embarrassment, and the way Cassandra was playing with her colleague's head.

He laughed outright. "Oh that, was that you?"

Cassy nodded and pointed at Worthy with her thumb. "In an earlier incarnation."

Swindel let him stew for a bit. The man looked almost psychotic with angst. "Tell me," he asked. "Why The Lie?"

"Uh, well, we are a PR and advertising firm," said Worthy. "It's what we do."

Baisch put in, "Kind of a little joke, Sir."

"Yes," said Cassandra smiling. "Like the ads we ran against your social program and dissolution of the Military—the ones with the dildos. Kind of a little joke, Sir."

Swindel frowned and Worthy visibly grimaced. He was about to pop. Then Swindel let him off easy.

"Yeah, I liked that one. Uncle Sam looked like a real sap, and the hyenas, man, they were soooo arch. No hard feelings of course. It's all part of the game here in Washington."

Worthy looked around him waiting for the other shoe to drop. It didn't.

After a long pause Baisch cleared his throat. "Ah, thank you, Mr. President, thank you very much." He turned to Worthy. "Tell me, have you met Senator Faircloth?"

"No, no I haven't."

"Ah well, step right this way and I'll introduce you. Excuse us please, Mr. President."

They started to move off into the crowd and Worthy pulled Cassy's sleeve to bring her along.

"I'll be along in a minute," she said.

Worthy looked worried as he receded. She winked at him.

"Thanks" she said. "He's starting to take himself a bit too seriously lately. I thought it would be fun to take him down a notch."

Swindel smiled. "Oh, happy to play along when I can. Those guys looked bad, real fear and loathing. I thought your buddy there was maybe going to check out on us. He looked like a blanched tomato."

They laughed.

"I think that it would take more than a little apoplexy to kill him, but maybe he will be slightly easier to live with for a while."

"Oh, by the way, I meant what I said about your work. I like it and I don't harbor any resentment about the earlier campaign. It really is par for the course around here."

"Thanks."

"Of course—I'll see that you never work again. You have paid your taxes haven't you?" He was po-faced.

It was like looking down the barrel of a pistol that is between your eyes. The blood pounded in Cassy's chest.

"What?!"

He waited a few fibrillating beats, and then said, "Got ya" and smiled.

Her face drained, she laughed nervously and said, "You have a very sick sense of humor."

"And you, Mam."

Worthy caught her eye from across the room. He motioned her over to him frantically.

"I think they want me," she said. "Excuse me please, Sir."

"See ya."

He liked that. It was fun to straighten people out, especially when they thought they were so clever. Usually people were too cowed by his office to engage him, but she had stepped right up and taken a swing. He had handed her, her ass, sure, but she did have pluck.

He made a mental note to have more punters to these affairs. He made a note also to have fewer and better parties. He made a note... His thoughts returned, and with them words.

"Certain fundamental truths that are immutable and accorded to every man, every_one_, are worth fighting for, and even worth dying for, if men, people, are to remain free. Cla-chink! Canopy? Oh, salmon! Dave, Dave come here for a moment, I want...It is to that end that this administration will commit itself, with your blessing. We will shed no blood that we don't...some guy with a meat axe! Hors d'oeuvre?"

It was like a vast inadvertent poem happening in and around his brain. It was a clanking, Frankenstein, brontosaurus of meaning wandering around the blue room. It was mad and beautiful. It was grotesque. It was..."Would you like an hors d'oeuvre, Mr. President? These are raw tuna and the square ones are truffle dumplings."

He took the sashimi. "Thank you."

He wondered where Michael was, he didn't see him at the moment, but he knew that he was circulating somewhere. The fish tasted good, rich and fatty, if a bit incongruous with the scotch.

The TV was chattering again, now about some news item. He would certainly be briefed on anything important and he tried to ignore it. He wondered why people always wanted to have the thing going, even in the middle of a cocktail party. It seemed like just plain bad manners to him.

Suddenly his mother was there in his mind, scolding him for some breach of manners. "Is that how you expect to function in the world?" she asked. "Well?" He couldn't for the life of him remember what she was mad about. "No Ann," he said silently.

"No?!!! What do you mean no?!"

"I don't know."

That was what stuck with him, his inability to determine what his demon wanted from him. It was like a frustration dream come true. And she had been true. She had been all too real in fact.

Ann filled his mind there in the White House, ranting and demanding and demeaning—savoring his inability to cope. She had been dead for 35 years and still he hated her as freshly as if she was in the next room, drinking alone.

The hate was like a wave washing over him. If he waited, it would pass, he knew. It always did and it never really quite did. There was always a tiny echo of it in everything he was.

He hated. He waited. She receded. He thought about his speech. She receded. He..."Milt, how are ya? Fine, fine. You know I was, Tingclink!!,...ing to Bob that we ought to get together." She was gone. "We have the opportunity to make the world a better, more fair place for all mankind. To insure that when petty evil little dictators take it into their heads to cause trouble for our allies, that there will be someone to answer to... I better take two. They're small. Here. Cleaner, brighter whites, even in cold water! Even blood!

"That's right even blood. New improved Omega powder gets

237

out really tough stains, even blood. That's why it is used by the US Marine Corps. When they get in a scrap, they need all the cleaning power they can get, so they call on the power of Omega powder." There was the sound of machine gun fire in the background and the whistle of incoming mortars. "Omega powder, wipes out stains."

Bill looked placidly at the screen. There was a time when he had openly enjoyed television, even the commercials. It had been a way of filling in the lonely spots between friends. But now that he was a television professional, and an ad man at that, Bill Crenshaw felt an obligation to himself and his colleagues, to stay hard and not like the stuff. He felt compelled to watch it still, but he took care to make it clear that he was not having a very good time doing it.

He stood there with a martini in one hand and cracker loaded with caviar in the other, watching, dead pan. He would occasionally furrow his brow just to let anyone who might see him know that this was not his idea of a good time. The soap jingle rattled on as he stood watching. He took a bite of the caviar and washed it down with the martini. "Dreck," he said.

The cocktail party flowed around him like a babbling sea. He too was experiencing the inadvertent poem of clinks and chitchat, but to him it was not a distraction from his train of thought but a generator of it. His mind wandered where the talk took it and he had no will at all to change the direction of it. It served to distract him.

He wanted to be distracted right then—to not be reminded of the sea change in the American will and his disastrous investments in the Maldives. And the worst part of it for him was that he was a part of the engine that drove it.

It was his smiling face and folksy way that had helped sell the idea that an army was a good and necessary thing to have around. He had gladly accepted the money and had put it into what seemed at the time like a great investment—a luxury hotel resort in the Indian Ocean—far from a troubled America, that was going down fast and would soon be bleeding millionaires like himself, eager to get away with their money intact. He had it all worked out, a tax haven hotel, with all the modern comforts and international banking facilities to boot. It was perfect!

Then those scheming politicians had reissued the dollar and his commercials had worked their magic, and the next thing he knew he was sitting on a half-paid-for white elephant in the middle of the, ever rising, Indian Ocean with not a customer in sight. He couldn't afford to quit then. When he thought about it, it made him sick and each day, the tide got a little higher. He looked at the TV. He listened to the poem. He drank his drink.

"...ever do that to me again! What? Omega po-u-wow-der. Yeah! ...esadent of the United States! Tinkle-e-dink Chill dude, it was just a...Margery Solomon how <u>have</u> you been?"

Trumpets blared as the NBC News logo rolled onto the screen. It was replace by anchorman Michael Salinger.

"Welcome back. Markets around the world were up today on heavy trading in New York, Berlin and Tokyo. Defense and industrials led the rally on Wall Street, and the average share price was up by over six dollars at the close. Today's big losers were leisure and travel stocks, as well as some mineral commodities for the third week running, on news of continued unrest in Eastern Sub-Saharan Africa and a new report on rising sea levels. The dollar was up against the euro to two dollar fifteen cents and down against the yen to twenty point four five. Last month the economy grew by a very healthy twenty percent according to the office of budget assessment."

Bill drained his glass and looked around for another. There was a tray passing and he set down his old one and grabbed the next in one smooth move. "Damn it!" he said.

Bill was right to be depressed, except for his Tokugowa stocks, his portfolio sucked. He was about the only one that was going broke from the economic boom. Most people had stock in defense systems and they were skyrocketing. Even people that had only a few dozen shares were seeing their stock split and big checks rolling in. It was great for the average guy. The Government was seeing to that, with huge injections of capital into the market and orders piling up day after day. That coupled with the hysteria they were trumping up was putting America to work and working people got paid and they spent their money on smart investments like defense stocks, that were subsidized by their Government. On and on it went. Up and up it went, in a delirious spiraling spending spree. America was arming herself to the teeth, and getting rich doing it.

The Europeans were buying, and the Japanese were buying too. It was great if you weren't Bill Crenshaw, the defeatist peacenik sap. Or, for that matter, someone trying to prosecute your own agenda in the world. Like, Pan-Arab Nationalism for instance. If your name happened to be Captain Mingetsu McDermott it wasn't great at all, in fact it was a pants filling, night sweating, balls up of unprecedented proportions.

239

The US was getting ready for war, but there was no one to declare it on. McDermott didn't give a tinker's damn about the States. He was in no position to challenge them on any single issue. He just wanted to be rid of a minor annoyance, Joshua Kabingga.

The US had no reason to turn on him, he had already met with the State Department officials and they had agreed that there would be no slowdown in the flow of minerals after he came to power. They had assured him that he was safe…

He felt like Damocles.

He was not alone. All over the world, in Asia, and South America, and other parts of Africa, there were people in positions that they had done all manner of despicable things to get and keep that felt the same. They had worked under a set of assumptions that had lasted for decades, and then was pulled out from under them in a little less than two months. They were the people in power and no one was more surprised than them. Frightened people do stupid things—they were terrified.

"Okay, just what exactly is your problem?" she asked him, out on the balcony.

Worthy shook his head in disbelief. How could she be so stupid?

"Look!" he said, "I know that you think that this is all just some kind of a game. That it doesn't really matter very much if you say things to embarrass people at a party, just for laughs. Hey, it's all just good fun. Right?"

"Exactly."

"No not exactly! Not at all! These are important people here tonight. What they think matters. Why can't you see that?"

"Listen to yourself," she said, sneering. "Do you know what you sound like? Do you? You sound like one of them. You sound like one of those soulless, gutless, nothings that are in there, sucking butt and drinking champagne. You sound like a fuck.

"This is not the Worthy I know. This is not the Worthy that did the bull spew radio campaign, or the lucky dog beer commercials, or even, so it seems, the Uncle Sam rearmament ads. This sounds like some dickless bureaucrat making apologies! 'Excuse me please, sorry. I have no dick. I beg your pardon.'

"I think you better strap a cucumber to your leg there, boy."

Now Worthy turned big and patronizing.

"Oh, figure it out, Cassandra. There is a lot at stake here, more than you can know. It is quite simply, a matter of

240

inappropriate behavior, plain and simple. Oh sure, you're right about me not being the same guy that did those early campaigns. You have, I trust, heard of the concept anyway, of growth. Well I have grown up a bit, that's all. Maybe you should take a page from my book. Then perhaps you could gain the perspective to see what's at risk here."

Cassy smiled. "Ah ha. That's what I thought it was—money. You have discovered money, and it has taken you by the nads and given you a good shake. Now you have 'grown up and taken an adult perspective'. Now you realize just what is at stake. Well I hope your money is a great comfort to you, it must be hard to live with no guts.

"They have beaten you with a bit of cash, some paper and some privileges, and up you go in smoke, like a pile of fermenting dung. You advertise Snakos!

"They are made out of pooh!" She was yelling now.

"Cassy, I would remind you that we are both now millionaires, whereas a year ago we weren't. We were nobody. Doesn't that count for anything with you. Maybe not. Maybe you would like to give your dough to charity. Hmm? No? What was that about guts?"

"Man, you figure it out!"

Cassy's smirk was almost outright laughter.

"It's not like they can take your precious money back off of you once they've paid the invoice. And you only made that money because you once had the gumption to stand up and take a chance. That's what it's all about—the risk. That's what makes it exiting. That's what makes it different than working in a bank.

"So you can get some more money, why bother to bend over for that? What's it going to get you? You think money's going to buy you happiness? It won't. It can't."

"That's were you are wrong, Honey," he said. Money can buy you happiness! Sure as shit. It's just really expensive, that's all."

-<>-

"What's my problem? What's my problem!? You got some fuckin' set on you, man!

"I'm going out of my fucking skull out here, 'cause I should be asleep now! At least I have the balls to whoop and holler about it! You're the guy with the stick up his ass, Tomlinson!"

"Yes. Can't be helped I'm afraid, you do whoop and holler a lot, you have me there————and blow yourself. That some sort of an elaborate practical joke or something, or is it a congenital thing that runs in the Snortom family?"

241

"It's something to do! You're just jealous 'cause you're not limber enough."

Tomlinson didn't even dignify this last with an answer. He checked his indicators one last time.

"Let's do this."

Knute turned his key. "Ready when you are."

"You know, just because I manage to maintain my discipline out here doesn't mean that I have a 'stick up my ass'."

Dave turned his key and started counting.

"Actually, you do."

As the bomb went and they were thrown back in their chairs, ringing, Knute said, "You know man, now you got me curious! I wonder if Grand Dad could blow himself!"

He sent an Email back about it later.

-<>-

"The purpose of advertising," said Mort impatiently, "is to let the world know, in a lively and informative manner, about your product or service, period."

Worthy smirked a patronizing little smirk and said this,

"That's what I thought. You see my friend, that's where you have it all so terribly wrong.

"It is the function of your product or service to have an artifact that the general public can actually hold in their hand after you have taken their money off of them. It's sort of like a consolation prize. It is the function of the public to generate real wealth, and be lied to and swindled, product and advertising are two sides of the same thing, a means to do that.

-<>-

What you see, if you look at the actual video tape that was broadcast, can you believe it, as I have, is a rather dark, out of focus picture of some soldiers sitting around a camp fire, someplace in the jungle. They are laughing and talking and eating a meal. It is really pretty hard to make out what is what at first, but this much is true, they are speaking Cantonese.

Then the camera moves in a little closer, and one guy has this bright red shoulder flash in the shape of a fat star, with a tiger. The 7th had just such a flash. The guy is eating a little arm. You can see for about 20 frames when he turns into the light, that there is a little hand on the end of it.

It could be chimp arm. I'm certainly no expert in these thing, but that's what I see, an arm. Some people say that there is a ring on one of the fingers, but I never saw that. I stopped watching pretty quickly.

-<>-

Faizel took his change and the burger and pulled away from the window. It wasn't halal, and he knew it, but what the hell. He pulled out into traffic.

The street was busy and he had to take a good deal of care negotiating the van through the traffic. There was a red light. He stopped. Faizel had a bite of the burger. He chewed, thinking about Egypt, in a dull sort of way. Sometimes he missed Egypt, sometimes. Sometimes he smelled a spicy smell and he remembered the bazaar, then he wondered what the hell he was doing, driving around the United States with an H-bomb. Sometimes in the summer, like today, it got up to 41˚C in the shade and then he remembered that that was a rather cool morning in Egypt and he smiled, knowing that he was not going to have to smell camel dung, rotting in the sun.

The light changed and he pulled away, down the ramp and on to I 10. The van bucked along over the concrete panel roadway with a steady rhythm. He checked his mirror to change lanes. There was a cop behind him. Faizel took another bite of his burger and made the lane change as smoothly as he could, watching the cop.

He could feel his heart start to pound and he wondered what would happen next.

Nothing. The cop stayed where he was and Faizel accelerated down the highway. He kept an eye on him in his mirror till he was far, far away down the road. Then he was okay again. Then he was lost in America.

Welcome to Snellville

The Umbutu River meandered through the lowland forests, taking its time to get to Lake Tanganyika. It was always a bit murky down in this part, particularly in the rainy season, when the silt washed down from the mountains above. The hippos didn't mind too much, the water was warm and there were plenty of waterweeds to eat, and besides, it was all part of the great cycle, it would pass in a few months.

But this year it didn't. This year there were men getting up to mischief in the mountains above them, and the water didn't clear at all. It was as thick as oil with light brown mud. The mud blocked the light, and so the waterweeds didn't grow, and fish died by the thousands.

Gustave's children, the crocodiles, that liked to eat the fish had to come to the edge of the bank that year, a lot more than they usually did, so that they could get wildebeests and children for their meals. This was not good. This made people come there with riffles to shoot the crocodiles for eating their babies, which was quite ridiculous of course.

-<>-

There was blackness, and there was pain. There was not much else, except thirst perhaps, but that too had become pain sometime long ago. He tried to stand, PAIN!!!!!!....

He awoke again. There was blackness and pain. He realized that he was completely alone, they <u>had</u> told him so. He didn't want to stand. His arms ached, and at the same time he couldn't feel his hands. He thought about his wife, Cindy—wondered where she was, if she was all right.

He tried to move his painful arms. This made them hurt a lot more, and he cried out a little, there in the dark. Others answered him. They too were hurting. They too were alone—and in the dark.

They were trussed up like meat monkeys, by the arms behind their backs, with their elbows tied together and then to a post. All their legs were broken. They could neither stand up nor sit down, but just hung there suffering. That was what was wanted of them—that they should hurt, and regret, and betray their friends.

Some had done this. Their legs were no less broken and their bonds no less tight. Others of them had not and they were no better or worse off for their courage. In the end it was a push, whether you talked was quite irrelevant to the people that did the leg breaking, they were just in it for the fun and the money, regardless of what you or they said.

They had broken his legs by putting them under the forks of a loading truck out at Snellville-Burundi International Airport and then put a floor jack under his calves and started asking him questions. Every time he gave them an answer they didn't like very much, they would pump the jack a little bit. It took a long time to break his legs that way. When they did finally go they made a sound like snapping an axe handle, like a pop and a crunch all at the same time.

His name was Forthright Kilawasi.

They had come for him, at work, where he was one of Snellville's third assistant secretaries to the Interior Ministry, so he was wearing a tie and a suit. The pant legs of his suit were stiff and stuck to his broken legs with his blood.

Forthright had not told the men that broke his legs what they wanted to know. He was ignorant of that information. In fact, he was the next best thing to innocent. He was only on the take to let a friend of his, a local business man, slip across the frontier at night and trade cigarettes for hashish, penicillin for whisky, gasoline for tennis shoes. As far as he was aware, none of this had altered the balance in a single firefight, and Forthright was in no way the traitor they said he was. He was just getting by, like everybody else.

The guys with the jack just smiled when he wouldn't give up his friend to them. It meant that they could pump the jack some more. They had bad teeth.

He raised his head a little, and looked around him. At first he thought that it was pitch black, but as he strained to see, he started to discern faint detail in the blackness. There were slightly less black masses around him. They were lumpy and upright, a few were moving a little. He realized that they were the other people he had heard in the dark.

"I am Forthright Kilawasi," he said.

There was no answer for a long time, as if the others couldn't hear him, or they didn't care at all who he was, then far away and very faintly he heard someone say, "You won't be tomorrow."

He thought about that, what the other person meant by it. He wasn't sure. He shut his eyes.

A long time later he awoke again, and now it was much lighter. The sunrise was painting the horizon baby blue and fuchsia. There were birds singing somewhere.

He looked around him now and he could see the others tied to their posts like meat monkeys, like him. Some were dead already, they hung very still, while others, he could see, labored hard just to breath. There were others there now too, moving among the meat. He couldn't see them but he could hear them behind him walking, and talking matter-of-factly together.

After a while there was a bit of commotion and they dragged one of his fellow monkeys past him, post and all and disappeared around the side of a hangar. There was a gunshot and then all was quiet again.

The meat monkeys hung there, and the sun climbed in the sky, making it very bright and tropical. It would have been a lovely spot to be on vacation, with lounge chairs arrayed around a swimming pool, and huge boat drinks sprouting archipelagoes of chopped fruit and little umbrellas so the ice didn't melt too fast.

Forthright thought about the pool, imagining it in every minutest detail. He felt the cool water against his skin and heard it lapping gently against the side. In his mind's eye the water was deep turquoise, and the stones at the pool's edge were white and smooth.

He was floating in the pool and he had a boat drink in his hand. He could feel the cold glass chilling his fingers and he could smell the luscious fruit sticking out of it. There was orange and mango and papaya, and just a hint of mint. Just a hint, mind you, to keep it all fresh, without overpowering it.

He looked up and there was Cindy swimming towards him, smiling her bedroom smile for him. Her eyes twinkled. He got a boner.

"Wake up you fucking pervert!" she shouted in a man's voice.

He was slapped awake.

There were three men standing there in front of him. Two he recognized as General Kabingga and his chief of security David Watson. The other one was a white man that he didn't know.

"What kind of a man has an erection at a time like this?" demanded Watson. His blue-black face was only inches from his. Forthright could smell the man's breakfast on his breath, eggs, sausage and coffee.

"Well?"

"I am Forthright Kilawasi," he croaked, "and I am an innocent man."

Kabingga nodded his head and then addressed the monkeys

en mass.

"Now hear this," he said, "we have just found out something very important from this man, this, Forthright Kilawasi, and that is this—an innocent man has an erection when he is trussed up like a monkey and tortured for treason, so if any of you can't manage a full and glorious tumescence when we come around to you, we will take that as an admission of your guilt! That is all."

The man next to Forthright managed to laugh a little at this bizarre joke. Kabingga stepped over to him and looked at the man.

"So," he said, leaning on the handle of the sledgehammer he had with him, "you find my words amusing, do you? Hm. I notice that you are flaccid at the moment my friend. Hm. Yes?"

He paused.

"I'm afraid I am going to have to make an example of you. Have a nice day."

With that he hefted the sledgehammer up into the air and swung it down in a smooth, practiced arc into the man's cranium with a squishy sounding crunch.

Blood sprayed out around the hammer's head where it imbedded in his dying brain. He twitched and danced for a few jabbering seconds, spattering Forthright and the others with gore.

He got a boner as dying men sometimes do.

At the end, when he hung limply from his post, Kabingga pulled his hammer out of the man's head. He looked at his fading erection and said, "Too late my friend, I'm afraid. Far too late."

He now turned his attention back to Forthright.

"Now then," he said, "we have a few questions that we would like answered. And I point out to you here, that it is your duty as a citizen of Snellville to answer them in a serious and timely manner.

"It's also a pretty good idea.

"First of all I would like to know if you have any information on the whereabouts of Mingetsu McDermott. Personally I mean. Where he sleeps at night and so on. What his likes and dislikes are. Does he have a dog?

"I hope for your sake, Mr. Kilawasi, that you do. I would hate to have to kill you in front of your wife."

"Cindy! Where is she?" he asked, looking out from behind his askew blindfold. "Is she alright?"

Kabingga let him stew for a bit.

"Is she alright!?"

"No," said Kabingga jovially. "I would say not. She is, after all, right behind you."

"Cindy?! Cindy?!"

Kabingga smiled at Kilawasi. "She can not answer you at the moment, she has a cane rat stuffed in her mouth.

"Come now, Kilawasi, let's not dawdle out here in the hot sun, I am beginning to perspire. Tell me or she will be next."

"But I don't know where McDermott is! I swear to you that that is the truth! All I did was take a little hand money to let a man trade a few non-essential goods across the frontier. Please don't hurt her. She is not involved in this at all. She is only my wife. I'm sorry I don't know…"

"I am sorry too," said Kabingga, "but someone here will talk. They always do."

He stepped back, spreading his legs shoulder width apart for a better purchase and then lifted his hammer again.

"Oh by the way," he said, "your wife is…"

He brought down the hammer.

Kabingga, Day and Watson moved on to the next guy after a few moments.

"You know," said Day. "Maybe we better get some Tyvek suits for this shit."

"Yes," agreed Kabingga, "and a bucket of warm soapy water. Will you see to it Dave?"

"I'll be back before you finish the next one," he said.

They went on like this all day, questioning and killing people in their Tyvek®[58] suites. It was a fairly effective way of obtaining information, most people that knew something talked, but it got to be pretty hard graft after a while, even for Joshua Kabingga, who was a big man.

At one point he offered Day a turn, but the State Department man declined.

"No, it's not really my style."

He looked around him. "I prefer the helicopter method.[59]"

---

[58] Tyvek® suites are the untearable white paper protective clothing worn for doing terrible things like entering the Chernobyl sarcophagus and cleaning up toxic waste dumps and bludgeoning people to death with sledge hammers and the like. Tyvek® is a trademark of the DuPont Corporation.

[59] The Helicopter method, first made popular in Viet Nam was similar, except that instead of bludgeoning your subjects to death, you took them up to 1000 meters in a Bell UH 135, (Huey) and threw the first one out the door. Then you asked the second

They all agreed, there under the hot African sun, in their gory white paper suites, that that way was much less messy, but in a pinch like this one, needs must.

At last they had interrogated everyone there and the only ones left alive were those who had talked. Kabingga had them thrown into a pile along with the dead, soaked, screaming, in gasoline and burned. They were traitors as well as snitches after all, and nobody likes a snitch.

This sort of thing was starting to happen quite often, there In Snellville the Lesser and Greater Burundi as his administration fell apart. Kabingga felt compelled to respond to treason harshly, and the information they gathered was vital if they were to defend themselves against the onslaught from without. It took his valuable time and he knew that he really should delegate such tasks, but he was a meticulous man and couldn't stand to see a job done badly. Also there was this. He liked it.

There was something very satisfying about looking into the eyes of someone that was against you, and everybody in the entire world was either for or against you as far as he was concerned, just before you killed them. It was just and ironic and sexual. It was total power. After a while he had somebody screw a whoopee whistle to the handle of his sledgehammer so that they could hear it coming. It sounded like this, "WHOOPEEE!!!"

Very festive.

A deal had been done and the cavalry was on the way, but he had to hold out for another few weeks. In that time, Day had asked him to get as much information as he could about McDermott and his IFI army. They needed a base line from which to anchor their satellite surveillance, as well as the establishment of links with sympathetic types within IFI. If they could do that, Day had said, they would be able to turn back IFI in a few relatively bloodless weeks.

Day was lying of course, but that's diplomacy for you.

And so it went. They got what information they could, and they eliminated many of their own weak spots in the process. It was difficult there for a while, what with the press and everything, but it was worth the effort. It was all going to be okay.

One morning Joshua stepped outside to pick up the paper. He looked toward Snellville Burundi International and there, arcing in out of the African sky, was a line of transports that

---

one a question, and so on. Remember, this was done by people a lot like you and me.

stretched into the infinite distance. They were coming in on each other's tails so thick that the ground crews could barely park them. The airport was in thinly controlled chaos, and there were parachutes blossoming like gray green daisies in the sky above him. He went inside and had his breakfast. He was ravenous.

There was a phone call for him a little later. He picked it up.

"Hello? Kabingga residence."

It was Swindel. "Hello, Joshua," he said. "How's the view this morning?"

"Dwayne, hello. It is beautiful. Thank you very much, my friend. When are you two coming back for a visit? There are chairs at our table for you."

"Soon, I hope, Joshua, very soon. And, don't thank me yet. This is just the beginning. In a year, no one will remember who Mingetsu McDermott was, or why he had such a huge bug up his ass in the first place. It's early days yet, Josh.

"Thank me————thank me in a year, when we start building Alpha 2, when there is a launch facility out at the air port and your place has a beach."

"A beach."

"You bet."

There was a pause.

"Tell me, Dwayne, am I moving the capitol or are you planning something unspeakable in Tanzania?"

"Neither, but I think you may want to look at expanding your border eastward as far as the Indian Ocean. Uh, should the opportunity arise, that is."

"Oh, I see," said Kabingga. "More help, even than we asked for."

"You bet."

"You bet," echoed Joshua.

After he hung up, Joshua had a full glass of whisky. He was just finishing it, in a long gulp, when there was a knock at the door. He went and opened it. There was an American soldier standing there, with a machine gun slung over her shoulder.

"Good morning, Sir," she said, saluting. "My name is Major Mortenson. I bring greetings from the president of the United States of America."

Joshua looked at her for a long time, thinking about the nature of Satan. It was like looking into the eyes of your enemy that was about to kill you. Then he said this, "Come in please, won't you. Welcome to Snellville."

Business As Usual

It was in the middle of prime time, on The Futterman Show, a talk show out of LA that Bill chose to make his ill-considered stand. This was something that the corporate bloc simply could not afford to overlook, people were watching.

The show was hosted by Francene Futterman, 'The Darling of Hollywood's Most Important People'. Bill was on there with other Celebs who had had a recent turn of bad luck. The show header for that night was 'Celebrities Who Pay For Their Principles'.

He was joined by several others, an actress who had resisted doing an enema scene, a couple of producers who had been blackballed for refusing to have car chases, Snakos bags and other product placement in their films, and, Bill was quite surprised to see, Harvey Washington Jr.

The Reverend Washington was up before him and he gassed on at length about how he had been singled out for auditing by the Internal Revenue Service because he was of African descent. It was common knowledge at the time that the IRS had no racial agenda at all. They were pragmatists, like Swindel and Kabingga. They would do anything to anyone to get what they wanted, which was, of course, the dough.

Francene Futterman teased him out as he went, giving him the perfect platform to rant from, and still he managed to fuck it up.

"So, tell us, Reverend Washington, how are things looking for your South Central Up and America Up projects while you are under the scrutiny of the IRS?"

"Well actually, Francene, they are doing quite well, in spite of this heinous injustice. Our numbers are looking quite good, especially in the white suburbs, where our fund raising efforts have almost doubled their return in the last quarter."

Francene smiled. "Wow, that's great! To what do you attribute this great success, Reverend Washington?"

Harvey grinned a big self-satisfied grin.

"Ah, I'm glad you asked that, Francene. These successes are due a great deal to my new incentive and accommodation programs that I have introduced over the last few months.

"Our marketing studies turned up a couple of interesting ideas that we have been capitalizing on lately. The first was, we found that volunteers, no matter how zealous they might be, are no match for commissioned salesmen as fund raisers. We decided that a 75% commission system would actually result in a higher return to our organization in the long run.

"The second thing we found out was that white people, even those with a high guilt quotient, were a lot more comfortable talking to other white people, and or people in uniform than they were with talking to people of African heritage, so we did that too."

Futterman looked a bit lost, as did everyone else there.

The actress cocked her head. "What?"

Washington looked at her suspiciously.

"We used white people in uniforms."

Francene nodded slowly.

"You used white people in uniforms to do fund raising?"

"That's right," said Harvey. "We tapped into an existing resource base of uniformed fund raisers and we let them keep 75 cents on the dollar."

"Who?" asked Bill.

"The Girl Scouts."

"Aren't there girl scouts of color?" asked Francene.

"Yes, but we don't use 'em!"

There was a long pause while everybody couldn't think of what to say.

"Uh, We'll be right back after this" said Francene, finally.

They went to the commercials and when they came back it was Bill's turn.

"So, Bill," she said. "What's new with you? The reissue of the dollar I guess annoyed you a bit."

Bill shook his head frowning sourly.

"You know, Francene, it's the damnedest thing I ever saw. A bunch bureaucrats in Washington can just do whatever their bosses tell them to do and we just have to take it, whether we like it or not.

"I thought all my life that this was a democracy, that we had a few rights around here, like free speech and no unlawful search and seizure, but that's not the case, I guess.

"It looks like the corporations are the real bosses here, and the average guy is just supposed to shut up and pay the bills.

"Capitalism, phooey! That's what I say! Phooey on the corporations. I think the average American is working 24 hours a day for some boss that he doesn't even know, and that they all have the power to stop it if they want to!"

Francene smiled at this.

"But surely, Bill, you can't mean that capitalism is at fault. It is the corporations that pay <u>your</u> salary too. And I'd guess that you make more than the average guy."

"Oh you're right there!" said Bill. "They do pay a hell of a lot for my endorsements.

"Don't you see? That's what's so sinister about it all. I am a populist icon. That's what they pay me for, to be the face of Joe average, the guy you can trust, the guy who won't lie to you. But I do! I guess I always have!

"The People that pay me to say that their cause is just or their food is yummy or their computer is amazing, they know that I don't know what the hell I'm talking about any more than the next guy. They know that I am a fraud, and they love that! They love that I can be bought for some money. It proves their point. If I can be bought, then anybody can! You can, Francene! You were, the same as any other talking head!!"

"Hey now hold on a minute, Bill! I believe in the products I endorse, or I wouldn't endorse them. You may have no integrity, but I do!"

"Sure! Make it good, sister! We all believe you! In a fucking pig's eye!!! You're as bad as me any day, you must be. You have your own show!"

He stood up and turned to the camera, addressing it directly.

"I say that it has to stop here and now! I'm through!

"You out there in TV land, you have the power to stop the corporate colossus! You can shut off the valve, right here and right now, and it's so easy, you couldn't imagine it.

"Just do nothing, that's all.

"Don't go to work, any of you. Just stay home and don't go to work, that's all you have to do! The machine will grind to a halt in a few days and that will be that! They can't do it without your labor. You can take the power back in just a few days if you have the will to do so!

Do it now!!

They cut the feed, but it was too late.

This went out live to half a billion people, and it raised the hair on the back of the necks of about fifty of them.

That was that. Those fifty people were the wrong people to piss off, and they were, damned sure the wrong people to scare.

-<>-

253

The Government of Greater Burundi invites all tenders for the provision of up to 20 helicopters, preferably Bell UH135 or similar...

The Economist, August 30, 2050

-<>-

Mr. Green passed through customs at Santiago airport with very little trouble. Of course, the purposefully badly faked Israeli and Chinese exit stamps were noted as well as the blatantly bogus Mongolian visa at the back, so the police put a tail on him, exactly as scripted. Green went about his openly covert business in the usual circumspect manner, taking great care to ask awkward questions of the wrong people and letting slip a phrase here and a name there. It was all according to plan and worked its magic much as it always did.

The taxi took him to the wrong side of town where he sat in a cafe' that was known by the authorities to be a hot bed of anti-Government activity. There he glanced around over his menu making spy signs and offering passwords to the waiters and other patrons. The police watched and waited and made notes of all this overt balderdash. They weren't particularly stupid policemen, as policemen go and if it had been their job to analyze whether this guy was really a spy or not, they would probably have had grave doubts about whether such a fucked up asshole could possibly live for more than a few minutes were he genuine. But that is not the way it works.

They were there just to observe and report back, and this they did. So when they made their superiors aware of his movements and actions they told a rather straight version of events. What were they supposed to do, say down their radio that there was this cardboard cut out of a spy, spying all over the place like a total spy and everything? They would have been assigned to garbage detail for making fun.

Their superiors, men of infinite self esteem, who had their jobs for mostly familial reasons, analyzed the data and came to the required conclusion—that this guy was here on 'business' from China—and it would serve them best, to let him make contact with his masters' proxies, the Shining Path before they whacked him. They told their operatives to keep an eye on him. So they did.

While Mr. Green was going about his business as usual, the other spooks, the real live honest to God scary people with cool obscure weapons and perfect Spanish blended in with the general Chilean populace and went to work. They did all manner of things, like renting rooms and engaging people in pleasant conversations in which they chatted about all sorts of interesting subjects. They gave money to some people and presents to others. Some people they met, they gave information to and gadgets to get more information off of the encrypted defense satellites of more than one country. Others they met were later found in back alleys with their faces blown off and their wallets gone. They, it seemed, were the victims of ordinary crime.

None of this was personal in any way. They just did it—killed people and helped them and were charming and deadly and evil and were cash customers to some, as a matter of course. It was business, and these were the tools—people. Some of the tools were sharp and useful, so they could be employed as they were. Others were useful in their absence. They were in the way, or knew something or someone, and they were set aside. To the people that did it, one action was no different than another.

Some of the people that they helped and bribed and gave information to were in the Chilean Government and then again some of them were members of the Shining Path. Some were even both, and some were apparently nothing at all to anybody. Likewise, so were some of the faceless destitute corpses that were dragged from back streets in plastic body bags. They too were a mixture of Government people and anti-Government people, and people of obvious significance and ignominious human beings that seemed useless to all but their fleas.

After about a week the "situation" in Chile was subtly different than it had been before. If you were a regular Joe you didn't even notice.

Even for many in the Chilean Government, things were normal. There was this weirdo from China acting like some kind of 'B' movie bad guy, but that was not a worry. He was known about and was being followed everywhere he went. If and when he tried to cause trouble he would be dealt with in the usual harsh manner. In the mean time, he was revealing interesting things to the authorities. All was as well as could be expected, really.

Then one day there was an article in Los Tiempos Del Santiago a local paper. It was not a very scathing piece as Chilean social criticism goes. It was a human interest story on Juan Sabastian Espanosa, and all it really said was that the Shining Path, whose leader in internal exile he was, had turned the corner from the purely terrorist bastards that they had pretty much always been, to a new way—that of the legitimate opposition in official absentia. It said that though they were still an outlawed organization, they had a mandate, however tentative from the agrarian peasantry.

Where it really dropped the Government's pants was where it dared to say that the interior minister should maybe open a dialog with Espanosa, just to see if they could agree on a ceasefire for Christmas. Man, did that blow fuses. It was one thing to say that the Shining Path had a point, that was opinion and could be ignored, but it was quite another to suggest that the Government should change its policy as regarded dialog. That was a call to action by Domingues' rivals within his own party, his brother the interior minster among them, to actually do something concrete about the situation. This would cause everyone in the country to notice that for the past seven years President Domingues had done nothing but suck up foreign aid and shunt it into his Swiss bank account, while there had been a ready solution staring him in the face the whole time. They would say, "Wow, you know you're right, the Emperor is balls naked! Hey, I know, let's hang him and vote for somebody else." This was Domingues' fear.

The journalist disappeared. So did his wife. So did the editor. Domingues had little to do with this, officially, but he knew how it would look, fortunately it was just a local incident, and it would blow over soon enough.

Then the US State Department called up, wanting to know what the hell was going on down there. Just what did Domingues think he was doing bumping off popular newspaper people? These were human beings! There was going to be outrage in Washington if and when they took notice. His friends could stave that off for a little while, but he better get his house in order and find a scapegoat fast, yada, yada, yada... Domingues denied any knowledge of the incident, but was not believed, unofficially.

Domingues paled at the thought of losing out on the money river, and at the suggestion of 'friends', decided to get the jump on his rivals and open a dialog himself. He called for a meeting in the center of Santiago at Plaza Simon Bolivar. This was a neutral ground of sorts. They would be out in the open where people could see them. Their supporters could all be there and witness their peaceful meeting. Espanoza, on the urging of 'friends', agreed. They would meet at Plaza Simon Bolivar.

Mr. Green had a room overlooking Plaza Simon Bolivar.

The police were aware of this and they duly reported it to internal security, where the information was channeled through someone who had just become much more wealthy through his

256

friendship with some of the scary people. They suggested that he forget about it, and gave him some more money. They also showed him two pictures. One of the pictures was of a faceless destitute corpse that he had known vaguely in life, there was smoke trailing away from where the face should have been. The other was of his wife and children in the park, playing. His new friends were not playing.

He forgot about it.

The days passed and Mr. Green spied around a bit. He talked furtively with students and social workers and nuns and labor organizers, a whole host of people, and they all went back to where they were supposed to and talked to whom they were supposed to under the watchful eyes of the ever more alarmed police.

The timed-release anodene-sulfoxilase capsule that was embedded under his skin was nearly gone now. It had done its job well and kept him functioning for a long time, but now that it was almost used up, his memory was beginning to falter again. Not in the big way it usually did, but in little peripheral ways. There were times when he had to refer to his notes about things that he felt he should know. This worried him and made him, if anything, even more paranoid than he usually was.

"Would you like more coffee, Sir?" asked the waiter.

Mr. Green looked up at him over his morning paper.

"Why?"

"Because, your cup is empty, Sir."

The waiter pointed at the empty cup.

They were used to him there at the Metropol. Like most waiters at top quality hotels, the staff at the Metropol was not very surprised by the eccentric behavior of any of their guests. That was just the way rich people were, odd. They got drunk and brought home goats as mistresses, and had the blood and scalp fragments hosed off the front of their Ferraris. So what? No eye is ever quite so blind as one that has been heavily tipped.

Green looked at his cup, trying to remember if he had drank it. He looked around him quickly, trying to catch people out.

"Okay, and this time see that you fill it, this time with shiny coffee."

"Yes, Sir."

He poured the coffee and went back to his station. The policeman put down the coffee pot and made a signal to his team mate the same as he did every morning.

Mr. Green finished his paper and his coffee and went back to his apartment. It was a lovely, clear day. The air smelled fresh and moist as he looked out his window into the plaza. It was a very pretty view. There were people down there setting up the stand and connecting power cables for the news people. This was to be an historic occasion, the meeting of the two sides in a struggle that had been going non-stop for over 80 years.

Green checked his watch—it was ten o'clock. He checked his notes. The meeting was at eleven o'clock. He had a little time yet, and he used it to observe the security procedures for the meeting. He pulled the scope out of its case and turned it on. It hummed for a moment and then the red light went out indicating that it was booted up and ready to go. He looked through it at the rooftops surrounding the plaza. He could only see three men up there, but he knew that there must certainly be more, they couldn't possibly be that naive. Next he looked at the floor of the plaza itself. There were the expected police units, set up at all the entrances, and several roving sentries spotting the workers. They would be involved with crowd control in case of trouble. Then he noticed something else.

There was a group of men on the band stand itself that were searching for something, a bomb perhaps, or maybe some other sort of mischief. He counted only fifty people in all. This was a handful compared to the importance of the guests, and he wondered why they were being so lax about the whole thing.

This was precisely what was going on in the mind of Domingues' security chief, Franz Estoban. He phoned repeatedly to the Interior Ministry asking what the hell they thought they were doing putting the president in such danger and was finally rebuffed by the minister himself. He was told that all was well in hand and that special arrangements had been made for the president's security—that even he, the security chief, was not highly cleared enough to be made privy to—and that if he wanted to keep his job he would just shut up and do his job, the usual shit.

He hung up the phone and instructed his snipers, Hallstead and McNeill on the roofs above the plaza to pay special attention to the Metropol, which was an ideally situated perch as well as where that jackass Green was staying.

Mr. Green shut off the scope and put it back in the case for the moment while he made all else ready. First he said "Screens on and lock."

This made the LCD screens that he had put in front of the windows snap on with an image of his empty room. It got a little darker. From a distance they were quite convincing and utterly opaque.

He pulled out the two tubular legs of his portable shirt rack that had matching screw threads cut into them. He screwed them together, and gently nestled them into their slot in the bottom of his electric razor. There was a minute click. Next he opened his suitcase and took out the two heavy, ornately worked bowling trophies he had brought with him. They too had round nestles cut into them that fit exactly against the screwed together tubes. Finally he locked the scope to the top of the whole affair with a twisting motion. He was ready.

Mr. Green checked his notes, as the square started to fill below. He was in place. It was nearly time and the target would arrive soon. He had his screens on. He had his escape planned and ready. He did not have the system powered up. Green reached down and switched on the gun. It chirped once and then was silent. He checked his watch and looked out the window through the scope, resting the muzzle on the windowsill.

There were people gathering now on the bandstand. They were sitting down in the ranks of chairs reserved for them and chatting. The two principals weren't there yet, but there was still a little time. He looked around at the crowd in the square. There were a couple of his people down there he knew, but he couldn't spot them, they were perfect.

There was a low chesty thumping sound that grew out of the distance. At first it was not much, but it built and he began to hear rather than feel it. That would be Domingues. He would arrive first.

Suddenly, over the top of his hotel the president's helicopter arched out over the square and then dove down steeply to land in the center. The notar wash sent papers swirling about as the pilot set down lightly to deposit Domingues. No sooner was the president clear than the chopper was up and away again. It came back over him. As it did, he could have sworn that the pilot looked straight at him, then it was gone.

Security moved the president up onto the bandstand to await Espinosa. It wasn't long. Almost as Domingues reached the top step another helicopter could be heard approaching. It was not the sleek new Sikorsky that had ferried the president with its whisper quiet approach and fast sure maneuvers. They all heard it and at once recognized the whumping thud of the antique Huey's flexing Kevlar rotor. It was the sound of botched imperialism.

That was why Espinosa had <u>it</u> and why Domingues had a brand new Sikorsky. Espinosa was the under dog and Domingues was the shit. Their choppers were their cowboy hats.

It took a long time for the old Huey to actually get there. The whumping went on and on getting louder and softer as the wind buffeted the sound around the city. At last, it appeared over the top of the Central Bank building then started to descend to the floor of the plaza below. At the bottom of its fall it flared and finally alighted with a slight forward skid. Espinosa un-strapped himself and climbed out onto the tiles of the plaza. He looked around at all the people.

Three of his security climbed out of the back and escorted him up the steps as the pilot wound up to leave. After a jerk, the Huey lifted off again and made a steady climb up out of the plaza. It thudded away into the distance.

Mr. Green watched through the scope as the old socialist[60] murderer made his way up the steps until he finally stood about ten feet from the thieving capitalist despot that he had opposed for so long. The two men looked at each other for a long time, as if neither one knew quite what to do next, then, almost on cue, they both stepped forward to shake hands.

A friend of his at the edge of the crowd turned and looked up at Mr. Green's window. He pushed a little button on his key fob, and the window turned transparent again.

Mr. Green looked at the president through his scope trying to get a perfect bead on him. He didn't notice the sun on his forehead at first, other than to feel a little more comfortable there gazing through the scope. Domingues pumped his hated rival's hand smiling falsely.

Gabriel McNeill scanned the top floor of the Metropol hotel through his scope. The windows were all the same as they had been a few minutes before. There was a couple making love in the first room, no one in the second, an old man asleep in the third, and so on down the line. The last three were unoccupied, and he thought about just skipping them, but he was well trained and checked them anyway, even though he knew full well that they were empty. The first was empty, the second was empty and

---

[60] Espinosa had been a socialist since his college days at the Sorbonne in Paris, where he had fallen in love with the idea of justice under the careful tutelage of his applied civics professor, none other than Son Hwang Htze, later the addled despot of China.

260

the third was also where the sniper was sitting looking through his scope.

!

"Silvan, look at the last room on the top floor of the Metropole, now!"

His teammate was quiet for a moment while he swung his gaze around that way. Then he spoke clearly and calmly.

"Sniper," he said. "I got him."

McNeill switched over to notify Estoban.

Domingues turned to gesture toward their seats for this historic meeting, and in so doing gave Mr. Green the clear shot he wanted. His back was square on to him and he was standing still.

Green exhaled, his heart beat, and he squeezed the trigger. There was a high-pitched whirring noise as the electromagnetic coils discharged and the gun rocked back with a loud 'TICK'.

Silvan Hallstead exhaled, his heart beat, and he squeezed the trigger. There was a louder bang.

Domingues' head exploded.

Green wondered who that guy was, and his head exploded too.

"Take him out," said Estoban.

Mr. Green's friend melted into the crowd and disappeared forever.

Later, when the crisis was over and Estoban stood looking down at Mr. Green, who was now just another faceless destitute corpse with little pieces of glass spread around him, he was bewildered to find such a sophisticated weapon on a supposedly Chinese agent. Usually their stuff was crap. This was brand new American spook kit. This didn't make sense. This was deeper. He started digging.

All over the world events like these were taking place, just as they pretty much always do. These seemed no more directed than usual. So some guys got bumped off and some others got rich, so what? Was that a conspiracy?

The Domingues hit was only one of many such actions that the Company carried out on a contract basis for the US Government. They were freelance. The people that did the job didn't know or care why they did what they did. It was above their pay grade to think about it. They were just working. Domingues died so Chile could fulfill her destiny as our enemy.

Mr. Green died because it was his job to die at that particular time. He would have been a confused and confusing puzzle piece if he had been left alive, but dead he was the perfect incriminator. So, he was spent, like a coin. He was a dead finger, pointing at Washington.

If Green had missed, someone else there that day, (there were dozens) would have got Domingues, and then they would have been sacrificed too. They would have been the finger pointing north, and either Domingues' successor would have had to make a stand against the Yankees and accuse them of murdering the president—provocation, (American nationals would be rounded up and shot), or else Espinosa would have come to the fore and nationalized the American interests there— more provocation.

If on the other hand they had all missed Domingues, then Green would have been exposed as both an agent of the Glowing Barbeque and their Chinese masters. This would have been a clear violation of the Western Hemisphere Co-Defense Pact by an Eastern power—again provocation. It would also serve to falsely incriminate the Glowing Barbeque which was on a peace offensive and thus force them back to outright war against the Chilean Government, which would then turn to the Yankees for their ready help and support against the now very rightly pissed off rebels.

Any way you sliced it, so the logic went, the Americans could be sucked into the situation, either as the saviors of their southern cousins from the onslaught of outside powers or as the rightful defenders of their vital interests overseas, or at the very least as a necessity to protect American lives. Whatever worked, whatever advanced the Lie, was fine.

Of course this was all based upon the rather naive assumptions that you could both predict human behavior and that people would not be as devious and resilient as you are. Let's not forget that by this time the spooks were buying a lot of their own bullshit. But let's also not forget that at some level they were not nearly as stupid as they looked and so they had many other scams running concurrently, so that if a dozen failed through untoward cleverness, then at least one or two might succeed by vent of those most human of virtues, venal self-interest and drooling stupidity. These were the corner stones of human society. If you couldn't trust people to be greedy morons what could you trust? In their narrow paranoid way they were right.

In Indonesia, a provincial mayor woke up to find his wife dead beside him in bed. Her throat was cut and the knife was in his hand. He was arrested, and someone else was in charge when the deal was cut with Amalgamated Mining.

In Paris, a particular woman was advanced over her comrades inside a minor terrorist cell. This was no big deal, one was as good as another, but now she owed. She would be a good girl for a little while. She would follow orders, without questioning them as hard as she usually did and would plant a bomb in the Mercedes of someone, that was not really a legitimate target, a certain industrialist that was supplying diamond paste to the Saudi fusion project, say.

In Memphis, a housewife received some pictures of her husband in her email. In the pictures he was doing things with his secretary that he never did with her. So she tied him to the bed for love play like they hadn't had in years. The feckless chump grinned at her over his throbbing boner, expecting a blowjob. Instead she jammed a KY® smeared stick of dynamite up his rectum[61], lit it and poured herself another scotch. She had to turn up the stereo.

He had been in charge of security at Amalgamated's plants world wide, and he would have known what pattern to look for in the movement of goods that would have indicated a risk, but he was not there to see.

And so it went, on and on around the world.

So McDermott's paymasters didn't get the supplies they needed, and they put pressure on him to get them from Snellville. And so, the terrorists in Paris got shafted by the French Internal Security for taking out the wrong guy. And the ones that were left, started hitting back at who they knew was behind it, the Americans of course. And so, Amalgamated started pushing people around in the Far East, desperately trying to fulfill their contracts with the Saudis, who were starting to threaten their representative in Riyadh.... It was beautiful. Everybody was going bananas.

-<>-

Tomlinson looked into the scope, wondering when he would notice it change. He found it odd. The view stayed the same for weeks and weeks. It was like someone had pasted a photo, over the scope. It was always the same.

And then, and then, he would notice a tiny change, like the relation of two stars, or a slightly different shape to the flair that the mirror supports caused in the scope itself, or Alpha's brightness.

---

[61] It went in pretty easily.

He tried to get off on the subtleties of it, to wallow in the nuance of the thing, like it was groovy and important. He stared very hard at Alpha, noticing it.

There was a beep from the incoming antenna array. They had mail. Dave looked at the screen.

"Computer, Status?"

"You have—1—piece of mail, it is the news."

"Computer, mail on screen."

This is what Dave saw on the screen:

Tax Revolt!

In a move that took Washington by complete surprise today, 90% of the American electorate put a freeze on their IRS accounts, following a speech by the president calling for further support of the failing Kabingga regime in East Africa, and a tax hike to pay for it. The Tax Hold started on the East Cost at around 12:00 noon EST and rolled across the country throughout the day, By 5:00 PM West Coast time, the Government was essentially bankrupt. Click page 6 for further details.

He got up and went to tell Snortom. As he walked toward the airlock, Dave wondered how the other crewman would react. He had become increasingly unstable, going to ever more outrageous extremes of behavior to needle him. He found it almost flattering, in a sick sort of way, that his shipmate would focus his entire narcissism on him.

The man was clearly going quite insane, and Dave hoped that he wouldn't have to take any 'action' against him. If he did, he would try to be as gentle as he could.

He came to the airlock, and looked in through the view port to where the other man was supposed to be checking the seals. He wasn't.

Snortom sat crouched in the corner, rocking. He had written several obscenities on the walls with his own feces. He rocked and rocked, and each time he rocked he bumped his head on the wall. There was a little bloodstain where his head hit each time.

Dave tapped on the glass. Snortom did nothing, showed no response at all. He tapped again, this time harder. Knute just rocked there for a while then he looked up at Dave, still rocking. Snortom looked like a mad chimp to Dave—like pictures he had seen as a child of zoos, before those nightmares had been abolished. Dave became very sad. Snortom looked away rocking.

Dave emergency cycled the airlock. There was a whooshing scream and in a moment, Snortom was gone.

Dave went and started waking the next person on the roster.

-<>-

The 'Compliance Tag Epidemic' as we call it today, eventually killed over a million people around the world. This is nothing compared to the influenza epidemic of 1918 that killed 50 million in a little over six months, but that was, as far as anyone has been able to prove anyway, a natural occurrence, part of the ecology of the Earth. The tag bug was made by people, and administered on purpose in an attempt to make the American taxpayers obedient to their Government. This in itself was treason of unprecedented proportions, but they fucked it up too.

People started to get sick from the tag. Not just the little mouse cold that Hirohito had had and in a few days they were all right again, they were dying! The thing was this, the bug mutated. It became something else. It became virulent. This would have been bad, but not too bad for the Government. Sometimes people get sick, that's all. But there was the leak.

It is not possible to prove just exactly where and how the leak occurred, but it has been pointed to again and again that the first verifiable place that the information was made public was in Chile in a communiqué from the Shining Path. You may infer from that, what you will.

But how it got out is far less important than <u>that</u> it got out. The message fragment that exists is as follows:

'...compare the virus DNA with US Patent Number 835,980,052 and you will find out something very interesting about the imperialist stooges in Washington.'

This went all around the world on the net, and people started checking it in their university labs, and what do you know?! The commies had a point! It was the same stuff!

These two items appeared the same day.

"Tokugowa Foods could not be reached for comment today following allegations that they were responsible for the flu epidemic that is sweeping the country. Joji Kakumatsu, a lawyer, that is often a spokesman for the company, said only that they were reviewing their options in light of the accusations and that a statement would be forthcoming. We reached him at his home in Nice."

And,

"The US Department of Agriculture and the Food and Drug Administration today started a joint investigation of Tokugowa Foods Industries, regarding the safety of its highly popular Snakos™ brand, and other 'irregularities' that the departments left un-stated. The new head of the Agriculture Department Aliesha Sarson said that they were, quote, 'going to get to the bottom of this thing, come hell or high water', end quote."

-<>-

"Tokugowa Foods only uses the finest ingredients in the production of our Snakos™ brand snack foods. Our flavorings are only USDA approved agents, and the base material is exclusively from US and Japanese collection points, and is sterilized under scrupulously clean conditions. No finer recycled food material exists in the world, or we would use it.

"These allegations are preposterous. There is no chance whatsoever that our processes have been compromised. The company stands behind its product 100%.

"I would like to take this opportunity to remind the public that there have been a number of cheap imitations coming on the market from Kwang Zu in China and some other manufacturers. They are not the same thing at all. They may even be using animal waste!

Snakos™, both original flavor and also the new flavors, including octopus-pesto and chipotle-capybara-meringue, are the one, the only, the original 100% recycled snack food from Japan, accept no substitute."

People kept buying them, even though they knew what they were eating. Think of that! But then who could blame them. They were, after all, 'Munchy-cruncha-licious good!'

-<>-

Yasad mounted the stairs with the heavy suitcase carried in both hands. It was three flights up and by the top of the stairs he was quite tired from the effort. He stopped to rest and catch his breath. Down the hall, his neighbor opened the door and stepped out. It was the Jew, Kohut. Yasad got into character. He grabbed the bag and started dragging it down the hall. He huffed and puffed a little.

"Oh darn this heavy old bag," he said mincingly.

Mort looked at him. "Would you like a hand with that, Youvel?"

Yasad looked up at him, hopefully. "Oh, would you please? Such a bag as this is so heavy, I wouldn't know what to do with it."

Mort came over to him and took one of the handles. He counted three and they both lifted it together. He had to admit that it was heavy.

"So tell me, what possesses you to set up a black smith's shop on the third floor, Mr. Goldberg?"

Yasad looked at him blankly.

"What do you have in here, an anvil?"

Yasad tittered. "Oh this. No. This is just a few things from LA, clothes and stuff."

"Some clothes horse."

"It's important for us to look good. Oy that's heavy."

They got to Yasad's door and set the bag down.

"Thanks," said Yasad. "I wouldn't know how to thank you."

"Don't mention it. We all have enough mishegas in our lives to not have to struggle with a bag," said Mort trying to return his new neighbor's strident self-conscious 'Jewishness'.

He had seen it before, but never to this degree. It was sort of a nervous tic that some people developed when they first came to New York, especially from Los Angeles. They wanted to fit in, but they got it all wrong and overcompensated. He'd settle down in a while. His boy friend was way worse.

Mort turned to go.

"Thanks," said Yasad, behind him, all thick and sappy.

"You bet."

Yasad watched the Jew go down stairs. He waited. Then he gave the coded knock, and entered using his key. He dragged the bag in behind him.

"Honey, I'm home," he said.

Dave was sitting at the kitchen table with electronic guts spread out all over it. He had a cup in his hand.

"Ah, *Youvel*, I was just having a cup of tea, will you join me, darling?"

"Yes my friend, I could use it." He shut the door.

Dave poured a cup and handed it to him. They both smiled.

They thought it was ironic and hilarious that they were posing as a gay, mixed race, Jewish couple as a cover.

"Everything go alright?" asked Dave.

"Yes, my associates are most thorough. They gave us plenty. Fortunately I got Kohut to help me with the last bit. Faizel is a bit useless. He'll do fine in Florida.

"How about yourself? Is your little electronics project advancing as planned?"

267

Dave eyed the pile of components on the table.

"Nearly," he said. "There are one or two things that I'm not quite clear on, but the bulk of the work is done. The timer works and the radio part seems to follow nicely."

He flicked some switches and jiggled the joystick on a model airplane radio controller. There was an audible tick in response to his movements. Yasad looked at the device. It was a bit cobbled together looking, for an atomic bomb. There were some rather sloppy solder joints and some of the components weren't aligned exactly. It would have to do.

"I will help you with that later."

They looked at each other for a moment. Then Yasad winked. "Do you want to see?"

"Lets open it," said Dave. They were like kids at Christmas time. They were evil monkeys.

They dragged the suitcase over to the middle of the room and Yasad fiddled with the combination. He looked at Dave dramatically and then flexed his thumbs. The latches popped and they carefully opened the case.

Inside there was a Styrofoam®[62] sheet on either side. They pulled these out and there they were, the machined components for the bomb. In one half of the case there was a sphere, about the size of a volleyball with a polished hole cut into the middle of it that would just about allow a cue ball to be put inside. In the other half there was what looked like a king-sized plutonium dildo with a mirror-polished head the size of the hole. Beside these where the two halves of the uranium outer jacket cupping the gallium dutieride middle jacket.

They knelt there beside their death shit, like a couple new fathers, ogling.

"Wow, I am definitely getting a boner here!" said Dave.

"Yes, it's quite exciting."

Dave reached out to touch the plutonium sphere. Like Dave, the Plutonium came ultimately from Africa, the upper Umbutu River valley in Greater Burundi to be precise.

"I wouldn't if I were you," said Yasad.

They had a look and then they quickly put back the Styrofoam sheeting and closed the lead lined case.

There was much to do, they washed their hands and got on

---

[62] The CIA once tried to classify Styrofoam, as it was an essential component of the early H-bombs. This was at a time when there was over a million tons a year being produced in the US alone!

with it.

-<>-

Mat knocked back his whisky with a sharp toss of his head. He could barely taste its delicate smokiness and it didn't bite his throat at all. It was his—he looked at the bottle, trying to focus—a bunchth one. Mat poured another one and a fresh sake for Hirohito.

Hiro swayed a little on his tiny mouse feet as he drank his sake. His ears were glowing like headlights. He was assholed.

Mat took a little surimi off his plate and offered it to his friend.

"Here," he said, "you should eat something, you are starting to lose your balance."

Hiro looked at the fish a bit blearily as it hung from the human's food sticks. He took it and started eating, wishing the room would stop spinning. Mat had some too.

They had just been fired from Tokugowa foods for single-handedly bringing the company into ill repute by both allowing a mouse virus to get mixed up with their genetic tagging system and, he wasn't sure how this part exactly worked, causing wide spread distrust of the Snakos™ line. He looked at Hirohito.

"It is all your fault," he said.

The mouse got into his wheel and started running. He got up to speed and then stopped, grabbing onto the wire below his feet. The wheel's momentum carried him on, around and around. He came almost to the top again, but not quite. The wheel reversed direction and he started sluing back and forth wildly. He barfed a little.

"You are a disgrace," said Mat.

-<>-

It was at the exact point that his car hit the top of its flaming arc that Bill got the message. He was retired, then and there. The car bomb was just a type of less deletable email.

That was fine with him. In fact, he wouldn't have it any other way. He had made that quite clear he thought, what with his last public speech and all. He watched as the car fell, flaming in pieces.

The day after, the day after the Futterman show speech, the market lost eleven and a half percent of its value in a single day. Apparently someone lost their nerve and thought that there was going to be a general strike, so they sold their stock. That made the price drop, and scared other people into selling too...

As always.

The car crashed down into the parking lot with a loud, crunching sort of a whack!

The valet landed a few feet closer to him. Bill could see where his legs should be. He shook his head, wondering what the guy's name had been.

He read an article on the net about it a few days later but it just mentioned Bill's name and referred to the valet only as that, the valet. Bill was at his beach resort drinking a piña colada at the time.

A Force Of Arms

It was inky black night, and they were driving through it down a twisting jungle road with the lights off. There was a reason for this seemingly insane and stupid behavior, they were trying to sneak up on the bad guys. In this case the 'bad guys' were Mingetsu McDermott's IFI guerrillas, and the 'they' were Major Tanya Mortenson and a gunnery sergeant by the name of Jeff Wetick. They were driving with the aid of night vision glasses, else the whole exercise would have been a rather short one in suicide. As it was, it was still pretty terrifying, Mortenson's arms ached from grabbing the roll cage, white knuckled.

Wetick was having fun. He liked to wind up the zeros and the idea of personal danger didn't really occur to him. He was just doing what he always did, what he was good at, acting crazy and killing people. Wetick loved war, as some people love sex or booze or work. He was a war-aholic.

Suddenly he whipped the wheel over and slid through an unexpected curve that just missed a huge banyan, saying, "Fuckin' eh! Big tree, Yee—Haw!" He straightened it out again. "You all right there, Sir?"

"Absolutely fine, Sergeant." Mortenson kept her voice level. "Tell me, Wetick, do you have any children?"

"No, Sir!" said Wetick sliding around another deadly curve.

"Good."

Mortenson was thirty-eight years old and had been a soldier her entire adult life. She didn't love war the way Wetick did, but she was as good at it as he was. She received a silver star for her bravery at the battle of Dearborn, and another for the Shan Shang campaign, though that had cost her her little toes. She was a professional killer whereas Wetick was a born one.

"How about you, Major?" asked the sergeant swerving into a gully. "Any kids?"

"No," she said, looking at his enhanced image. "I bought myself a hysterectomy for my twenty-first instead."

"Good."

"Fuck you too, Sergeant." They both laughed.

Baisch was due in the day after tomorrow and she wanted to have something interesting to show him. For weeks the IFI had been skirmishing across the border, trying to nudge it back a little every night, and every day Mortenson and her troops pushed it back the other way. In the slightly longer view the Snellvillans and Americans had been making some progress. The dumbbell shape that was Snellville the Lesser and Greater Burundi was getting fatter across the 'bar' section. They had pushed the IFI back by three miles so far on either side and that was something at least. It meant that the Snellville-Burundi Super Highway was once again safe to travel, at least in broad daylight, but she wanted something more dramatic to show him. He gave her this assignment based on her past performance and while that was a hard act to follow she fully intended to do so.

The satellite showed a build up on both sides of the bar that had been trickling in over the past fortnight. It was clear that IFI was planning a pincer attack to try to separate the country into two halves and would attempt to do so in the next month or so. She was going to try to throw a monkey wrench into McDermott's plans tonight and get some kind of a trophy for the general.

So far no American troops had been killed in anger. So far the political implications of the Military Expeditionary Advisory Force's presence in Snellville were simple. So far the plan wasn't working.

They came up to the top of a hill that looked down onto the plain of Snellville and stopped. From there they could just see the glow of the highway off to the extreme right and the black hole of scrubland where IFI was, straight in front of them. Mortenson sent a query out from her laptop. The satellite bounced it back to her subordinates. There was a few moments wait and then they sent their replies. All was ready. She sent a green light.

"Sergeant, you may continue," She said.

They drove away into the night.

All over the plain small units now advanced on the IFI positions. They were able to move precisely, and not take wrong turns using a combination of satellite data and night vision aids. They had the best weapons in the world at their disposal and they were trained like no other fighting force in the history of warfare. Against McDermott, in a fair fight, they would win every time. This was not going to be fair.

First of all, because IFI had a whole load of new Chinese equipment, including their new 'Smart' land mine that wouldn't go off unless you were wearing US/NATO anti-infra-red clothing, and secondly because IFI was intercepting all of Mortenson's communications on a decoder that the spooks had slipped them.

!

What was supposed to happen was, that the Americans would sneak up on them, a few at a time and take them out as quietly as possible. The IFI were spread out along a broad swath of land that approximated the border, the satellite data showed their positions very clearly. It was expected that there would be a few shots fired and that eventually they would catch on, but that was only supposed to happen after they were already stitched up. When they did figure out that this was not just another minor harassment, so the plan went, they would do the standard guerrilla thing and fade into the bush, leaving a hole for the Americans to fill and hold. In the bush and on the run, they would be easy meat for the American's smart weapons.

That was the plan.

What actually happened was this.

As the first point men made contact with the IFI, they met only token resistance. In fact, they didn't actually manage to even kill anybody. It was all just a lot of noise and flashes and the occasional round to make them keep their heads down. The enemy that they were supposed to just walk over, that their sophisticated reconnaissance told them were sitting ducks, dozing under cover, turned out to be both, nearly invisible and also a lot more mobile than they were supposed to be. It was almost like they'd seen them coming.

The assault teams pushed on, trying to get an engagement that they could sink their teeth into but there was very little there to fight and what little fire they were getting seemed to all come from the middle of the area, where it seemed there were a few of them dropping back as fast as they could. This was reported to Mortenson, and she drew the logical conclusion, that the recon was wrong and that there were actually many fewer IFI than they had been led to believe. It was a rout—they were romping all over the scum! She gave orders to press on, and try to pocket them by sending teams out on either end in a pincer movement of her own. It was looking like Baisch was going to be quite pleased after all.

They ran them back almost three miles into the open country beyond the border before she started to get reports back from the satellite that there was something going on behind her. Then and only then did it occur to her what had happened.

What was going on behind her was that McDermott's men

were pulling off their new Chinese Satiflage[63] nets, and blooming out onto the veldt like cockroaches. There were twenty thousand of them, all armed with brand new Chinese kit, including rockets and even a few light artillery pieces. They came out all around her in a huge ring. She was trapped and she knew it.

Now it was a firefight. Now it was mayhem. They shot the shit out of her guys forcing them back into the center, where they eventually made a stand of it. She had gone in with three hundred soldiers, some of the best in the US Army, and as they stood, there were still nearly two hundred left.

She called for air support, and that helped a little, what finally got there. It didn't arrive until almost 4:00 AM, and when it did finally get there the pilots couldn't target the IFI directly with any effectiveness in the bush, and because their instruments were running off the satellite, about all they had to go on were muzzle flashes and her calls, which were best guesses at best.

As the sun rose that morning they were down to forty people, many of them badly wounded. In the light, the pilots could see the IFI and they put a ring of napalm between Mortenson and them. Now she had a chance.

Tanya heard the thudding of a chopper blade above her as she called in an air strike to her southern flank. She looked up to see the Osprey coming in almost on top of her. It flared, sending up a dense cloud of dust that choked her. She curled into a ball trying to avoid the flying chaff. She thought that she was being relieved at last—then she thought about leaving her troops in someone else's hands, and she resolved to stay. Tanya reached down and cocked her pistol. She would shoot the fucker that tried to relieve her!

Bob Ryan and his camera-crew jumped from the bird, without it even landing. It hung there for a moment longer and then skedaddled, taking hits all the time from the surrounding IFI.

Ryan dove in to the hole with her, followed closely by his crew.

"Hi," he said. "Bob Ryan, associated news."

Tanya looked at him like he was a hallucination.

"What!?"

"We're here to get your story!"

Tanya looked at him for a long moment.

---

[63] This was the first use of anti-satellite reconnaissance camouflage in the history of warfare.

"My story? What the fuck's a matter with you? I'm in the middle of a firefight, and I'm getting my ass handed to me! Get the fuck out of here, you're gonna' get killed, you fucking idiot!!"

Bob motioned over his shoulder to Frank to get all this on card.

Tanya re-assessed the situation. She still needed that air strike on her flank and she punched up air command.

"Big eye, big eye, come back? Over."

"Big eye, Over," crackled in her earpiece.

"Where's that fuckin' boom boom, man? I need it at 90 ASAP! Copy? Over."

There was a pause, and then, "Copy. In route—ETA three minutes—Over."

"Roger. Over."

Bob looked into the camera and put on his sincere voice.

"I'm here on the front lines of the fighting, at extreme personal risk to myself, in order to bring you the stories that matter most to you, first hand. We are in what was yesterday part of Greater Burundi, but which has been over-run by IFI commandos, pinning down this unite of the American Expeditionary Force. We are with the commander.

"What's you name, soldier?"

He stuck the mic in Tanya's face and Frank zoomed in on her.

"Fuck you."

A mortar round hit a hundred feet away, killing somebody.

She switched channels.

"Ackerman, find that mortar and kill it!"

Bob hated to do this to her, but he did have a story to get.

"Look," he said, "I hate to do this to you but I can pull rank on you and order you to do an interview if I want to. So instead, I am asking you. Will you please give me an interview, now?!"

He pulled out his shiny new Military ID card that identified him as a non-combatant with the rank of colonel and handed it to her. Tanya took it and examined it. It was genuine. She threw it back at him like it was a weapon.

"I have work to do, Sir."

"So do I."

He stuck the mic in her face again.

"What's you name soldier?" he asked.

"Major Tanya Mortenson."

He turned back to the camera.

"I'm here with Major Tanya Mortenson, who has found

herself in charge of a unit that got itself pinned down sometime last night, out here in the bush. They are surrounded by enemies and are losing the battle for their lives. Lets see what she has to say."

He turned back to Tanya.

"So tell me, Major Mortenson, what do you intend to do about your situation?"

She looked into the camera.

"I intend to kill my way out of it."

The air strike arrived and there was whoosh, and a great wall of flame burst out to her right. She could hear her guys cheer.

Tanya smiled. "And here's where we start."

She switched to the address channel.

"Okay, everybody listen up! On my order everybody who can move, makes for those trees to the south. There's an LZ on the other side and we can get picked up there. Work in teams and move your wounded with you.

"Okay, on my three!"

Frank spoke to Bob. Bob thought for a moment. Then he made a little square out of his fingers and wagged it around in front of him. He shook his head.

"Uh, Major Mortenson? It would actually be better for us if you could move off to the left."

"What!?"

Bob made the little square again.

"You know, for screen direction."

Frank interjected, "If you go to the right, it won't cut with our other footage!"

Tanya looked at them.

"You really are a couple of prize winning cunts. Aren't you?"

She looked around at her troops. They were ready.

"Okay, on my three! One, tw…"

Bob reached down and switched off her radio.

"Alright," he said, "if that's the way you want to play it, I order you to exit screen left. Is that clear, Major Mortenson?!"

Tanya turned on her radio again. She rather meticulously stood up and said, "THREE!!!!" into her mic.

She shot Bob in the leg, and stepped on his chest as she walked over him, where he fell. Wetick was behind her a little and as he passed by, he grabbed the camera away from Frank and threw it down onto the ground. Frank reached down for it and so the IFI round that would have killed him caught the soundman's head, instead.

Tanya made it to the trees along with most of her remaining people, just as the choppers dropped in to pick them up. She was badly wounded by that point and was delirious with pain and blood loss. Wetick threw her into the chopper and went back for more wounded.

The IFI overran Bob Ryan's position and they stood him and Frank up with guns to their head to execute them.

"Hang on a second here!" said Bob, waving his ID card around like it was a magic talisman. "We are with the media, you can't touch us!"

The IFI commander looked at their IDs. He pointed to the camera with his pistol.

"How do you run this thing?" he asked.

"The red button, push the red button," said Frank.

The commander picked up the camera and pointed it at the two Americans. He pushed to red button.

"Maybe you would like to say a few words for our viewing audience," he said.

Bob started protesting and invoking the sacrosanct name of the press and so on. They let him go on for a while, and then the commander gave a cue to his lieutenant with his black, pink nailed, hand.

Bob and Frank's heads fragmented into fountains of goo as the machine guns barked out for a moment.

"Cut," said the commander. "That's a keeper!"

He pushed the red button again.

They got Tanya out, but just, and that day, in broad daylight, McDermott gave a press conference in the fast lane of the Snellville-Burundi Super Highway with Bob Ryan's camera, in which he stated that he would 'barbeque and eat' Kabingga's children.

He also urinated in an American Army helmet and poured it over Sergeant Wetick, whom he'd had bound and gagged with an American flag and was using as a footstool.

Now there was provocation!

The news stories started flying right and left. There were special investigative summaries and late night what-the-hell-are-we-going-to-do-now shows. They even dragged out old Dagmar Veets from the slam. He was doing a year at the country club[64] for inciting the attempted overthrow of the American Government, but that didn't make him ineligible to broadcast

---

[64] The Federal Minimum Security Prison at Lompoc California.

over the airwaves. He ranted and railed about our brave young fighting men who were being put at risk by not being given the tools to do the job right. He called for that man loving brigand the president to pour the gasoline of the American arsenal onto the righteous fire of the battle to defend our Christian brothers in the enclave of Snellville the Lesser and Greater Burundi, yada yada yada. And away they went!

Where before, there had been what you would call a hell of a lot of American soldiers in Snellville, there was now just about no room to lie down in the place. They poured into the airport and poured back out into the bush, forcing the IFI back like a gray-green flood that killed just about anything that moved, except endangered species, they had strict orders about that, it would have been terrible PR.

Baisch and Kabingga gave Mortenson a gold star for conspicuous bravery during a special prime-time slot, live from her hospital room. She tried to salute them with the stump of her arm and that was it, America sucked it up like serotonin ice cream. Support at home was tremendous. People bought the God damned rearmament bonds as fast as they could print them and America began to bristle.

Then, there was this.

A company of Marines on patrol in the upper Rusizi River valley managed to get itself wiped out without a word on the radio said about it. They just never came back, and when air intelligence went to look for them, they were all dead in the middle of a clearing and stacked in a pile like cordwood. This was eerily familiar.

Then a few days later a similar incident took place, and this time one guy got away because he stopped to relieve himself. He said that he had heard an enormous burst of fire and when he went to have a look, about an hour later there were, so he claimed, a full battalion of Chinese regulars stacking his comrades corpses up in their usual manner.

Well, I don't need to tell you that eyebrows were raised at this. Since when did the Chinese Army get involved in Africa? Oh, they supplied weapons to their Arab Nationalist allies to be sure, but this guy claimed that he had seen the arm flash of the dreaded 7th Kowloon[65]. If he was telling the truth then things were getting really interesting.

---

[65] The 7th Kowloon were the point men at the butcher of Alma-Ata, 350,000 dead and 110,000 eaten.

The soldier was thrown in jail, just in case he was lying for about a week until somebody actually managed to capture one of the 7th—his anti-capture charge malfunctioned—and sure enough he eventually divulged that they were indeed at battalion strength in aid of McDermott.

-<>-

"Clearly there is a fundamental difference between Snakos and the other competing products. That difference lies in the quality of the base material, and the flavor ingredients. It is not merely a difference in the marketing practices of each company, or one of alternate processing techniques, but rather a basic difference in the stuff from which they are made..."

New York Times Columnist and federal prisoner, Dagmar Veets

-<>-

Dave Tomlinson and Fran Watson sat eating their dinner together on the bridge. They had the news from Earth up on the screens. It was the usual stuff, and being seven months old they didn't pay all that much attention to it anyway. They had almost lost touch with Earth completely now.

Now, they were a tiny island, creeping through the night.

Dave was happy with Fran as a crewmate and as a lover. This was good—they had a long trip ahead of them still.

At the end of the news there was a show with highlights and analysis of the pony speech from the president. They didn't give it much notice.

-<>-

"The main thing is this—if you eat Cruncheez with beer you can get an upset stomach, particularly if you are lactose intolerant like me. But if you eat Snakos you can drink beer all day long. But they cost more and that is a concern for all city dwellers, regardless of race. In my opinion, the extra money is worth it, considering that you're going to be putting it in your body. And I can recommend the Cilantro Chicken flavor over all others, except maybe Bar-B-Q, if you like that kind of thing."

Washington Post Columnist and federal prisoner, Harvey Washington Jr.

-<>-

"Phone, open."

Billy's face popped onto the screen. "Ambassador Ziow? I

have a call from the president of the United States."

Ziow nodded. "Of course."

"One moment please."

She was replaced by Swindel. The president looked out at him for a long moment before Ziow spoke.

"Mr. President, hello, how are you?"

"Pissed off. Just what exactly do you people think you are doing?"

"Mr. President?"

"Well? I asked you a question, Zow."

"I, I don't understand, Mr. President. Is there some problem that I'm not aware of?"

"Yes, I suppose that you could say that, though I doubt that you are at all unaware of it. What the fucking problem is—is that the 7th Kowloon has slaughtered almost a thousand of our advisers in Snellville! What do you think you are playing at, Dickweed?!"

Ziow looked genuinely surprised at this revelation. He looked most concerned.

"Mr. President," he blinked. "I, I don't know what to say. As far as I am aware the 7th Kowloon regiment is on training exercises with units of the Zaire Freedom Front. Where exactly, if you don't mind me asking, did this alleged incident take place?"

Swindel smirked sarcastically to himself.

"You really got a pair on you, man. You know perfectly well that it was in the Rusizi River valley. Stop bullshitting me, Ambassador, we have one of your people alive and talking."

Ziow shook his head, still looking surprised.

"Mr. President, please you must believe me, your facts are somehow incorrect. First off the Rusizi River is in Islamic Free Africa, and has been for almost six months now and secondly, if you had captured one of the 7th, which is very unlikely, they would never talk to you about operations. Never.

"If your advisors are in the Rusizi, that is a clear violation of protocol on international borders and unfortunately sometimes these accidents will occur, especially in a military exercise zone. If you will furnish us with a list of the names of the dead we will, of course, issue letters of condolence to the service personnels' families, without admitting any responsibility, of course. I can assure you that we are no happier about this than you are.

"What, if I may ask, were these advisors doing inside our allies territory in the first place? Advising, I presume?"

"The Rusizi is part of the enclave of Snellville the Lesser and

280

Greater Burundi. That has been established for over fifteen years and just because your lapdog McDermott has recently over-run the place doesn't mean that it is a free fire zone for your fucking cannibals!"

That got him. Dwayne could see it in his face. The Ambassador hated him personally.

"Mr. President," he said mustering calm, "on behalf of my Government and people, and in the name of Son Hwang Htze, I must protest this last insult. The People's Republic of China does not have dogs of any kind, they are filthy, tough animals, and very difficult to digest, we abhor them. And furthermore, it was the actions of America along with your evil allies, NATO and the Russians that forced our troops to turn to cannibalism in some rare isolated cases in the Shan Shang valley campaign, of the last great conflict. It is you that has the blood of the Kazaks as well as my own countrymen on your hands and not us. We will not engage in dialog with you if you persist in this insulting and degrading manner."

"Yeah, you're damned right. It's not going to be dialog that we are engaging in if this shit keeps up."

"Just what exactly are you threatening my country with, Mr. President?"

"Push me and see, asshole! Phone hang-up"

The screen went blank.

Swindel sat back and crossed the first one off his list. This was fun. He went on all morning sticking thorns in the side of various and sundry governments around the world, paying special attention to McDermott's pan-Arab Nationalist buddies.

And they, in their turn, were calling American ambassadors on the carpet in their capitals and demanding to know just what the hell we thought we were doing, first wading into what had been a very nicely run campaign in Africa and messing it up, and secondly then letting our lunatic president go calling people up and rubbing their faces in it. Didn't we know that there were channels for this sort of thing? Weren't we aware that this was the height of bad manners, as well as being an outrage in principle?

A note needs to be made here about the Chinese—Arab bloc. They, left to their own devices, would much rather have had peace, and not been in Africa paired off against the US. They would much rather have let McDermott take the hit and bided their time till they were far stronger, before starting trouble again. It was the Americans that were pushing the issue, as far as they were concerned. This was really outrageous Yankee aggression.

Even Washington's allies were looking askance at the goings-on coming out of the White House.

This was only the latest out of Swindel as well. He had taken of late to pushing policies on people that they didn't like and would not stand for—like demanding a special tariff on Chilean goods, in spite of the fact of over three centuries of reciprocal agreements and telling the Japanese that they had to start buying 20% more of their light metals from the US for Floatkyo than they had planned to—without bothering to outline that this was because of the expected difficulties in moving them out of Snellville directly for the duration of the conflict and so on. This was tantamount to calling everybody's mothers sluts.

This sort of thing was not only going down like fish hooks in foreign countries, but also at home. You diss the Pan-Arab Alliance, you also ruffle the feathers of every Arab-American. They take it personally. The Chilean-American sub-population and there were over three million of them believe it or not, were rightly outraged. They started marching in the streets of major cities and the kids started turning over cars and burning convenience stores. They were soon joined by other Hispanics as well. They didn't really have that big a beef, but the opportunity was far too much fun to pass up! New York City was starting to boil.

Mayor Fienbalm called the president personally to complain that his behavior was threatening the very security of his citizens. He said that he wanted to impose martial law if Swindel didn't back down on his rhetoric, and that he expected the Federal Government to pay for it.

By which he meant, 'Come on dude, you are starting to piss people off, how about a break for a little while?'

Swindel said this to him, "Mayor Fienbalm, don't worry about a thing. Everything is going according to plan, and if you need to impose martial law, you can go ahead and do so, we will back you up, but the Federal Government can not be held to ransom by the civil population."

!

By which he meant 'That's your problem pal, we are going ahead with our agenda regardless of the political fall out and you better just keep your end sweet or else we will come in and straighten everybody out ourselves. You included. Do I make myself clear?'

Then he called General Baisch, and asked him about the logistics of such a plan.

282

This is what the general said, "Mr. President, you can count on the full cooperation of the Army. We have a contingency plan for this as you know, and we are ready at 24 hours notice to implement it on your orders."

Two days later there were checkpoints at the bridges coming into Manhattan.

Anna handed her snotty little kid[66] to Mort and threw her arms around Sergei's massive neck. She hugged him hard and he could feel her tears dripping onto his shoulder. It felt good, he was sad, her hair smelled clean.

He had last shaved a week ago and his stubble rasped against her cheek like a mill bastard.

"Anna darling, don't be so sad. You are only going to California, is not the moon."

"I know, Sergei," she said in his ear. "I know. But no one there will think up something more depressing to cheer me up when I am blue."

"And this makes you sad."

"Yes, this makes me sad," she said looking into his lapis eyes.

"Yes. But just think, someone on this bus has cold, so you will be sick as fucking dog when you get to the beach. Besides, you don't have a problem. You were just renting, and now you are going to surfing, I have now to sell my place! I will be lucky to get hundred thousand bucks for it!"

Mort looked at Sergei quizzically. "You are selling your house? Now?"

"Da!" interjected Nadia who was standing next to Sergei. "Is stupid fucking Hezbollah making threats everyday, well, and so. Maybe we come out to visit sooner you think."

"Please come," said Anna, taking Louis back from her husband. "We will have plenty of room for you all."

"All?" asked Stan, who had been standing behind his brother in law smoking as usual.

"Yes, even you and your brother," said Mort. "Though we would appreciate it if you would refrain from political arguments while you are there."

Stan stared at him like he was crazy. "Sergei," he said, "you explain."

"Their political arguing is type of weather, it can be predicted with some accuracy using super computers, but nothing actually can be done about it." He shrugged.

Now Igor could be heard coming through the crowd, saying, "Excuse me please," over and over again. He made slow progress

---

[66] We had the bug.

through the dense throng dragging a big suitcase with him, and after a long time he squeezed past a fat myopic guy that was eating Snakos, obviously, and appeared next to his brother, panting in the stifling August heat.

"Hello," he said. "Sorry to take so long. First I missed your train and then they searched your bag twice, like I am looking some kind of terrorist!"

Everyone looked at him, and no one spoke for a long moment.

"Don't push your luck," said Stan.

The bus depot was jam packed with people trying to get out of New York City, anyway they could. Both Hezbollah, and the BCA, in the name of all Pan-Arab Nationalists everywhere had been threatening major terrorist actions there for the past week and one of them had given what they both called a little teaser, by bombing the United terminal at JFK the night before, killing sixty people.

Now most flights were canceled and with the increased unrest on the streets, not helped by the imposition of martial law, people were starting an orderly sort of panic.

It was a widely held belief that Hezbollah was capable of anything and then the FBI came out and said they assigned a no greater than 40% chance that they could get together a nuclear device, so as to calm the situation.

!

The authorities were stuffing people onto buses and trains, trying to get them out of the city as fast as they could, to just about anywhere they could.

This bus, the one that the Kohuts were about to board, was headed for Chicago, where the airline promised they would be sent on to LA at the earliest possible time. The bus was six hours late.

A soldier walked down the lines of waiting people looking at them. He had a billy club and was sort of strolling along intimidating people from misbehaving. He was met by another soldier with a box and they conferred a few yards away from the group. Then, the one with the box stood up on top of it and addressed the crowd with a bullhorn. He was from the Bronx.

"Okay, people, listen up! You too, Mr. poop eating coprophage." he said, pointing at the Snakos guy.

"This bus," he pointed, "number one-sixty-four is about to load for Chicago. If you do not have a ticket for Chicago, then do not try to board this bus.

"If you do try to board this bus, without a ticket for Chicago, you will be arrested for being an asshole. If, on the other hand, you do have a ticket for Chicago, you may bring one, and only one suitcase on this bus. Leave your suitcase next to the bus with your name on it and it will be loaded for you. Do not try to bring two cases with you, thinking that we won't notice, because we will.

"If you do this, then we will think that you think that we are stupid. This will annoy us, and you will again be arrested, for being an asshole!

"All people being arrested for being assholes will be taken down town and incarcerated with their own kind. What do <u>you</u> think are the odds, of <u>you</u> being the biggest asshole in New York City?" He paused for effect.

"We will now begin boarding this bus. That is all."

Several people stepped out of line and started grumbling. The line tightened up and started boarding the bus. Mort and Anna kissed and shook hands with everybody. Nadia gave Louis a rattle that she had made for him[67]. His ears glowed a little, and Sergei smiled big and confident. He said this, "Buy me surfboard, I see you next month!"

Mort said, "OK, Dude, I'll—like totally see ya later."

The people behind shoved and they turned and boarded the bus. Sergei and his family were moved away to let the bus out and Mort couldn't find them again in the crowd.

The bus pulled away into traffic and was gone. Sergei's family went to the park. That was the last time my parents ever saw them.

-<>-

Snakos, they <u>are</u> the shit!

© The Lie Inc. 2050 Manhattan billboard campaign.

-<>-

In later years, this was the seminal event, the, to use the nauseating catch phrase of the time, defining moment, that historians would point to as the cause of World War III.

The historians were full of shit of course—wars don't really have clear-cut causes that can be easily pointed to with a little stick. They are vast indifferent things, stuck together with scotch tape and murdered children, but this, they said, was the straw—this speech, given on this day, by this man—that broke the

---

[67] I still have it.

camel's back.

He was really just a tiny fractal node of an immense four-dimensional lie space that stretched for eons, but they would blame him, as was their right and convenience.

America, according to the opinion polls was solidly behind his remarks. War stocks were up and Joe public was feeling scrappy. The place was in NBC's Washington studios, the time was 7:30 PM, Friday, August 28th, 2050 Eastern Daylight Time, and the man was Dwayne Swindel, the 55th president of the United States of America.

Dagmar Veets had been flown out from California for a very special edition of America Tonight. He adjusted his chair as they waited for the cue light that would indicate that they were on the air. He could still do the do. He had been listening to tapes of his old shows to brush up so that he would be utterly convincing and all that but inside, Dagmar Veets was as different a man as could be, from the bellicose self-sure ass-bite that had called, after the fact, for the Hold and all the rest of it. He had seen too much, he had lost friends, and been shot, albeit grazingly, in the head by Nathan Mornette. Most importantly he had been betrayed by the American political system for speaking what he saw as the truth. He was frightened now, and doubted even his own perceptions.

That was okay with the soulless pricks that ran NBC, they had never really cared about his convictions, they were only interested in his outward cockiness, and deep voice. That was what they paid him for.

If he held controversial views, well, that was all the better, but if he hadn't then they would have come up with some for him.

"Three minutes," said the disembodied voice of an engineer.

They waited in silence not looking at each other. Then Swindel said, "So tell me, Veets, how's the chow out in Cali?"

Veets looked at him calmly, his heart pounding with apprehension. "Fine, Sir," he said. "A little monotonous."

"Good."

The lights dimmed and they could hear the intro music fading up. The cue light came on and a spot came up on Dagmar.

"Hello, and welcome to a very special edition of America Tonight. This evening we have the entire broadcast dedicated to only one man. That is appropriate, as he is the single most powerful human being on the face of the Earth. Ladies and gentlemen, Mr. Dwayne Swindel, the 55th president of the United States."

287

They brought up a spot and applause on the president.

"Good evening, Mr. President, and welcome to the show."

"Thanks, Dag, and you. Tell me, how's the chow out on the West Coast?"

Veets stumbled a little. "Ah, fine, Sir. First class!" he ended a little too loudly.

"Good, we like our federal prisoners to be comfortable, not too comfortable, but comfortable enough."

"Yes, Sir." He cleared his throat.

"Mr. President, first let me thank you for coming on the show tonight, it is a great honor for me and I think a great opportunity for the American people to hear what you have to say about the events of late. Particularly the United bombing.

"Sir, there are those in the country that are saying that this sort of thing was inevitable, considering the high tone of the rhetoric coming out of Washington in general and out of your office in particular. They contend that the days of American hegemony are in the distant past and that we, as a nation, cannot just go around doing as we please anymore. Well, Sir, how do you answer these allegations?"

Swindel looked at him for a second before he answered.

"Well first thing, Dag, I want to make clear that this sort of criminal behavior is neither inevitable nor acceptable and I have the assurance of the FBI that they will be picking up some suspects imminently. The United States will not tolerate this sort of thing, and there will be appropriate action taken, when the time comes, more on that later, but first I want to say this. The United States Government, in its various branches, has been pursuing and will continue to pursue, a set of policies that have been arrived at by consensus, and no amount of murder will deter those actions.

"A necessary part of government is implementation of policy through words, and if those words are sharp, then they are meant to be so, because they are the organs of very pointed policies.

"You know, we just don't sit up there on the hill and try to come up with statements that will anger our adversaries. We are not reacting—we are acting. Some of those acts will inevitably rankle people that have a different agenda from ours. That's alright we don't ask their cooperation on this.

"As for the days of American hegemony being in the distant past, let me tell you, they are in the near future. We have not yet begun to lay down the law to these people. It is high time that the less civilized half of the world realizes that though we are patient, our patience is not boundless. We are through waiting for these other countries to start playing the game by the rules."

"Yes, Mr. President, but whose rules?"

"Our rules, my rules if necessary. We, the Western world, have the ability to annihilate anybody we so choose, and it is our civility and education and liberal ideals that keep us from doing so at the drop of a hat. Well that is about to change. We have waited and asked nicely and made trade pacts and done a thousand other velvet gloved things to try to get these people to come around and see the light—to realize that they need to play ball with us as much or more than we need them to.

"We are talking about countries that still gobble up endangered species, practice slavery, and cannibalism and that subjugate their women like cattle. These are not the good guys here, or some quaint backward tribal people that can be forgiven their shortcomings because they still need time to grow. These are advanced industrial powers that have been cheating the system for years. Well here is where we draw the line. Right here, and right now."

"And what," asked Dagmar, "do you intend to do, Sir. That is what a lot of Americans would like to know."

Swindel smiled a big arrogant smile, intended to really needle his critics.

"What we are going to do is this—we will state to the Chinese, and the Pan Arab Nationalist governments throughout the fertile crescent, and even those flaky half assed little dictators in Chile, who, by the way, had the audacity to call me up an hour ago and accuse the United States of assassinating their President Domingues two weeks ago, that there are certain rules of both internal and external conduct that must be complied with. We will read them off to them once and only once, and give them 24 hours to comply."

"And if they don't comply? What then?"

Dwayne Swindel, the president of the United States put out his hands like he was holding two watermelons and went "BOOOOOM!!!!!!"

"Boom? Just what, exactly, do you mean by boom, Mr. President?"

Swindel smirked. "What are you, thick? We will do them in. We will take them out. We will, to use the colloquial, 'slap they bitch asses up'. This might mean war in some cases, and something else entirely in others. This is what I was saying earlier about appropriate action, and consensus.

We have conferred with our NATO allies, the Russian Federation, and the Japanese along with a handful of other decent, civilized countries, and we have agreed to a plan, where by to attack one is to attack all, and in which we will pool our resources to bring these other people into line. This might be, well, for instance in Chile, to just go in and eliminate a few hundred individuals at the top of their corrupt Government. They would never know what hit them. They would just wake up in the morning as a headless chicken. The next guys that come to power there, whether they are democratically elected or if they are the Glowing Barbeque is irrelevant. They will be read their rights and responsibilities and given 24 hours to comply.

Now, if we are talking about the Chinese Government that is a very different thing. They have over ten million key people in their Government, all of whom will have to be eliminated, so that would probably mean a preemptive nuclear strike on Beijing, and then a small land war to root out all those that remain. There will then be camps established and so on, I think you get the picture."

Veets was completely aghast by this lunatic frankness on the part of the president, He literally couldn't believe his ears.

"Bu..., but—surely, Mr. President, you are talking about Armageddon. This—will be the end of the world!"

Swindel made reasonable, spreading his hands.

"Doesn't have to be. Not if compliance is utter and complete. After all, as I have just said, they have had more than a fair chance. Much more than fair. We are slow to anger as a people, but once you have managed it, and they have, just about, we are unstoppable. We will not quite once started, we can not be dissuaded by pictures of crying mothers holding the burned corpses of their children. There is no amount of reason that will change our minds. We will smash the crap out of anybody that doesn't capitulate. I am afraid that it has come down to that, capitulation, pure and simple.

"Gone are the days when we tried to get them to see our side. Now they will have a simple, brute, choice to make. Do it our way, and God help your family if you try to cheat, or die in a world of shit."

"You can't be serious, President Swindel. What you are talking about is total fascism! It is as undemocratic a stance as I can imagine. You are no countryman of mine, Sir."

Swindel waved him down patronizingly.

"I am deadly serious, Dag. And yes you are right, what I am

saying is utter fascism. That's the whole deal with fascism—it's total. As I have said, we have already tried to be the good guys, now we are going to just stuff it down their throats and see if they gag on it. Cool eh?

"And yes, it will be undemocratic, for those who don't play ball, that is. For them, it will be as bad as we can possibly make it. There will be trade embargoes and we will cut off the electricity and poison their ground water. And we will have a really good laugh about it all, too. It will be great, just think, Westerners will be able to walk the streets of any country in the world and know that they will be safe, because the police of that country will see to it, knowing that if they don't, they will be exterminated like the vermin they are. We will institute a world language program. There will be one world language, English. All people in the world will learn English or be eliminated. We welcome their cultural diversity, and we don't want them to stop speaking Urdu or whatever, but they will all have to speak English, politely, to Westerners.

"There will be one world law, our law. No more of this bullshit like you can smoke dope in Oman but women can't drive a car there. And there will be freedom of worship everywhere, not just in the States and Europe and Japan.

"It will be great, Dag, you will love it. Just think. There will be greater freedom in the world, than at any other time in history! The West will be free as it has been now for a long time and those other places, where people have not been free, where they have been suffering under the tyranny of decrepit old men, with vested interests to look after will become free, or sterile as they so choose. We say choose life. We say go west old man."

Dagmar tried to say something else, but Swindel stopped him with an open hand.

"As to your last point, that I am no countryman of yours, well, you can say what you like—this is a free country, Dag, but not only am I your countryman, I am your president, elected fair and square, and you can't undo that, without impeachment, till the next election. So, you have about a year and a half to wait. And as your president I am empowered to speak on your behalf, as well as the rest of our citizens, and here is what I have to say."

He turned toward the camera and they zoomed in to frame his face, nice and full, he was the picture of authority.

"For more than a century now all the problems of the world have been blamed on the US by the ungrateful people that we have been giving money to, in order to help them. Well, that's

291

fine, that's history after all, and we can do nothing about it, regardless of how unjust that has been.

"What we can do, however, is to make a new start, here and now. This is it, this moment, the start of a new world order, in which the West starts playing for itself, and for keeps. We are going to get the blame for everything anyway, well okay, we have broad shoulders, but we are going to exact a price for that service, and that is this. Whatever you accuse us of, we will then really do to you. If you say we are colonialist bastards, then look out, because there is going to be an American family moving into your house, next week. You will be given the choice of being their servants, or you will be executed. Simple. If you say we are the great Satan, we will be. And you have seen absolutely nothing yet. If you think I am an asshole now, stick around!

"On behalf of the American people, I put it to you all. To each and every despot, dictator and mullah. We are going to wipe our asses with you, and too damn bad if you don't like it. You want a piece of me? Okay, let's do it! I say, bring it on, cunt!! Right fucking here and right fucking now!"

He concluded his remarks with a stiff little finger pointed at the floor and his upper teeth biting into his lower lip.

They cut to an ad for feminine napkins.

-<>-

It was really hot that Saturday afternoon, and everybody who could be was either out at the beaches or doing whatever else, to stay cool and calm. Hezbollah's rhetoric was reaching a fevered pitch and since Swindel's speech, even the legitimate governments in the Middle East were starting to make some rather feisty public statements. People were on edge.

At Rockefeller Center they had the ice on and a few hundred people had come down to glide around like swans on the cool hard rink. Many of them were stiffly graceful and silent, and some were awful yowling catastrophes scuttling around on quivering bruised limbs.

And then there was one woman that was obviously trained as a world-class figure skater. She pumped her legs hard, sending her around a great arc, faster and faster, till she pulled into a tight curve and leapt into a triple axle, that came out into a back facing eight, perfect. She was exhaustingly beautiful, and had some fans with her that sat at the edge of the ice, drinking house-made beer and clapping for her. They were wildly enthusiastic about her stylish maneuvers, and called out requests to her in Russian English. She was Nadia Molotov.

292

"Do Salchow!" said Igor.

"Da!" she nodded, gliding through the crowd.

Nadia got to a clear spot and looked around for a path through the punters. They cleared after a moment and she started her run. She drove fast for the outside edge of the ice, pushing herself around it at about 25 miles an hour, then she weaved back into the center, past Dave and Yasad, and headed straight for Sergei. Again the crowd parted, exactly where she figured they would and she executed a perfect double Salchow, ten feet in front of them. They all cheered and raised their bottles to her, as she shot past, grinning in the glow of their adulation.

Dave stood next to Yasad, who was kneeling down next to the suitcase that he had just opened. He was peering into the guts of the 5-megaton hydrogen bomb that they had spent the last week kludging together. He was angry—it wasn't working. He poked at the control board with his finger.

"It is a dry solder joint, I am sure of it," said Yasad. "Why didn't you learn to solder correctly!?"

Dave just looked at him, not speaking.

"Well!?" demanded Yasad.

"Can you fix it?" asked Dave.

Nadia glided past them. She was curious about their activities there in the middle of the ice. She tried to spy on them as she went around for another axle.

Yasad tried bending the power lead, where it joined the board and the little confidence light blinked off and on erratically.

"A ha! There, you see? It is a dry solder joint, just exactly as I have said," he said pointedly, pointing, as if blame would fix it.

Dave leaned over and looked at the board for a long time.

"A dry solder joint," he said.

"Yes, there is no question about it."

"Well, what can we..." started Dave.

"Do about it?" finished Yasad tersely for him.

Yasad's persnickety attitude was starting to needle Dave. He had enough trouble, not killing light skinned people who fucked with him, under normal circumstances and now this rag head was yanking his chain, while they were busy trying to blow up New York City. What did he think he was going to accomplish?

Dave kept cool for the moment.

"Okay," he said. "So what can we do about it?"

Yasad snorted derisively.

"What can we do about it? Well—," he spread his hands

theatrically. "I don't know, Dave. Do you have a soldering iron in your pocket, and if so where do you suppose we can plug it in around here, the ice?"

"Well..."

"Well! Yes my friend. If you had not bungled this simple soldering job then we would not be in this predicament would we? And <u>well</u> so there you go. We are stopped because of your incompetence!"

Dave raised a staying hand, trying to smile off this insult, in a patronizing sort of way.

"Okay, hold it right there, Yasad. First of all, I have to say that you are not going to address me in that tone of voice and secondly, I am a revolutionary not an electronics expert. I assembled the control board from <u>your</u> plans and <u>you</u> inspected my work. Now, I think that you share some responsibility in this.

"And, come to think of it, I think it was you who actually soldered the power leads onto the board in the first place, while I was making spaghetti. In fact, I'm sure of it."

"Yes, you and your endless spaghetti," snapped Yasad, rising. "You can't do that either!"

As far as Dave was concerned, Yasad was going down in flames now.

"Look," he said. "I am not going to stand here and take this kind of shit from you or any other honky dickweed. I made spaghetti and you ate it. What, I suppose you were crippled all of a sudden. You could have gone out for a pizza you know, or made some of, what ever it is that they eat in Arabia!"

"Iran!"

"Oh well fine, fuck, Iran then, like I give a damn! Some kind of egg plant bullshit?! You were the one that made this solder, weren't you? Admit it!"

He pushed Yasad to emphasis his point.

Nadia glided past, watching them argue. She clocked her head and did an axle.

Both men slid back away from the suitcase, trying to keep their balance. Dave was not as nimble as Yasad but he had the advantage of rubber-soled shoes, whereas the Iranian was wearing patent leather loafers that were as smooth as plums. Yasad lost his balance and tried to catch himself. His feet shot out from under him and he landed hard on his coccyx.

Yasad looked around. There were people starting to take an interest in them now and that was the last thing they wanted. He got up painfully, first onto his knees and then up onto his feet.

The two men regarded each other across the hydrogen bomb, both keenly aware of the eyes on them from the edge of the ice.

They both made there way back to the suitcase in sullen silence. Yasad knelt down and held the offending control board in his hands, thinking.

"What we need," he said, "is a clip of some kind to hold this wire to the board, at the incompetent solder joint."

Dave thought about this, looking at the people around them. He shrugged.

"I'll see what I can find," he said.

Dave walked gingerly toward the edge of the ice. There was a group of people sitting there watching the woman skate figures. They had food and drink in grocery bags with them, perhaps they might have something that would help. It took him a while to get there, walking slowly and deliberately, through the gliding skaters.

"Excuse me, please," he said.

The big, stubble faced man, in the middle of the group looked up at him.

"Excuse me, please," repeated Dave. "We have a little problem with our, peace display, and I was wondering if you could help us out."

Sergei looked at him openly.

"Sure, what I can do to help you?"

"Oh, you're Russians, aren't you?"

They all looked around at each other and then they shook their heads.

"No," said Stan, pointing at Sergei. "He is Chechen. We are Russian. Would you like a beer, Mister?"

He held up a bottle.

Dave hadn't had a beer in twenty-eight years. This might be his last chance.

He took the beer saying, "Thank you."

The beer was cool and delicious, it tasted like sour wall nuts and bread.

"Wow, that's great."

There was no label on the bottle. He looked at it.

Sergei inclined his head.

"Thank you, my wife, Nadia, made it. She is one skating."

Dave looked over his shoulder at her, out on the ice.

"Oh," he said. "She's very good."

"Yes, now tell me, Mister...?"

Dave thought about this. Who was he, really? It didn't matter what he told this man, he would never live to tell it to anyone.

"Islam. My name is, Islam Africa, people call me Dave, though."

Sergei shrugged. "So tell me, Dave, what is the problem with this 'peace display' of yours?"

Dave took another drink of the delicious beer. In spite of their being in an ice rink, it was hot with the sun straight overhead.

"Well, it seems that my friend made a dry solder joint on the control board that drives the display. It is on the positive rail and we don't really have time or the inclination for that matter, to drag the whole megillah back across town to fix it, especially in this weather. Man, it's hot!

"What we need, really, is —some kind of a clothes pin or —a clip or something, that we can just clip the wire on with. I don't suppose that you would have anything like that with you."

They looked around their bags for something appropriate but no luck.

Sergei thought for a moment, and then he stood up and whistled to Nadia. She looked at him and he motioned her over. She glided toward them.

"What does this 'display' of yours, do exactly?" Sergei asked Dave. "I presume it lights up or somethink?"

Dave nodded his head. "Yes, that's it. It lights up, very bright in fact. You'll see it about two hours from now. It's on a timer."

Igor shrugged. "Unfortunately, we will be not here then. We will be uptown."

Nodia skated up to them.

Dave said, "Oh, you might be able to see it form there, even, for a few seconds anyway."

"Da?" asked Nadia.

Sergei looked at his beautiful wife. She had her mane of auburn hair up in a bun, held in place with several clips.

"Please, Nadia, may I have one of your hair clips?" He pointed. "That one there, one of the Walgreens' ones."

She reached up and grabbed the cheap plastic clip, handing it to him.

"Thank you very much," said Sergei.

Nadia asked, "Is it—"

"Yes, thank you."

"Okay…?" She smiled at Dave and pushed off again, out onto the ice. They all watched her go. Who could not?

"She is an excellent skater," said Dave.

"Yes," Sergei smiled. "She would have gone to the Olympics—instead she became artillery captain. Your clip."

Dave took it.

"If you think my sister is graceful on skates," said Stan, "you should see her commanding tank assault!"

They laughed.

Dave drained his beer, thanked them for the clip and started making his precarious way back across the ice to Yasad. Nadia passed him once on the way. She winked at him when he smiled at her, did an axle and flowed away into the crowd, like an impossible swan.

As Dave made his way back out across the ice, it struck him how amazing life was, how the beer had tasted, how beautiful the Russian skater, Nadia, was. A sense of irony filled him, at how he was about to blow New York to smithereens, and here he had just met some really great people—people that were kind and generous and funny—and they were going to get blown up along with the rest of the shit that lived there, just because they happened to be in the wrong place at the wrong time. It seemed really unfair to him.

He thought back to his days as Islam Black Africa—to the running street battles and the justice they had dolled out to the racist monsters in the suburbs of Dearborn, Chicago and Detroit. Justice, that's what it had all been about—finally getting back some of their own from their tormentors. They had stood up and said that above all else, there must be justice in America, before there could be peace. It had all been so clear back then. There was us and them.

He had executed dozens of pleading white people for the crime of property, and never thought twice about it, (they would have done the same to him, given the chance), and now, on the cusp of the new era who should he meet but some really good white people. This was difficult for him, the lines were beginning to blur.

He got to Yasad without falling down and at last stood there with the clip held out in front of him.

"A clip," he said.

"A clip," repeated Yasad.

"Yes, a hair clip, this should work to hold the wire to the board."

Yasad took the clip and looked at it like it was a piece of shit.

"Very well," he said at last.

Yasad bent down and started trying to attach the wire onto

the control board with the hair clip.

Dave watched Nadia glide across the ice, in a great graceful sweep.

"You know," he said, "it seems ironic to take out everybody in New York, when at least half of them are the victims of the system, and not a part and parcel of it, necessarily."

Yasad didn't look up at this, but his ears were just about shaking with the strain to catch every nuance of what was said next.

"The people that gave me the clip—they were Russians. They were really nice people."

Yasad knew that this would happen. He had been waiting for it, in fact. This Yankee nigger was losing his nerve at the last minute. Westerners were all the same. They talked a great game, but then, when it came down to it, they were all pussies, unable to go through with it. They all just wanted to live a long, rich life and die in their sleep.

"Yes," he said conversationally. "I saw you enjoying a beer with them and talking. They look like a nice bunch of people. Maybe you could start putting up the dove."

Nadia twirled.

"Oh, right."

Dave started folding together the big cardboard dove that they had made as a cover to hide the bomb from prying eyes, while they made their escape in the chopper that Yasad had waiting on the roof above. It was a tab and slot job, decorated in bright sloppy paint. It had 'Peace On Earth' written across it.

Yasad set the clip in place and threw the switch. The confidence light went on and stayed bright. It was fixed. He thought about 'plan B'.

It really didn't matter very much if they died of cancer in a year or two, as they both surely would from handling the plutonium hemispheres, he thought. The world was going to change beyond recognition anyway and they had certainly done their part…

He unplugged the servo switch and threw it over into the 'armed' position. He fished his keys out of his pocket.

Nadia shot past them, traveling backwards. She swung her leg up like a pendulum to propel herself through a triple axle. Dave smiled at her. She smiled back at him.

Yasad found pins 6 and 19 on the male DB 25 connector at the bottom of the board.

"It just seems wrong somehow," said Dave.

Yasad said this, "Quick, Dave, go to sleep!"
Nadia swung her leg, leapt and twirled.
"What?"
He shorted across the pins.

-<>-

While Dave said, "What?"—

Across the key went the electrons and on down the wire to the detonator. Inside the detonator a minute speck of a chemical called lead azide detonated. This detonation caused a much larger piece of the chemical pentaerythritol tetranitrate to explode inside the small canon that housed the plutonium dildo—the 'plunger'.

The plunger, being restricted in all but one direction shot down into the heart of the plutonium sphere—into its 'nestle'. The nestle was machined to fit exactly with the surface of the plunger, so there was a great deal of contact between the two unstable radio active parts and their combined mass was greater than their super-critical limit.

The plutonium sphere fissioned into the lighter and yet still radioactive elements, strontium^{90}, iron^{54} and arsenic^{118} and converted about 13 grams of its mass into 10^{12} watts of energy.

This energy in turn caused the gallium deuteride middle jacket to deteriorate, giving up free deuterium that underwent fusion into helium^5 and so kicked the uranium^{238} outer jacket into a really big, sustained fission reaction. This was a 5 megaton F-F-F type H-bomb.

For a moment there was a tiny piece of the sun in the middle of the skating rink at Rockefeller Center.

The light shone through Yasad—and then through Dave—and then through Nadia. They ceased to exist, except as memories.

The others there were illuminated too and then ceased to exist and then Rockefeller Center ceased to exist and Midtown and the Park and Worthy, who was in town on business ceased to exist, along with the New World Trade Center and Harlem and Queens and Brooklyn and parts of New Jersey and Staten Island. They all disexisted in that one terrible instant.

If you had been standing behind a four foot thick, reinforced concrete wall at the southern tip of Staten Island, with your head screwed on sideways, as Senator Daniel Failsworthy was in his garden, you might just have made it and been able to pick yourself up as he did, in time to see, albeit tiltedly, the great mushroom cloud rising over what had been the greatest city that the world had ever known. He was wearing a T-shirt that said this on it, 'No one knows I'm a lesbian'. In a few days, you probably would have died too.

-<>-

The Bomb, as it would later become known, killed 24 million people in three seconds starting at 13:23:17 EDT on August 29th 2050. Some of them would take weeks to die, visibly, but from that moment, they were as dead as bricks.

From the outside, America appeared to do nothing for a day. The world held its breath.

And then, at 12:00:00 EDT on the 31st of August there were little pieces of the sun in some of the major cities of the world. A list follows.

Addis Ababa	Baghdad
Beijing	Cairo
Chongqing	Damascus
Kabul	Kinshasa
Pyongyang	Riyadh
Santiago	Shanghai
Tehran	And just in case, Rio de Janeiro

The US Military didn't really know who had bombed them, but they had to show a response, so they just hit everybody they could think of that had openly hated the United States. They had carte blanche after all.

Those who could, like the Chinese and Iranians launched counter attacks as soon as they could and some of their missiles got through the US defense network. A list follows.

Washington DC	Detroit
Atlanta	Boston
Las Vegas	Santa Monica
Fort Worth	Petaluma[68]
Louisville	Charlotte

---

[68] A near miss intended for San Francisco.

Almost everybody in this book is now dead, including the following.

Dwayne Swindel[69]	Michael Farber[70]
Cassandra Robertson	General Harlan Baisch
Dagmar Veets	Harvey Washington Jr.
Rick Stern	Dan Carstairs
Joshua Kabingga	Pablo
Matsune Suzuki	Hirohito

There were an additional 1 billion 360 million or so people killed, all told but there isn't really room to list them all here. Besides, most of them weren't celebrities like Bill Crenshaw.

He watched it all on CNN from the verandah of his resort in The Maldives along with his charming neighbor, Joshua Kabingga. Bill died in his sleep in 2058 from a stroke.

My wife, Yoko and I live in what is left of Beverly Hills, California along with my parents, Anna and Mort Kohut.

In researching this book, I had occasion to visit the upper Umbutu River. The water there is in a crisp hurry, and it is so clear that it is almost invisible. Later, it slows down and warms up for the hippos. They send their regards.

When I make love, and when I am playing a joke my ears glow a little. Yoko says, that that is why she fell in love with me in the first place.

Thank you Hirohito.

---

[69] Suicide by gunshot
[70] Murdered by Dwayne Swindel

Mark Weatherbe lives with his wife, Mary Elizabeth McNeill in London and Los Angeles.

Errors and Omissions
I am sure that I have missed something. No one is perfect—yet. If you have typos, misspellings, mistakes and the like that you want to report, please write them out in long hand on ripe fruit and send them to:

Miguel Garcia Balfadore´
Special Spanish Envoy to Guam
136 Aspinall Ave.
Hagatna, Guam
96910

Made in the USA
Charleston, SC
16 December 2011